Quarkus Cookbook
Kubernetes-Optimized Java Solutions

Alex Soto Bueno and Jason Porter

Beijing · Boston · Farnham · Sebastopol · Tokyo

Quarkus Cookbook

by Alex Soto Bueno and Jason Porter

Copyright © 2020 Alex Soto Bueno and Jason Porter. All rights reserved.

Published by O'Reilly Media, Inc., 1005 Gravenstein Highway North, Sebastopol, CA 95472.

O'Reilly books may be purchased for educational, business, or sales promotional use. Online editions are also available for most titles (*http://oreilly.com*). For more information, contact our corporate/institutional sales department: 800-998-9938 or *corporate@oreilly.com*.

Acquisitions Editor: Suzanne McQuade
Development Editor: Jeff Bleiel
Production Editor: Daniel Elfanbaum
Copyeditor: Piper Editorial
Proofreader: Amanda Kersey

Indexer: Potomac Indexing, LLC
Interior Designer: David Futato
Cover Designer: Karen Montgomery
Illustrator: Rebecca Demarest

July 2020:   First Edition

Revision History for the First Edition

2020-07-14:   First Release

See *http://oreilly.com/catalog/errata.csp?isbn=9781492062653* for release details.

978-1-492-06265-3

[LSI]

Table of Contents

Foreword

Red Hat, and JBoss before it, have been at the forefront of helping to shape the evolution of enterprise Java since the early 2000s. With an emphasis on open source and growing communities, these two companies have collaborated with other vendors, consultants, individuals, and standards organizations to ensure Java and some of its most popular frameworks have been developed to address new technological waves and to keep Java one of the most popular programming languages around. As a result, you can find Java being used in areas as diverse as IoT applications, web services, health care, and financial services. Yet when the cloud came along it presented some problems that traditional Java frameworks and even the Java Virtual Machine struggled to match.

Red Hat was the first vendor to marry a Java Enterprise Edition application server with the cloud through OpenShift. It continued this trend with all of its Java portfolio of projects and products. However, when the world moved to Linux Containers and then to Kubernetes, the entire application development paradigm for all programming languages moved toward immutability. Java has always been about enabling dynamic applications, and the frameworks built over many years take advantage of that aspect. Addressing this problem space and ensuring that Java remains a viable option for cloud developers requires a change of mindset, new tools, and new frameworks.

When we started to work on Quarkus in early 2018, the team had carte blanche to go back to the drawing board and consider all options. Working with various groups, including the Red Hat OpenJDK team, and seeing the opportunity that GraalVM represented for creating immutable native images from Java, resulted in Quarkus. In the intervening years, Quarkus has taken the Java community by storm and has grown faster and become more popular than we could have imagined back then. We firmly believe that it represents a view of the future for Enterprise Java in the Kubernetes clouds. We've re-architected many of the most popular Java frameworks and have written others from scratch, all with an eye toward ensuring that Quarkus is the preeminent Kubernetes-native approach for Java developers, including for new areas such as Serverless and Knative.

The authors of this book have been actively involved with Quarkus and have been part of the team for quite a while. They have insights into developing applications with Quarkus that few others have today. They've written this book to take advantage of their experiences and to help the reader build Quarkus applications and get Developer Joy! Whether you're new to Quarkus or already familiar with it, you will find this book to be exactly what you need. It covers a lot of ground, including taking you through the following: basic Quarkus applications; testing those applications; adding advanced concepts from Eclipse MicroProfile; reactive programming, which is a core part of Quarkus and not just an afterthought; how to build with Spring; and more. This is a great book to add to your developer library and use to increase your knowledge and skills. You'll enjoy working your way through it and will hopefully find yourself wanting to learn more and join the growing Quarkus community. Enjoy! Onward!

—Dr. Mark Little
VP, Engineering, JBoss CTO

Preface

We're excited to have you with us on this journey of learning and using Quarkus! Unlike traditional Java frameworks, which can be big, cumbersome, heavy-weight, and take months to learn, Quarkus builds on knowledge you already have! It uses JPA, JAX-RS, Eclipse Vert.x, Eclipse MicroProfile, and CDI, just to name a few technologies you're already familiar with. Quarkus then takes your knowledge and combines it into a compact, easy-to-deploy, fully Kubernetes-optimized container targeting either OpenJDK Hotspot or GraalVM. This allows you to pack your Kubernetes cluster as tightly as possible, making use of every resource on the machine as your application scales to meet demand. Regardless of where you are on your migration to Kubernetes, you'll find something useful with Quarkus, and this book will give you the tools and resources you need to succeed.

Who Should Read This Book

Obviously, we want everyone to read this book! However, we have made some assumptions about the reader:

- You are already familiar with Java and application development within that space.
- You understand traditional software development practices.
- You regularly deploy services into a cluster of machines or into the cloud.

Why We Wrote This Book

Quarkus is a relatively new framework in a new space (native Java and GraalVM). We wanted to dive into some more examples and how-to sections than what you will find on the internet. Also, we wanted to give you as much substance with this book as possible. There's no large application to understand or remember. All the examples in this book are self-contained and ready to be used. We hope you keep this as a reference for all your Quarkus development!

Navigating This Book

The organization of the chapters is fairly loose, but it basically flows as follows:

- Chapters 1 and 2 introduce you to Quarkus and get your basic project set up.
- Chapters 3 through 6 introduce the bread-and-butter portion of Quarkus: RESTful applications built using concepts from CDI and Eclipse MicroProfile. These chapters also show you how to package your application.
- Chapters 7 through 14 relate to harder, though just as important, concepts such as fault tolerance, persistence, security, and interaction with other services. You will also learn about additional integrations Quarkus has with Kubernetes.
- Chapters 15 and 16 talk about reactive programming using Quarkus and some additional functionality of the framework such as templating, scheduling, and OpenAPI.

Conventions Used in This Book

The following typographical conventions are used in this book:

Italic
    Indicates new terms, URLs, email addresses, filenames, and file extensions.

`Constant width`
    Used for program listings, as well as within paragraphs to refer to program elements such as variable or function names, databases, data types, environment variables, statements, and keywords.

`Constant width bold`
    Shows commands or other text that should be typed literally by the user.

`Constant width italic`
    Shows text that should be replaced with user-supplied values or by values determined by context.

 This element signifies a tip or suggestion.

This element signifies a general note.

This element indicates a warning or caution.

This element indicates an important item to remember.

Using Code Examples

Supplemental material (code examples, exercises, etc.) is available for download at *https://oreil.ly/quarkus-cookbook-code*.

If you have a technical question or a problem using the code examples, please send email to *bookquestions@oreilly.com*.

This book is here to help you get your job done. In general, if example code is offered with this book, you may use it in your programs and documentation. You do not need to contact us for permission unless you're reproducing a significant portion of the code. For example, writing a program that uses several chunks of code from this book does not require permission. Selling or distributing examples from O'Reilly books does require permission. Answering a question by citing this book and quoting example code does not require permission. Incorporating a significant amount of example code from this book into your product's documentation does require permission.

We appreciate, but generally do not require, attribution. An attribution usually includes the title, author, publisher, and ISBN. For example: "*Quarkus Cookbook* by Alex Soto Bueno and Jason Porter (O'Reilly). Copyright 2020 Alex Soto Bueno and Jason Porter, 978-1-492-06265-3."

If you feel your use of code examples falls outside fair use or the permission given above, feel free to contact us at *permissions@oreilly.com*.

O'Reilly Online Learning

 For more than 40 years, *O'Reilly Media* has provided technology and business training, knowledge, and insight to help companies succeed.

Our unique network of experts and innovators share their knowledge and expertise through books, articles, and our online learning platform. O'Reilly's online learning platform gives you on-demand access to live training courses, in-depth learning paths, interactive coding environments, and a vast collection of text and video from O'Reilly and 200+ other publishers. For more information, visit *http://oreilly.com*.

How to Contact Us

Please address comments and questions concerning this book to the publisher:

O'Reilly Media, Inc.
1005 Gravenstein Highway North
Sebastopol, CA 95472
800-998-9938 (in the United States or Canada)
707-829-0515 (international or local)
707-829-0104 (fax)

We have a web page for this book, where we list errata, examples, and any additional information. You can access this page at *https://oreil.ly/quarkus-cookbook*.

Email *bookquestions@oreilly.com* to comment or ask technical questions about this book.

For news and information about our books and courses, visit *http://oreilly.com*.

Find us on Facebook: *http://facebook.com/oreilly*

Follow us on Twitter: *http://twitter.com/oreillymedia*

Watch us on YouTube: *http://youtube.com/oreillymedia*

Acknowledgments

Jason Porter: What do you do during quarantine? You write a book, of course! Thank you to all those brave people on the front lines of health care. I'd like to thank the team behind both Quarkus and GraalVM for giving us an amazing tool and fun development experience. I've been developing software for over 20 years, and Quarkus brings back the enjoyment I had back when first learning about software development. A great thanks goes out to Georgios Andrianakis and Daniel Hinojosa for providing us with a technical review of the book! Your work has helped us create something that is accessible, useful, and hopefully enjoyable to those learning Quarkus. I would also like to thank Red Hat for allowing me the opportunity to write the book. Alex, thank you for asking me once again to work with you on a book! Lastly, thank you to my five children (Kaili, Emily, Zackary, Nicolas, and Rebecca) and wife, Tessie, for putting up with me writing another book, despite me saying I wouldn't do it again. Love you all!

Alex Soto Bueno: This book was finished during the COVID-19 pandemic, so first of all I'd like to thank all the health care workers who are taking care of all us. I would also like to thank the Red Hat Developers team, specially Burr Sutter, for allowing me the opportunity to write the book. Jason, as always, it was a pleasure to write a book with you. Lastly, thank you to my parents; my wife, Jessica; and my daughters, Ada and Alexandra; for their patience while I was writing the book, because there is no one without two. Thank you very much for everything.

Quarkus Overview

Kubernetes is becoming the de facto platform to deploy our enterprise applications nowadays. The movement to containers and Kubernetes has led to changes in the way we code, deploy, and maintain our Java-based applications. You can easily get yourself in trouble if you containerize and run a Java application without taking proper measures. Containers in Pods (a Kubernetes term) are the basic units in Kubernetes, so it is very important to have a good understanding of how to containerize a Java-based application correctly to avoid pitfalls, wasted work, and extra hours of frustration.

Quarkus is a cloud-native framework with built-in Kubernetes integration. It is an open source stack, released under the Apache License 2.0, that helps you create Kubernetes-native applications tailored for GraalVM and OpenJDK HotSpot. It is built on top of popular libraries and technologies such as Hibernate, Eclipse Micro-Profile, Kubernetes, Apache Camel, and Eclipse Vert.x.

The benefits of Quarkus include easy integration with Docker and Kubernetes, quick startup time, low resident set size (RSS) memory, and increased developer productivity. In this introductory chapter, we'll take a quick look Quarkus—what it is, the problems it solves, how it integrates with Kubernetes, why developers enjoy working with it, and some of its most noteworthy features.

Developer-Friendly

Quarkus allows you, the Java developer, to be more productive, and it helps you stay relevant in the fast-paced area of microservices and cloud-based applications.

Quarkus will enable your applications to scale better, to more tightly fill up a Kubernetes cluster utilizing fewer resources overall, and to make use of decades of community work in open source Java.

To start developing with Quarkus, you won't need to learn a new technology. If you're already familiar with dependency injection, JAX-RS, Hibernate, and Eclipse Micro-Profile concepts, there's nothing new here. All the knowledge you have built up over the course of your career will map directly into Quarkus. Whereas it might take weeks to learn other frameworks, you can get started with Quarkus and be productive in a matter of days or even hours.

Quarkus is designed to be an optimized choice for the next generation of application development and deployment. It supports you through the entire application life cycle from application scaffolding and live reloading in dev mode (a save-and-refresh workflow), all the way through to deployment in a cloud-based Kubernetes cluster. As a developer, Quarkus will keep you productive and solving problems, instead of shaving yaks.

Integration with Kubernetes

We said that Quarkus is meant to run within Kubernetes. That sounds great, but we know lots of things can run within Kubernetes. Throw your application in a Docker container, and it will run on Kubernetes. While this is true, there are a number of things that traditionally have to be done to properly tune, size, and configure your application to run efficiently within Kubernetes. You also have to pull out your text editor of choice and craft multiple YAML files—and let's be honest, no one really enjoys doing all that.

Quarkus eliminates that work by having a number of enhancements for deploying to and using Kubernetes with your application. When you bootstrap a Quarkus application, it comes with some Dockerfile files used to generate the Docker containers for your application. That is a great first step. These files are optimized for running with the OpenJDK JVM or running as native executables with GraalVM. They contain what is necessary to run the application, thereby eliminating as much duplication and unnecessary bloat from the container image as possible.

Next, when you use the Kubernetes extensions, Quarkus can generate the resources (YAML files) for a vanilla Kubernetes or OpenShift deployment! No more having to wade through YAML files and make sure you have the right indentation. After all, you'd prefer to be writing code than looking for that one line of YAML that isn't formatted correctly. Quarkus can also push your image to a registry before deploying to the Kubernetes cluster. All of these application images can be further enhanced and customized via the Quarkus application configuration, which you'll learn about in Chapter 4. For example, in Quarkus 1.4 and later, ConfigMap and Secrets can be read from the API server—you don't need to mount any of the files in the Pod!

Memory and First Response Time

Quarkus is known as the "supersonic, subatomic" Java framework. That may set off marketing alarms with developers, but when you break it down and understand what Quarkus is doing, you'll see that you really are getting a very small, quick, and productive execution. With Quarkus, you can deploy a native application optimized to be run on Kubernetes. For example, let's say you want to deploy a native application, optimized to be run on Kubernetes, where the container image is around 200 MB or smaller. In Quarkus, this application will start up and be ready to accept requests within a fraction of a second, and it will use less than 50 MB of memory.

When deploying to a Kubernetes cluster, you want to pack in as many instances of your application as possible so you are able to scale to meet unexpected load yet still utilize as many of the resources as possible. When scaling up you want your new application instances up and running quickly—this is where a native executable shines. Quarkus does as much pre-boot of your application and the frameworks it uses as possible during the native executable build process. This helps your application start quickly and be ready to service requests without having to do additional class loading, runtime scanning, or other warm-up the the JVM typically does.

Naturally, available memory is a finite resource. Understanding exactly how much memory is being used by your application, and not starving the JVM while trying to keep that number low, is key to deployment density. Quarkus succeeds in helping you achieve that with the native executable, which is small and memory efficient.

A Basic Quarkus Workflow

While reading this book and going through the recipes, you'll be introduced to the Quarkus ecosystem. You'll learn about extensions, integrations, and design decisions. You will also see the basic workflow used throughout to help you be productive. In a nutshell, this workflow is as follows:

1. Scaffold
2. Launch dev mode
3. Code
4. Test
5. Package
6. Deploy

Scaffolding your application, or adding an extension to an existing start, gives you a solid foundation to build upon. You'll become familiar with this in Chapter 2. Following scaffolding, you will be asked to run your application in dev mode, which is also introduced in Chapter 2. You will then learn about typical tasks for an application: creating RESTful services, completing the basic programming model, and performing application configuration. Dev mode will give you near instant feedback without the bothersome dance of compile, package, and deploy that you've become familiar with. In Chapter 5 you'll see how to test a Quarkus application that targets both the JVM and native executable, giving you reassurance that your application runs correctly and meets your standards. Creating the final deliverable is covered in Chapter 6, as is learning how to package your application for your particular deployment strategy. The last piece of that workflow, deployment, is covered in Chapter 10. Exploring further, you'll learn how to make your application more fault resistant, how to interact with various persistence engines, and how to communicate with external services. We will also explain additional integrations to aid you in leveraging existing knowledge from other libraries and programming paradigms. We'll walk you through setting up the Kubernetes optimizations that are necessary for your application, building Kubernetes resources, and pushing it all live.

CHAPTER 2

Scaffolding

In this chapter, you'll learn about creating the project structure of Quarkus. Quarkus comes with some different ways to scaffold a project.

You'll learn how to do the following:

- Scaffold a project in different ways, from Maven to VSCode IDE
- Improve developer experience with the live reloading
- Serve static resources with Quarkus

2.1 Scaffolding a Quarkus Project with Maven

Problem

You want to start quickly in Quarkus by generating a simple project.

Solution

Use the Quarkus Maven plug-in.

Discussion

Using the Quarkus Maven plug-in creates a simple project that is ready to be deployed and contains the following:

- A *pom.xml* file with minimal Quarkus dependencies
- A simple JAX-RS resource
- A test for the JAX-RS resource

- A native test
- Dockerfiles to generate a container
- An empty configuration file

We assume you've already installed Apache Maven (*http://maven.apache.org*). Open a terminal and execute the following command:

```
mvn io.quarkus:quarkus-maven-plugin:1.4.1.Final:create \
    -DprojectGroupId=org.acme \
    -DprojectArtifactId=getting-started \
    -DclassName="org.acme.quickstart.GreetingResource" \
    -Dpath="/hello"
```

The project has this structure:

```
├── mvnw
├── mvnw.cmd
├── pom.xml
└── src
    ├── main
    │   ├── docker ❶
    │   │   ├── Dockerfile.jvm
    │   │   └── Dockerfile.native
    │   ├── java
    │   │   └── org
    │   │       └── acme
    │   │           └── quickstart
    │   │               └── GreetingResource.java ❷
    │   └── resources
    │       ├── META-INF
    │       │   └── resources
    │       │       └── index.html ❸
    │       └── application.properties ❹
    └── test
        └── java
            └── org
                └── acme
                    └── quickstart ❺
                        ├── GreetingResourceTest.java
                        └── NativeGreetingResourceIT.java
```

❶ Dockerfiles

❷ JAX-RS resource

❸ Static resource

❹ Configuration file

❺ Auto-generated tests for JAX-RS resource

2.2 Scaffolding a Quarkus Project with Gradle

Problem

You want to get started quickly in Quarkus by generating a simple project, and you are a Gradle user.

Solution

Use the Quarkus Maven plug-in (yes, the Maven plug-in).

Discussion

You can scaffold a simple Quarkus project by using the Quarkus Maven plug-in; you just set the output as a Gradle project. The resulting project is ready to be deployed and contains the following:

- A *build.gradle* file with minimal Quarkus dependencies
- A simple JAX-RS resource
- A test for the JAX-RS resource
- A native test
- Dockerfiles to generate a container
- An empty configuration file

We assume you've already installed Apache Maven (*http://maven.apache.org*). Open a terminal and execute the following command:

```
mvn io.quarkus:quarkus-maven-plugin:1.4.1.Final:create \
    -DprojectGroupId=org.acme \
    -DprojectArtifactId=getting-started \
    -DclassName="org.acme.quickstart.GreetingResource" \
    -Dpath="/hello" \
    -DbuildTool=gradle
```

Unlike in Apache Maven, this command will create the structure in the *current* directory.

The resulting project has the following structure:

```
.
├── README.md
├── build.gradle
```

```
├── gradle
│   └── wrapper
│       ├── gradle-wrapper.jar
│       └── gradle-wrapper.properties
├── gradle.properties
├── gradlew
├── gradlew.bat
├── settings.gradle
└── src
    ├── main
    │   ├── docker
    │   │   ├── Dockerfile.jvm
    │   │   └── Dockerfile.native
    │   ├── java
    │   │   └── org
    │   │       └── acme
    │   │           └── quickstart
    │   │               └── GreetingResource.java
    │   └── resources
    │       ├── META-INF
    │       │   └── resources
    │       │       └── index.html
    │       └── application.properties
    ├── native-test
    │   └── java
    │       └── org
    │           └── acme
    │               └── quickstart
    │                   └── NativeGreetingResourceIT.java
    └── test
        └── java
            └── org
                └── acme
                    └── quickstart
                        └── GreetingResourceTest.java
```

2.3 Scaffolding a Quarkus Project with the Quarkus Start Coding Website

Problem

You want to start quickly in Quarkus by generating a simple project without having to install Maven or Gradle.

Solution

Use the Quarkus Start Coding website by visiting *https://code.quarkus.io* to generate a simple Quarkus project.

Discussion

At the time of writing, the home page looks like what's shown in Figure 2-1.

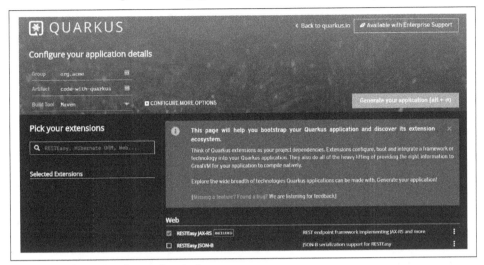

Figure 2-1. https://code.quarkus.io homepage

When the page is loaded, push the "Generate your application" button to download a ZIP file with the generated project inside.

Open a terminal and uncompress the generated project:

```
unzip code-with-quarkus.zip
cd code-with-quarkus/
```

The scaffolded project is the same as the one you generated in Recipe 2.1, with the following elements:

- A *pom.xml* file with minimal Quarkus dependencies
- A simple JAX-RS resource
- A test for the JAX-RS resource
- A native test
- Dockerfiles to generate a container
- An empty configuration file

See Also

We have not yet discussed Quarkus extensions, but notice that you can generate a project with any of the Quarkus extensions registered. You'll see more about extensions in the next sections.

Extensions are added either by selecting them in the checkbox that contains every extension in the page or by using the search box.

2.4 Scaffolding a Quarkus Project with Visual Studio Code

Problem

You want to start quickly in Quarkus by generating a simple project in Visual Studio (VS) Code.

Solution

Use the Quarkus VS Code extension.

Discussion

A Quarkus extension is developed for Visual Studio Code IDE to integrate some of the features of Quarkus into the IDE. The following are some of these features:

- Commands to scaffold a project
- A command to add extensions
- Auto-completion for configuration file (properties and YAML formats) Snippets

To install the plug-in, open VS Code, and push the "Extensions" button, as seen in Figure 2-2.

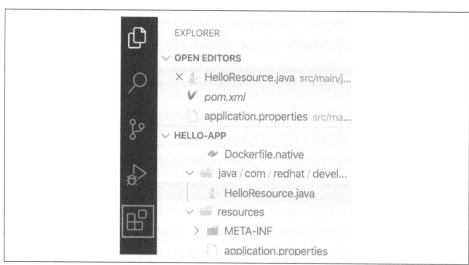

Figure 2-2. Clicking on the extension button in VS Code allows you to install the Quarkus Extension

Then search for `quarkus` and select the `Quarkus Tools for Visual Studio Code` by Red Hat. Your search should populate similar to Figure 2-3.

Figure 2-3. The Quarkus extension is available for free from the VS Code marketplace

After the installation process, restart the IDE, and you can start using the extensions.

To generate a new Quarkus project, open the Command Palette and select "Generate a Quarkus Project." The available options at the time of writing are shown in Figure 2-4.

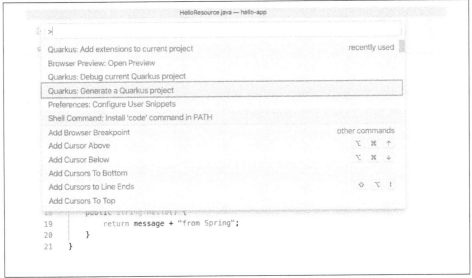

Figure 2-4. Generate a new Quarkus project from the Command Palette

The next step, shown in Figure 2-5, will ask you about which build tool you will be using. There are also some questions about `groupId`, `artifactId`, and so on.

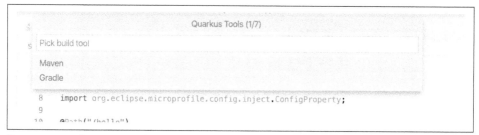

Figure 2-5. Selecting your building tool

Extensions can be added by using the `Add Extension` command from the console, as shown in Figure 2-6.

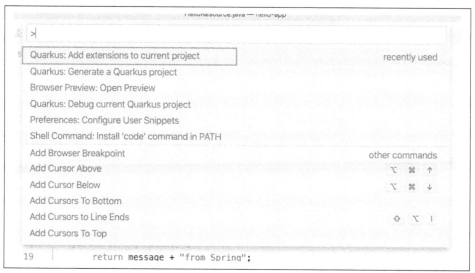

Figure 2-6. The `Add extension` command

And select any Quarkus extension that you might want to add to the project. A sample of available extensions can been seen in Figure 2-7.

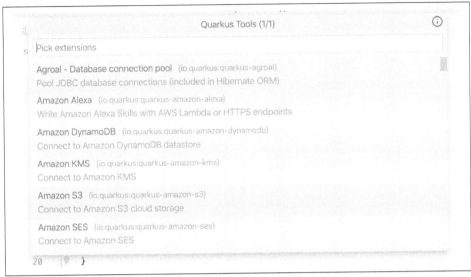

Figure 2-7. You can see a list of available extensions for your application that could be installed

In the following figures, you can see some of the features that are provided by the Quarkus extension.

Figure 2-8 shows the auto-completion of configuration properties that help you correctly configure the application.

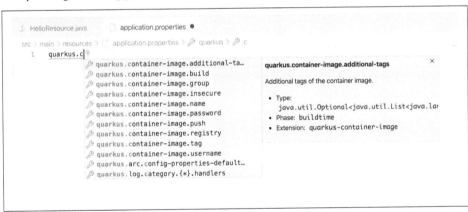

Figure 2-8. Auto-completion and type information of configuration property keys

Figure 2-9 shows the description of a configuration property when you mouse over it.

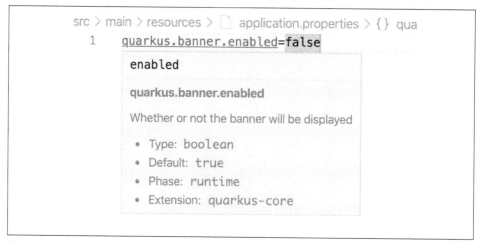

src > main > resources > ☐ application.properties > {} qua
```
1    quarkus.banner.enabled=false
```

enabled

quarkus.banner.enabled

Whether or not the banner will be displayed

- Type: `boolean`
- Default: `true`
- Phase: `runtime`
- Extension: `quarkus-core`

Figure 2-9. Hovering over a configuration property gives you more information about that property

Figure 2-10 demonstrates how to detect unused properties in your application.

```
⚙ HelloF  Unknown property 'greetings.message' microprofile(unknown)

src > ma  Peek Problem (⌥F8)    Quick Fix... (⌘.)
1        greetings.message=Hello
```

Figure 2-10. Detect unused configuration properties

Figure 2-11 shows the URL representing the endpoint. If you click it, a new browser window is opened, pointing to the given URL.

```
8     @Path("/hello")
9   ∨ public class HelloResource {
10
11        @GET
12        @Produces(MediaType.APPLICATION_JSON)
          http://localhost:8080/hello
13  ∨     public String hello() {
14  💡        return "Hello";
15        }
16  }
```

Figure 2-11. A clickable URL endpoint is generated by the VS Code extension for each endpoint method

See Also

The Quarkus extension is available for several IDEs:

- Visual Studio Code (*https://oreil.ly/rL1Md*)
- Eclipse (*https://oreil.ly/3Ais_*)
- IntelliJ (*https://oreil.ly/Whvdj*)

2.5 Live Reloading with Dev Mode

Problem

You want to review the result of a change in the project without having to repackage and redeploy the full application.

Solution

Use *development mode*, which enables hot deployment with background compilation, which means that when you modify your Java files and/or your resource files and refresh your browser, these changes will automatically take effect.

> Each of the scaffolding methods default to Java 11. You will need a Java 11 VM, or you will need to modify the project to use a different version of the JVM.

Discussion

To start an application in development mode, run the `quarkus:dev` command in the root of your project. For this example, you are using the project created in Recipe 2.1:

```
./mvnw compile quarkus:dev

[INFO] Scanning for projects...
....
[INFO] --- quarkus-maven-plugin:1.4.1.Final:dev (default-cli) @
      getting-started ---
Listening for transport dt_socket at address: 5005
INFO  [io.qua.dep.QuarkusAugmentor] (main) Beginning quarkus augmentation
INFO  [io.qua.dep.QuarkusAugmentor] (main) Quarkus augmentation
    completed in 946ms
INFO  [io.quarkus] (main) Quarkus 1.4.1.Final started in 1.445s.
    Listening on: http://[::]:8080
INFO  [io.quarkus] (main) Installed features: [cdi, resteasy]
```

When the application is up and running, open a new terminal window and run the following command:

```
curl http://localhost:8080/hello

hello
```

Now *without* stopping the `quarkus:dev` mode, do this next modification in `org.acme.quickstart.GreetingResource.java`:

```
@GET
@Produces(MediaType.TEXT_PLAIN)
public String hello() {
    return "hola";
}
```

Then run this again:

```
curl http://localhost:8080/hello

hola
```

It is really important to note that you've done a change in your source code and that without any recompilation, repackaging, or redeployment, the change has been automatically populated in your running instance out of the box—without any special setup.

Now, instead of *write code → compile → deploy → refresh → repeat*, you are simplifying your development workflow to *write code → refresh → repeat*.

Development mode detects changes for Java files, application configs, and static resources.

To stop development mode, go to `quarkus:dev` terminal and push Ctrl+C.

To run development mode in Gradle projects, you can run a `quarkusDev` task:

```
./gradlew quarkusDev
...
```

2.6 Serving Static Resources

Problem

You want to serve static resources such as HTML, JavaScript, CSS, and images.

Solution

In Quarkus, any resource copied into *src/main/resources/META-INF/resources* is served from the root path.

In some situations, you might want to serve static resources to your callers. These could be static downloadable content or an HTML page.

By default, Quarkus comes with an *index.html* file as a static resource.

Start the application:

```
./mvnw compile quarkus:dev
```

Open a browser and enter the following URL: *http://localhost:8080/index.html*.

And you'll see something like what's shown in Figure 2-12.

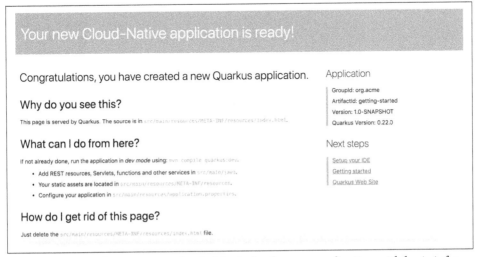

Figure 2-12. Quarkus creates a placeholder index for your application with basic information and next steps to help you after scaffolding

 Live reloading also works with static resources.

CHAPTER 3

Developing RESTful Services

Quarkus integrates with RESTEasy, a JAX-RS implementation to define REST APIs. In this chapter, you'll learn how to develop RESTful web services in Quarkus. We'll cover the following topics:

- How to use JAX-RS for creating CRUD services
- How to enable CORS for requesting resources from other domains
- How to implement reactive routes
- How to implement filters to manipulate requests and responses

3.1 Creating a Simple REST API Endpoint

Problem

You want to create a REST API endpoint with CRUD operations.

Solution

Use the JAX-RS `GreetingResource` resource generated previously and fill it with JAX-RS annotations.

JAX-RS is the default framework used in Quarkus to define REST endpoints. All of the JAX-RS annotations are already correctly on your classpath. You will want to use the HTTP verb annotations (@GET, @POST, @PUT, @DELETE) to declare the HTTP verb(s) that the endpoint methods will listen to. Of course, you will need the @Path annotation to define the URI relative to the rest of the application for your endpoint.

Open `org.acme.quickstart.GreetingResource.java`:

```java
package org.acme.quickstart;
import javax.ws.rs.GET;
import javax.ws.rs.Path;
import javax.ws.rs.Produces;
import javax.ws.rs.core.MediaType;

@Path("/hello")  ❶
public class GreetingResource {
    @GET  ❷
    @Produces(MediaType.TEXT_PLAIN)  ❸
    public String hello() {
        return "hello";  ❹
    }
}
```

❶ Identifies the URI path of the current resource

❷ Responds to HTTP GET requests

❸ Defines the media type(s) that are returned

❹ Returns plain text

Let's create the remaining methods for creating, updating, and deleting a message:

```java
@POST  ❶
@Consumes(MediaType.TEXT_PLAIN)  ❷
public void create(String message) {  ❸
    System.out.println("Create");
}

@PUT  ❹
@Consumes(MediaType.TEXT_PLAIN)
@Produces(MediaType.TEXT_PLAIN)
public String update(String message) {
    System.out.println("Update");
    return message;
}

@DELETE  ❺
public void delete() {
    System.out.println("Delete");
}
```

❶ Responds to HTTP POST requests

❷ Defines the media type(s) that are accepted

❸ Body content of the request

❹ Responds to HTTP PUT requests

❺ Responds to HTTP DELETE requests

The following are valid HTTP methods: @GET, @POST, @PUT, @DELETE, @PATCH, @HEAD, and @OPTIONS.

3.2 Extracting Request Parameters

Problem

You want to extract request parameters using JAX-RS.

Solution

Use some of the built-in annotations provided by JAX-RS specification.

Open the `org.acme.quickstart.GreetingResource.java` class and change the `hello` method with the request parameters to look like the following extract:

```
public static enum Order {
    desc, asc;
}

@GET
@Produces(MediaType.TEXT_PLAIN)
public String hello(
            @Context UriInfo uriInfo,                           ❶
            @QueryParam("order") Order order,                   ❷
            @NotBlank @HeaderParam("authorization") String authorization  ❸
            ) {


    return String.format("URI: %s - Order %s - Authorization: %s",
                    uriInfo.getAbsolutePath(), order, authorization);
}
```

❶ Gets `UriInfo` of the request; `UriInfo` is part of JAX-RS and allows you to obtain application and request URI information

❷ Gets query parameter named `order` as `Enum`

❸ Gets header parameter named `authorization` integrated with bean validation

Try it by opening a new terminal window, starting the Quarkus application, and sending a request to the GET method:

```
./mvnw clean compile quarkus:dev

curl -X GET "http://localhost:8080/hello?order=asc" \
    -H "accept: text/plain" -H "authorization: XYZ"
URI: http://localhost:8080/hello - Order asc - Authorization: XYZ

curl -X GET "http://localhost:8080/hello?order=asc" \
    -H "accept: text/plain" -v
HTTP/1.1 400 Bad Request
```

Other request parameters can be extracted using annotations such as form parameters (`@FormParam`), matrix parameters (`@MatrixParam`), or cookie values (`@Cookie Param`). Also, using the `@Context` annotation, you can inject other elements related to JAX-RS, such as `javax.ws.rs.core.SecurityContext`, `javax.ws.rs.sse.SseEvent Sink`, or `javax.ws.rs.sse.Sse`.

Discussion

In Recipe 3.1, you saw how to create REST API endpoints using JAX-RS, but you usually need to extract more information from a request rather than just the body content.

One of the important things that you need to take into consideration when using Quarkus and JAX-RS is that, under the covers, Quarkus uses RESTEasy working with Vert.x directly by default, without using anything related to the `Servlet` specification.

Generally speaking, everything you might need for developing REST API endpoints is well supported, and Quarkus offers alternatives when you need to implement custom `Servlet` filters or get the HTTP request directly into the code.

But, if it is a requirement, you can configure Quarkus to use RESTEasy while working with the `Servlet` specification instead of Vert.x by adding the `quarkus-undertow` extension:

```
./mvnw quarkus:add-extension -Dextensions="quarkus-undertow"
```

```
./gradlew addExtension --extensions="quarkus-undertow"
```

See Also

To learn more about JAX-RS, visit the following websites:

- Eclipse Foundation: Jakarta RESTful Web Services (*https://oreil.ly/Tgn5d*)
- RESTEasy (*https://oreil.ly/WpJ3x*)

3.3 Using Semantic HTTP Response Status Codes

Problem

You want to use HTTP response status codes to correctly reflect the result of a request.

Solution

The JAX-RS specification uses the `javax.ws.rs.core.Response` interface to return the correct HTTP response status code as well as to set any other required information like response content, cookies, or headers:

```
package org.acme.quickstart;

import javax.ws.rs.Consumes;
import javax.ws.rs.POST;
import javax.ws.rs.Path;
import javax.ws.rs.Produces;
import javax.ws.rs.core.MediaType;
import javax.ws.rs.core.Response;
import javax.ws.rs.core.UriBuilder;

@Path("/developer")
public class DeveloperResource {

    @POST
    @Produces(MediaType.APPLICATION_JSON)
    @Consumes(MediaType.APPLICATION_JSON)
    public Response createDeveloper(Developer developer) {
        developer.persist();
        return Response.created( ❶
            UriBuilder
                .fromResource(DeveloperResource.class) ❷
                .path(Long.toString(developer.getId())) ❸
                .build()
            )
            .entity(developer) ❹
            .build(); ❺
    }

    public static class Developer {

        static long counter = 1;

        private long id;
        private String name;

        public long getId() {
            return id;
```

```
        }

        public void setName(String name) {
            this.name = name;
        }

        public String getName() {
            return name;
        }

        public void persist() {
            this.id = counter++;
        }
    }
}
```

❶ Sets response status code as 201 created with the Location header as the URI

❷ Sets path from the resource class

❸ Sets the developer ID in the Location header

❹ Sets the created developer as response content

❺ Builds the Response object

 You will need the quarkus-resteasy-jsonb or quarkus-resteasy-jackson extension in your project if you are returning JSON from your endpoints.

Try it by opening a new terminal window, starting the Quarkus application, and sending a request to the GET method:

```
./mvnw clean compile quarkus:dev

curl -d '{"name":"Ada"}' -H "Content-Type: application/json" \
  -X POST http://localhost:8080/developer -v

< HTTP/1.1 201 Created
< Content-Length: 21
< Content-Type: application/json
< Location: http://localhost:8080/developer/1
<
{"id":1,"name":"Ada"}
```

Notice that the Location header contains a valid URI to get access to the created resource.

Discussion

When defining a RESTful Web API, it is really important to follow some conventions that are provided by the underlying technology that is used; for RESTful web services, it is the HTTP layer.

Another critical part of defining your API is using the correct response status codes, which are sent back to the client to indicate whether the request has been completed. There are five classes of status codes:

- Informational responses (100–199)
- Successful responses (200–299)
- Redirects (300–399)
- Client errors (400–499)
- Server errors (500–599)

By default, Quarkus tries to offer out-of-the-box responses with the correct HTTP status codes. For example, it offers a 400 Bad Request in case of constraint violations and a 500 Internal Server Error in the case of server exceptions. But there is one use case that it is not covered by default: the creation of a resource in which an HTTP 201 Created status response code should be sent back to the client with the new resource in the body of the message and the URL of the new resource set in the Location header.

See Also

Full HTTP response status codes are summarized at the following website:

- MDN Web Docs: HTTP response status codes (*https://oreil.ly/Gq02d*)

3.4 Binding HTTP Methods

Problem

You want to bind methods to HTTP verbs that do not have a dedicated annotation provided by the JAX-RS specification.

Solution

Use javax.ws.rs.HttpMethod annotation to create your HTTP method annotation.

JAX-RS specification provides seven annotations to specify the HTTP method that a method should respond to. These annotations are @GET, @POST, @PUT, @DELETE,

@PATCH, @HEAD, and @OPTIONS. But there are many more HTTP methods, and JAX-RS provides javax.ws.rs.HttpMethod annotation to support these other methods.

The first thing to do is create a meta-annotation. We're going to use the LOCK verb, defined at RFC-4918 (*https://tools.ietf.org/html/rfc4918#section-9.10*). The LOCK verb locks access or refreshes an existing lock to a resource. Our annotation will be named LOCK, and it is annotated with @javax.ws.rs.HttpMethod:

```
package org.acme.quickstart;

import java.lang.annotation.Documented;
import java.lang.annotation.ElementType;
import java.lang.annotation.Retention;
import java.lang.annotation.RetentionPolicy;
import java.lang.annotation.Target;

import javax.ws.rs.HttpMethod;

@Target({ElementType.METHOD})
@Retention(RetentionPolicy.RUNTIME)
@HttpMethod("LOCK") ❶
@Documented
public @interface LOCK {
}
```

❶ Binds the LOCK HTTP method to the annotation

Finally, use this annotation in a resource method to bind it to the LOCK HTTP verb.

Open the org.acme.quickstart.GreetingResource.java class and create a LOCK method:

```
@LOCK ❶
@Produces(MediaType.TEXT_PLAIN)
@Path("{id}")
public String lockResource(@PathParam("id") long id) {
    return id + " locked";
}
```

❶ Bind to LOCK HTTP method

Try it by opening a new terminal window, starting the Quarkus application, and sending a request to the LOCK method:

```
./mvnw clean compile quarkus:dev

curl -X LOCK http://localhost:8080/hello/1
1 locked
```

See Also

A complete list of HTTP methods can be found at the following GitHub page:

- KNOW YOUR HTTP methods WELL (*https://oreil.ly/DC9Wi*)

3.5 Enabling Cross-Origin Resource Sharing (CORS)

Problem

You want to request restricted resources from another domain.

Solution

Use `quarkus.http.cors` configuration property to enable CORS.

Discussion

Cross-origin resource sharing (CORS) is a mechanism that allows restricted resources to be requested from another domain outside the domain from which the first resource was served. Quarkus provides a set of configuration properties to configure CORS.

To enable CORS in Quarkus you need to set the `quarkus.http.cors` configuration property to `true` in the *application.properties* file.

An example of CORS configuration could look like the following:

```
quarkus.http.cors=true
quarkus.http.cors.origins=http://example.com
quarkus.http.cors.methods=GET,PUT,POST,DELETE
quarkus.http.cors.headers=accept,authorization,content-type,x-requested-with
```

You can view the output and headers using `curl`:

```
curl -d '{"name":"Ada"}' -H "Content-Type: application/json" \
    -X POST http://localhost:8080/developer \
    -H "Origin: http://example.com" --verbose
```

The output should show the `access-control-allow-origin` header:

```
upload completely sent off: 14 out of 14 bytes
* Mark bundle as not supporting multiuse
< HTTP/1.1 201 Created
< access-control-allow-origin: http://example.com
< access-control-allow-credentials: true
< Content-Length: 21
< Content-Type: application/json
< Location: http://localhost:8080/developer/5
```

See Also

You can find more information about CORS at the following Wikipedia page:

- Cross-origin resource sharing (*https://oreil.ly/iSiqh*)

3.6 Using Reactive Routes

Problem

You want to implement HTTP endpoints using reactive routes.

Solution

Use the Vert.x `io.vertx.ext.web.Router` router instance or the `io.quarkus`
`.vertx.web.Route` annotation.

There are two ways to use reactive routes within Quarkus. The first way is to register
routes directly using the `io.vertx.ext.web.Router` class.

To retrieve the `Router` instance at startup, you need to observe the creation of the
object using Contexts and Dependency Injection (CDI).

Create a new class named `org.acme.quickstart.ApplicationRoutes.java`:

```
package org.acme.quickstart;

import javax.enterprise.context.ApplicationScoped;
import javax.enterprise.event.Observes;

import io.quarkus.vertx.http.runtime.filters.Filters;
import io.quarkus.vertx.web.Route;
import io.vertx.core.http.HttpMethod;        ❺
import io.vertx.ext.web.Router;              ❺
import io.vertx.ext.web.RoutingContext;      ❺

@ApplicationScoped ❶
public class ApplicationRoutes {

    public void routes(@Observes Router router) { ❷

        router
            .get("/ok") ❸
            .handler(rc -> rc.response().end("OK from Route")); ❹

    }
}
```

❶ Instantiates the object into CDI container with *application* scope

❷ Provides the `Router` object to register the routes

❸ Binds the `GET` HTTP method to `/ok`

❹ Handles the logic

❺ Imports used later in the example

Try it by opening a new terminal window, starting the Quarkus application, and sending a request to the new method:

```
./mvnw clean compile quarkus:dev
```

```
curl http://localhost:8080/ok
OK from Route
```

The second way to use reactive routes is a declarative approach with the `io.quarkus`
`.vertx.web.Route` annotation. To have access to this annotation, you need to add the
`quarkus-vertx-web` extension:

```
./mvnw quarkus:add-extension -Dextensions="quarkus-vertx-web"
```

Then you can annotate methods with `@Route`. These methods must be defined within a CDI bean.

Open the `org.acme.quickstart.ApplicationRoutes.java` class and define a route:

```
@Route(path = "/declarativeok", methods = HttpMethod.GET) ❶
public void greetings(RoutingContext routingContext) { ❷
    String name = routingContext.request().getParam("name"); ❸

    if (name == null) {
        name = "world";
    }

    routingContext.response().end("OK " + name + " you are right"); ❹
}
```

❶ Sets the HTTP path and method

❷ `RoutingContext` to get request information

❸ Gets query param

❹ Handles the logic

Try it by opening a new terminal window, starting the Quarkus application, and sending a request to the new method:

```
./mvnw clean compile quarkus:dev

curl localhost:8080/declarativeok?name=Alex
OK Alex you are right
```

Discussion

Quarkus HTTP is based on a nonblocking and reactive engine. Under the covers it is using Vert.x and Netty. When a request is received, it is managed by *event loops* that may either rely on a worker thread, in case of servlet or JAX-RS, or use the I/O thread, in case of reactive route, to handle the logic of the invocation.

It is important to note that reactive routes must be either nonblocking or explicitly declared as blocking; if not, because of the nature of reactive event looping, you are going to block the loop, thus preventing further loops from being processed until the thread unblocks.

Within the same project, you can mix JAX-RS endpoints with reactive routes without any problem.

See Also

You can learn more about reactive routes in Vert.x on the following web page:

- Basic Vert.x-Web Concepts (*https://oreil.ly/kznp9*)

3.7 Intercepting HTTP Requests

Problem

You want to intercept HTTP requests to manipulate requests or responses.

Solution

Sometimes you need to manipulate the request before reaching the endpoint logic (i.e., security checks) or before the response is sent back to the caller (i.e., compressing response). With Quarkus you can intercept HTTP requests by using either Vert.x `Filters` or JAX-RS filter interfaces.

Let's see how to implement a filter using `io.quarkus.vertx.http.runtime.fil ters.Filters`.

To retrieve the `Filters` instance at startup, you need to observe the creation of the object using CDI.

Open the `org.acme.quickstart.ApplicationRoutes.java` class and add a method named `filters`:

```java
public void filters(@Observes Filters filters) { ❶
    filters
        .register(
            rc -> {
                rc.response() ❷
                    .putHeader("V-Header", "Header added by VertX Filter"); ❸
                rc.next(); ❹
            },
            10); ❺
    }
```

❶ Provides `Filters` object to register the filters

❷ Modifies the response

❸ Adds a new header to the response

❹ Continues the filter chain

❺ Sets the order of execution

It is important to note that these filters are applied for servlets, JAX-RS resources, and reactive routes.

Try it by opening a new terminal window, starting the Quarkus application, and sending a request to the new method:

```
./mvnw clean compile quarkus:dev

echo Reactive-Route
curl localhost:8080/ok -v
< V-Header: Header added by VertX Filter
< content-length: 13
OK from Route

echo JAX-RS
curl -X GET "http://localhost:8080/hello?order=asc" \
    -H "accept: text/plain" -H "authorization: XYZ" -v
< V-Header: Header added by VertX Filter
< content-length: 65
URI: http://localhost:8080/hello - Order asc - Authorization: XYZ
```

Notice that both requests (the reactive route and JAX-RS endpoints) were modified by the registered filter and by adding a new header.

That said, you can also use the javax.ws.rs.container.ContainerRequestFilter/
javax.ws.rs.container.ContainerResponseFilter interfaces to implement a filter.

Create a new class named org.acme.quickstart.HeaderAdditionContainerRespon
seFilter.java:

```java
package org.acme.quickstart;

import java.io.IOException;

import javax.ws.rs.container.ContainerRequestContext;
import javax.ws.rs.container.ContainerResponseContext;
import javax.ws.rs.container.ContainerResponseFilter;
import javax.ws.rs.ext.Provider;

@Provider ❶
public class HeaderAdditionContainerResponseFilter
                implements ContainerResponseFilter { ❷

    @Override
    public void filter(ContainerRequestContext requestContext,
                    ContainerResponseContext responseContext)
            throws IOException {
                responseContext.getHeaders()
                    .add("X-Header", "Header added by JAXRS Filter"); ❸
    }
}
```

❶ Sets this class as an extension interface

❷ Applies changes in response

❸ Adds a new header to the response

This filter is applied only to JAX-RS resources, and not in reactive routes.

Try it by opening a new terminal window, starting the Quarkus application, and
sending a request to the new method:

```
./mvnw clean compile quarkus:dev

echo Reactive-Route
curl localhost:8080/ok -v
< V-Header: Header added by VertX Filter
< content-length: 13
OK from Route

echo JAX-RS
curl -X GET "http://localhost:8080/hello?order=asc" \
    -H "accept: text/plain" -H "authorization: XYZ" -v
< V-Header: Header added by VertX Filter
```

```
< Content-Length: 65
< Content-Type: text/plain;charset=UTF-8
< X-Header: Header added by JAXRS Filter
URI: http://localhost:8080/hello - Order asc - Authorization: XYZ
```

Discussion

Notice that in the case of the reactive-route endpoint, only the V-Header header is added, and not the X-Header header. Meanwhile, in the JAX-RS endpoint, the request is modified by both filters by adding both HTTP headers.

See Also

To learn more about JAX-RS and Vert.x, you can visit the following websites:

- Eclipse Foundation: Jakarta RESTful web services (*https://oreil.ly/xioAv*)
- Vert.x Documentation (*https://vertx.io/docs*)

3.8 Secure Connections with SSL

Problem

You want to secure connections so as to prevent an attacker from stealing sensitive information.

Solution

Enable Quarkus to use SSL to secure connections.

Securing communication between a client and the application is important when the information that is going to be transmitted is sensitive (password, account numbers, health information, etc.). For this reason, it is very important to protect the communication between services using SSL.

To secure the communications, two elements must be provided: a certificate and an associated key file. Both can be provided individually or in the form of a *keystore*.

Let's configure Quarkus to use a keystore that contains an entry with a certificate:

```
quarkus.http.ssl-port=8443 ❶
quarkus.http.ssl.certificate.key-store-file=keystore.jks ❷
quarkus.http.ssl.certificate.key-store-file-type=jks
quarkus.http.ssl.certificate.key-store-password=changeit ❸
```

❶ Sets HTTPS port

❷ Type of keystore and location relative to *src/main/resources*

❸ The password to open the keystore

Start the application and send a request to the HTTPS endpoint:

```
./mvnw clean compile quarkus:dev
```

```
curl --insecure https://localhost:8443/hello
hello
```

As the certificate has been self-signed, the `--insecure` flag is provided to skip the certificate validation. In an example in which the certificate is not self-signed, the `insecure` flag should not be provided. The flag was used in this example for simplicity.

 Providing the password as plain text in the configuration file is a bad practice. It can be supplied by using an environment variable `QUARKUS_HTTP_SSL_CERTIFICATE_KEY_STORE_PASSWORD`, as you read at the beginning of the book when the MicroProfile Config spec was introduced.

Discussion

For the busy developer, this is how to generate your own key cert for Quarkus:

1. Go to *src/main/resources*.
2. Execute the following command:
   ```
   keytool -genkey -keyalg RSA -alias selfsigned \
       -keystore keystore.jks -storepass changeit \
       -validity 360 -keysize 2048
   ```

See Also

To learn about how to generate certificates, key stores, and trust stores, see the following web page:

- Oracle: Java Platform, Standard Edition Tools Reference: `keytool` (*https://oreil.ly/ mwOSH*)

CHAPTER 4

Configuration

In this chapter, you'll learn the following about setting configuration parameters:

- How to configure a Quarkus service
- How to inject configuration parameters in the service
- How to apply values depending on the environment
- How to correctly configure the logging system
- How to create customizations for the configuration system

4.1 Configuring the Application with Custom Properties

Problem

You want to configure the Quarkus application with custom properties.

Solution

Quarkus makes use of a number of the Eclipse MicroProfile specifications. One of those is the Configuration specification; however, to simplify configuration, Quarkus uses just one file for all configurations, *application.properties*, which must be placed in the root of the classpath.

This file can be used to configure Quarkus properties such as logging or default path, Quarkus extensions like data source or Kafka, or custom properties that you define for the application. You are going to see all of them in the book, but in this recipe, you'll see the latter one.

Open the *src/main/resources/application.properties* file and add the following property:

```
greeting.message=Hello World
```

You can inject the property value defined in *application.properties* by using the `org.eclipse.microprofile.config.inject.ConfigProperty` annotation in a field.

Open `org.acme.quickstart.GreetingResource.java` and inject `greeting.message` property value:

```
@ConfigProperty(name = "greeting.message") ❶
String message; ❷

@GET
@Produces(MediaType.TEXT_PLAIN)
public String hello() {
    return message; ❸
}
```

❶ Injects the value of `greeting.message` property

❷ Places fields in package-protected scope

❸ Returns the configured value

> For performance reasons when using GraalVM and reflection, we encourage you to use *protected-package* scope on fields that will be injected at runtime. You can read more about it in the Quarkus CDI Reference Guide (*https://oreil.ly/8e1Sd*).

In a new terminal window, make a request to `/hello` to see that the output message is the configured value in *application.properties*:

```
curl http://localhost:8080/hello
```

```
Hello World
```

If you want to make a configuration field not mandatory and provide a default value, you can use the `defaultValue` attribute of `@ConfigProperty` annotation.

Open the `org.acme.quickstart.GreetingResource.java` file and inject the `greeting.upper-case` property value:

```
@ConfigProperty(name = "greeting.upper-case",
                defaultValue = "true") ❶
boolean upperCase;
@GET
@Path("/optional")
```

```
@Produces(MediaType.TEXT_PLAIN)
public String helloOptional() {
    return upperCase ? message.toUpperCase() : message;
}
```

❶ Sets the default of `greeting.upper-case` property to true

And in a terminal window, make a request to /hello/optional to see that the output message is in upper case:

```
curl http://localhost:8080/hello/optional
```

```
HELLO WORLD
```

Multivalue properties are supported—you need to define only the field type as one of Arrays, `java.util.List` or `java.util.Set`, depending on your requirements/preference. The delimiter for the property value is a comma (,) and the escape character is the backslash (\\).

Open the *src/main/resources/application.properties* file and add the following property with three values:

```
greeting.suffix=!!, How are you???
```

Open *org.acme.quickstart.GreetingResource.java* and inject `greeting.suffix` property values:

```
@ConfigProperty(name = "greeting.suffix")
List<String> suffixes;
@GET
@Path("/list")
@Produces(MediaType.TEXT_PLAIN)
public String helloList() {
    return message + suffixes.get(1);
}
```

And in a terminal window make a request to /hello/list to see that the output message contains the second suffix:

```
curl http://localhost:8080/hello/list
```

```
Hello World How are you?
```

The YAML format is also supported for configuring the application. In this case, the file is named *application.yaml* or *application.yml*.

To start using the YAML configuration file, you need to add the config-yaml extension:

```
./mvnw quarkus:add-extension -Dextensions="config-yaml"
```

Given the following configuration file using the `properties` format:

```
greeting.message=Hello World

%staging.quarkus.http.port=8182

quarkus.http.cors=true
quarkus.http.cors.methods=GET,PUT,POST
```

The equivalent in YAML format follows:

```
greeting:
  message: Hello World ❶
  "%staging": ❷
    quarkus:
      http:
        port: 8182
quarkus:
  http:
    cors:
      ~: true ❸
      methods: GET,PUT,POST
```

❶ Simple properties are set as a structure

❷ Profiles are supported wrapped in quotation marks

❸ When there are subkeys the ~ is used to refer to the unprefixed part

Discussion

Eclipse MicroProfile Configuration comes with the following built-in converters to map a configuration value into a Java object:

- `boolean` and `java.lang.Boolean`; the values for true are `true`, `1`, `YES`, `Y`, and `ON`, while any other value is considered `false`
- `byte` and `java.lang.Byte`
- `short` and `java.lang.Short`
- `int` and `java.lang.Integer`
- `long` and `java.lang.Long`
- `float` and `java.lang.Float`
- `double` and `java.lang.Double`
- `char` and `java.lang.Character`
- `java.lang.Class` based on the result of the call of `Class.forName`

If a built-in converter or custom converter does not exist, then the following methods are checked in the target object. If a built-in converter or custom converter *does* exist, the discovered/found method is used to instantiate the converter object and the string argument is passed for conversion:

- Target type has `public static T of(String)` method
- Target type has `public static T valueOf(String)` method
- Target type has public constructor with a `String` parameter
- Target type has `public static T parse(CharSequence)` method

4.2 Accessing Configuration Properties Programmatically

Problem

You want to access configuration properties programmatically instead of injecting them using the `org.eclipse.microprofile.config.inject.ConfigProperty` annotation.

Solution

Inject the `org.eclipse.microprofile.config.Config` class in the object for which you want to access properties programmatically.

The Eclipse MicroProfile Configuration spec allows you to inject `org.eclipse.micro profile.config.Config` to get properties programmatically instead of injecting directly with `ConfigProperty`.

Open `org.acme.quickstart.GreetingResource.java` and inject `Config` class:

```
@Inject ❶
Config config;
@GET
@Path("/config")
@Produces(MediaType.TEXT_PLAIN)
public String helloConfig() {
    config.getPropertyNames().forEach( p -> System.out.println(p)); ❷

    return config.getValue("greeting.message", String.class); ❸
}
```

❶ Use `Inject` CDI annotation to inject the instance

❷ You can now access the list of properties

❸ Property needs to be cast to final type

You can access the `Config` class without using CDI by calling `ConfigProvider.get Config()` method.

4.3 Overwriting Configuration Values Externally

Problem

You want to overwrite any configuration value at runtime.

Solution

You can overwrite any property at runtime by setting it as a system property or environment variable.

Quarkus lets you overwrite any configuration property by setting a configuration as a system property (`-Dproperty.name=value`) and/or as an environment variable (`export PROPERTY_NAME=value`). System properties have more priority than environment variables.

Examples of externalizing these properties can be a database URL, username, or password because they are known only in the target environment. But you need to know that there is a trade-off because the more runtime properties are available, the less build time prework Quarkus can do.

Let's package the application used in Recipe 4.1 and override the `greeting.message` property by setting a system property:

```
./mvnw clean package -DskipTests
```

```
java -Dgreeting.message=Aloha -jar target/getting-started-1.0-SNAPSHOT-runner.jar
```

In a new terminal window, validate that the property has been overridden from `Hello World` to `Aloha` by running:

```
curl localhost:8080/hello
```

```
Aloha
```

In the case of environment variables, three naming conventions for a given property name are supported. This is because some operating systems allow only alphabetic characters and underscores (_) but no other characters, like dots (.). To support all possible cases, the following rules are used:

1. Exactly match (`greeting.message`).

2. Replace nonalphanumeric characters to underscore (`greeting_message`).

3. Replace nonalphanumeric characters to underscore and convert the rest to upper case (`GREETING_MESSAGE`).

Here is the *application.properties* file:

```
greeting.message=Hello World
```

You can override its value using any of the following environment variable names because all of them are equivalent:

```
export greeting.message=Aloha
export greeting_message=Aloha
export GREETING_MESSAGE=Aloha
```

There is also a special place where you can put the *application.properties* file outside the application itself, inside a directory named *config* where the application runs. Any runtime properties defined in that file will override the default configuration.

 config/application.properties works in development mode as well, but you need to add it on your build tool output directory to make it work (in case of the Maven, the *target* directory; in case of Gradle, *build*), so you need to be aware of the need to re-create it when running the `clean` task.

Apart from environment variables and the *application.properties* file, you can also place a *.env* file in the current working directory to override configuration values, following the environment variables format (`GREETING_MESSAGE=Aloha`).

4.4 Configuring with Profiles

Problem

You want to overwrite configuration values depending on the environment in which you are running Quarkus.

Solution

Quarkus supports the notion of configuration profiles. These allow you to have multiple configuration values for the same property in the same file and enable different values to suit the environment in which you are running the service.

The syntax for configuration profiles is `%{profile}.config.key=value`.

Discuss

Quarkus comes with three built-in profiles.

dev

Activated when in development mode (i.e., `quarkus:dev`).

test

Activated when running tests.

prod

The default profile when not running in development or test mode; you don't need to set it in *application.properties*, as it is implicitly set.

Open *src/main/resources/application.properties* file and set to start Quarkus at port 8181 in development mode:

```
%dev.quarkus.http.port=8181
```

After this change, start the service to again check that the listening port is 8181 instead of the default one (8080):

```
./mvnw compile quarkus:dev

INFO  [io.qua.dep.QuarkusAugmentor] (main) Beginning quarkus augmentation
INFO  [io.qua.dep.QuarkusAugmentor] (main) Quarkus augmentation completed
    in 671ms
INFO  [io.quarkus] (main) Quarkus 1.4.1 started in 1.385s. Listening on:
    http://0.0.0.0:8181
INFO  [io.quarkus] (main) Profile dev activated. Live Coding activated.
INFO  [io.quarkus] (main) Installed features:
    [cdi, hibernate-validator, resteasy]
```

Notice that now the listening address is *http://0.0.0.0:8181* instead of the default one.

Finally, rollback to 8080 port, remove `%dev.quarkus.http.port=8181` line in *application.properties* to align with the port that is used in the rest of the book.

4.5 Changing Logger Configuration

Problem

You want to change the default logging configuration.

Solution

Quarkus uses a unified configuration model in which all configuration properties are placed in the same file. In the case of Quarkus, this file is *application.properties*, and you can configure many aspects of logging there.

For example, if you want to change the logging level, you just set `quarkus.log.level` to the minimum log level.

Open *src/main/resources/application.properties* and add the following content:

```
quarkus.log.level=DEBUG
```

Now start the application to see that a lot of new logging messages are printed in the console:

```
./mvnw compile quarkus:dev


...
[INFO] --- quarkus-maven-plugin:0.22.0:dev (default-cli) @ getting-started ---
Listening for transport dt_socket at address: 5005
DEBUG [org.jbo.logging] (main) Logging Provider: \
    org.jboss.logging.JBossLogManagerProvider
INFO  [io.qua.dep.QuarkusAugmentor] (main) Beginning quarkus augmentation
DEBUG [io.qua.run.con.ConverterSupport] (main) Populate SmallRye config builder
    with converter for class java.net.InetSocketAddress of priority 200
DEBUG [io.qua.run.con.ConverterSupport] (main) Populate SmallRye config builder
    with converter for class org.wildfly.common.net.CidrAddress of priority 200
```

We had to span multiple lines for formatting in the book; we have used the backslash to indicate this.

You can also enable storing logs in a file by using `quarkus.log.file.enable` property. The output is written by default to a file named *quarkus.log*:

```
quarkus.log.file.enable=true
```

While you are in development and working out of the source directory, your logging file will be in *target* directory.

4.6 Adding Application Logs

Problem

You want to add log lines to your application.

Solution

Most of the time, your applications need to write their own logging messages and not rely solely on the default logs provided by Quarkus. Applications may use any of the supported APIs for logging, and the logs will be merged.

Quarkus supports these logging libraries:

- JDK java.util.logging
- JBoss logging
- SLF4J
- Apache Commons Logging

Let's see how to use JBoss Logging to log content. Open org.acme.quickstart.Gree tingResource.java and log a message when an special endpoint is called:

```
private static org.jboss.logging.Logger logger =
                org.jboss.logging.Logger.getLogger(GreetingResource.class); ❶

@GET
@Path("/log") ❷
@Produces(MediaType.TEXT_PLAIN)
public String helloLog() {
    logger.info("I said Hello"); ❸
    return "hello";
}
```

❶ Creates the logger instance

❷ Endpoint subpath is */log*

❸ Logs at info level

Now start the application:

```
./mvnw compile quarkus:dev
```

In a new terminal, window make a request to /hello/log:

```
curl http://localhost:8080/hello/log
```

If you inspect the terminal where you started Quarkus, you'll see the next logline:

```
INFO  [org.acm.qui.GreetingResource] (executor-thread-1) I said Hello
```

Discussion

Logging is done on a per-category basis. A configuration that applies to a category also applies to all subcategories of that category, unless there is a more specific matching subcategory configuration.

Categories are represented by class location (i.e., the package, or subpackages, where they are defined). For example, if you want to set Undertow security logging to trace level, you need to set the quarkus.log.category."io.under tow.request.security".level=TRACE property in *application.properties*.

Following the previous example, let's restrict log lines from classes residing in `org.acme.quickstart` (and subclasses) so the minimum log level is `WARNING`:

```
quarkus.log.category."org.acme.quickstart".level=WARNING ❶
```

❶ Double quotes are mandatory to set the category

If you repeat the request to *http://localhost:8080/hello/log*, logline is no longer written down.

4.7 Advanced Logging

Problem

You want to centrally log all your services.

Solution

When working with microservice architectures and Kubernetes, logging is an important thing to take into consideration because each service is logging individually; but as a developer or operator, you might want to have all the logs centralized in one place so they can be consumed as a whole.

Quarkus logging also supports JSON and GELF output.

These logs can be written in JSON format instead of plain text for machine processing by registering the `logging-json` extension:

```
./mvnw quarkus:add-extension -Dextensions="logging-json"
```

Use the GELF extension to produce logs in GELF format and send them using either TCP or UDP.

Graylog extended log format (GELF) is understood by three of the most centralized logs systems that are used nowadays:

- Graylog (MongoDB, Elasticsearch, Graylog)
- ELK (Elasticsearch, Logstash, Kibana)
- EFK (Elasticsearch, Fluentd, Kibana)

To start logging in GELF format, all you need to do is add the `logging-gelf` extension:

```
./mvnw quarkus:add-extension -Dextensions="logging-gelf"
```

Logging code is not changing, so the same interfaces are used:

```
private static org.jboss.logging.Logger logger =
        org.jboss.logging.Logger.getLogger(GreetingResource.class); ❶
```

```
@GET
@Path("/log") ❷
@Produces(MediaType.TEXT_PLAIN)
public String helloLog() {
    logger.info("I said Hello"); ❸
    return "hello";
}
```

❶ Creates the logger instance

❷ Endpoint subpath is */log*

❸ Logs at `info` level

The GELF handler must be configured in *application.properties*:

```
quarkus.log.handler.gelf.enabled=true ❶
quarkus.log.handler.gelf.host=localhost ❷
quarkus.log.handler.gelf.port=12201 ❸
```

❶ Enables extension

❷ Sets host where log messages are sent

❸ Sets the endpoint port

> If you are using Logstash (ELK), you need to enable the Input plug-in that understands the GELF format:
>
> ```
> input {
>   gelf {
>     port => 12201
>   }
> }
> output {
>   stdout {}
>   elasticsearch {
>     hosts => ["http://elasticsearch:9200"]
>   }
> }
> ```

If you are using Fluentd (EFK), you need to enable the Input plug-in that understands the GELF format:

```
<source>
  type gelf
  tag example.gelf
  bind 0.0.0.0
  port 12201
</source>

<match example.gelf>
  @type elasticsearch
  host elasticsearch
  port 9200
  logstash_format true
</match>
```

Discussion

Quarkus logging also supports syslog format by default without the requirement of adding any extension. Syslog format can be used in Fluentd as an alternative to GELF format in Quarkus:

```
quarkus.log.syslog.enable=true
quarkus.log.syslog.endpoint=localhost:5140
quarkus.log.syslog.protocol=udp
quarkus.log.syslog.app-name=quarkus
quarkus.log.syslog.hostname=quarkus-test
```

You need to enable the Input plug-in that understands the syslog format in Fluentd:

```
<source>
  @type syslog
  port 5140
  bind 0.0.0.0
  message_format rfc5424
  tag system
</source>

<match **>
  @type elasticsearch
  host elasticsearch
  port 9200
  logstash_format true
</match>
```

If you are using Kubernetes, the simplest way to log is to log to the console and install into the cluster a central log manager that collects all log lines.

See Also

To learn more about advanced logging topics, visit the following website:

- Logstash/Gelf Loggers (*https://oreil.ly/Mj9Ha*)

4.8 Configuring with Custom Profiles

Problem

You want to set different configuration values for the custom profiles you've created.

Solution

So far, you've seen that Quarkus comes with built-in profiles so that you can set different configuration values for the same property and enable them to suit the environment. But with Quarkus, you can also set your own profiles.

The only thing you need to do is specify which profile you want to enable by either using the `quarkus.profile` system property or the `QUARKUS_PROFILE` environment variable. If both are set, the system property takes precedence over the environment variable.

Then the only thing you need to do is create the property with the profile name and set the current profile to that name. Let's create a new *staging* profile that overwrites the listening port of Quarkus.

Open *src/main/resources/application.properties* file and set to start Quarkus at port 8182 when the `staging` profile is enabled:

```
%staging.quarkus.http.port=8182
```

Then start the application with `staging` profile enabled:

```
./mvnw -Dquarkus.profile=staging compile quarkus:dev

INFO  [io.qua.dep.QuarkusAugmentor] (main) Beginning quarkus augmentation
INFO  [io.qua.dep.QuarkusAugmentor] (main) Quarkus augmentation completed
    in 640ms
INFO  [io.quarkus] (main) Quarkus 0.23.2 started in 1.300s. Listening on:
    http://0.0.0.0:8182
INFO  [io.quarkus] (main) Profile staging activated. Live Coding activated.
INFO  [io.quarkus] (main) Installed features: [cdi, hibernate-validator,
    resteasy]
```

In this case, the system property approach is used, but you could also set it using the `QUARKUS_PROFILE` environment variable.

Discussion

If you want to set the running profile in tests, you only need to set the `quar kus.test.profile` system property to the given profile in your build script—for example, in Maven:

```
<groupId>org.apache.maven.plugins</groupId>
<artifactId>maven-surefire-plugin</artifactId>
<version>${surefire-plugin.version}</version>
<configuration>
    <systemPropertyVariables>
        <quarkus.test.profile>foo</quarkus.test.profile>
        <buildDirectory>${project.build.directory}</buildDirectory>
    </systemPropertyVariables>
</configuration>
```

or, in Gradle:

```
test {
    useJUnitPlatform()
    systemProperty "quarkus.test.profile", "foo"
}
```

Also, you can change the default production profile. The built-in profile in Quarkus is `prod`, so when you are running your application without any profile, this is the default one where the values are taken. But you can change that at build time so that, without specifying any profile, your profile is the default one when the application is running.

The only thing you need to do is build the application using the `quarkus.profile` system property with the profile value you want set as the default:

```
./mvnw package -Pnative -Dquarkus.profile=prod-kubernetes`
./target/getting-started-1.0-runner ❶
```

❶ The command will run with the `prod-kubernetes` profile enabled by default

4.9 Creating Custom Sources

Problem

You want to load configuration parameters from any other source instead of/apart from *application.properties* file.

Solution

Quarkus uses the Eclipse MicroProfile Configuration spec to implement all the logic regarding configuration. The specification offers `org.eclipse.microprofile .config.spi.ConfigSource` Java SPI (*https://oreil.ly/o0A51*) interface to implement a custom way to load configuration properties instead of/apart from the default one provided by Quarkus.

For example, you could load configuration properties from a database, an XML file, or a REST API.

Let's create a simple *in-memory config source* that gets configuration properties from `Map` populated at instantiation time. Create a new class called `org.acme.quick start.InMemoryConfigSource.java`:

```java
package org.acme.quickstart;

import java.util.HashMap;
import java.util.Map;

import org.eclipse.microprofile.config.spi.ConfigSource;

public class InMemoryConfigSource implements ConfigSource {

    private Map<String, String> prop = new HashMap<>();

    public InMemoryConfigSource() {  ❶
        prop.put("greeting.color", "red");
    }

    @Override
    public int getOrdinal() {  ❷
        return 500;
    }

    @Override
    public Map<String, String> getProperties() {  ❸
        return prop;
    }

    @Override
    public String getValue(String propertyName) {  ❹
        return prop.get(propertyName);
    }

    @Override
    public String getName() {  ❺
        return "MemoryConfigSource";
    }

}
```

❶ Populates map with a property

❷ Used to determine the importance of the values; the highest ordinal takes precedence over the lower-priority ordinal

❸   Gets all properties as Map; in this case it is direct

❹   Gets the value for a single property

❺   Returns the name of this config source

Then you need to register this as a Java SPI. Create the *services* folder at *src/main/resources/META-INF*. Next, create a file inside *services* named *org.eclipse.micropro-file.config.spi.ConfigSource* with the following content:

```
org.acme.quickstart.InMemoryConfigSource
```

Finally, you can modify the `org.acme.quickstart.GreetingResource.java` class to inject this property:

```
@ConfigProperty(name = "greeting.color") ❶
String color;

@GET
@Path("/color")
@Produces(MediaType.TEXT_PLAIN)
public String color() {
    return color;
}
```

❶   Inject the value of the property defined in the `InMemoryConfigSource`

And in a terminal window make a request to `/hello/color` to see that the output message is the configured value in the custom source:

```
curl http://localhost:8080/hello/color

red
```

Discussion

Each `ConfigSource` has a specified ordinal, which is used to set the importance of the values taken from the `ConfigSource` in the case of multiple config sources defined for the same application. A higher ordinal `ConfigSource` is used over a `ConfigSource` with a lower value. Using the defaults in the following list as a reference, a system property will be used over everything, and the *application.properties* file in the *src/main/resources* directory will be used if no other `ConfigSources` are found:

- System properties to 400
- Environment variables to 300

- *application.properties* at *config* directory to 260
- *application.properties* at project to 250

4.10 Creating Custom Converters

Problem

You want to implement a custom converter.

Solution

You can convert a property from `String` to any kind of object by implementing the `org.eclipse.microprofile.config.spi.Converter` Java SPI.

Quarkus uses the Eclipse MicroProfile Configuration spec to implement all the logic regarding configuration. The specification offers the `org.eclipse.micropro file.config.spi.Converter` Java SPI (*https://oreil.ly/kcqQw*) interface to implement the conversion of configuration values to a custom type.

For example, you could transform a percentage value (i.e., 15%) to a `Percentage` type, wrapping the percentage as `double` type.

Create a new POJO class `org.acme.quickstart.Percentage.java`:

```
package org.acme.quickstart;

public class Percentage {

    private double percentage;

    public Percentage(double percentage) {
        this.percentage = percentage;
    }

    public double getPercentage() {
        return percentage;
    }

}
```

And then create a class `org.acme.quickstart.PercentageConverter.java` that converts from `String` representation to `Percentage`:

```
package org.acme.quickstart;

import javax.annotation.Priority;

import org.eclipse.microprofile.config.spi.Converter;
```

```
@Priority(300) ❶
public class PercentageConverter implements Converter<Percentage> { ❷

    @Override
    public Percentage convert(String value) {

        String numeric = value.substring(0, value.length() - 1);
        return new Percentage (Double.parseDouble(numeric) / 100);

    }

}
```

❶ Sets the priority; in this specific case it might be optional

❷ Generic type that sets the type to convert to

Then you need to register this as a Java SPI. Create the *services* folder at *src/main/resources/META-INF*. Next, create a file inside the *services* folder named *org.eclipse.microprofile.config.spi.Converter* with the following content:

```
org.acme.quickstart.PercentageConverter
```

Then, you can modify the `org.acme.quickstart.GreetingResource.java` class to inject this property:

```
@ConfigProperty(name = "greeting.vat")
Percentage vat;

@GET
@Path("/vat")
@Produces(MediaType.TEXT_PLAIN)
public String vat() {
    return Double.toString(vat.getPercentage());
}
```

Lastly, you will need to add a new property into the *application.properties* file in your *src/main/resources* directory:

```
greeting.vat = 21%
```

And in a terminal window, make a request to `/hello/vat` to see that the output message is the transformed vat as double:

```
curl http://localhost:8080/hello/vat

0.21
```

Discussion

By default, if no @Priority annotation can be found on a converter, it is registered with a priority of 100. Quarkus converters are registered with a priority of 200, so if you want to replace a Quarkus converter, you should use a higher value; if you don't need to replace a Quarkus converter, then the default one is perfectly fine.

A list of Quarkus core converters has been shown in Recipe 4.1.

4.11 Grouping Configuration Values

Problem

You want to avoid setting the common prefix of a configuration property over and over again.

Solution

You can group common properties (those with the same prefix) using the @io .quarkus.arc.config.ConfigProperties annotation.

When you are creating ad hoc configuration properties in your application, typically these properties will have the same prefix (i.e., greetings). To inject all these properties, you can use the @ConfigProperty annotation (as shown in Recipe 4.1), or you can use the io.quarkus.arc.config.ConfigProperties annotation to group properties together.

Using the *application.properties* file:

```
greeting.message=Hello World
greeting.suffix=!!, How are you???
```

let's implement a class that maps the configuration properties into Java objects using the io.quarkus.arc.config.ConfigProperties annotation. Create a new class org.acme.quickstart.GreetingConfiguration.java:

```
package org.acme.quickstart;

import java.util.List;
import java.util.Optional;

import javax.validation.constraints.Max;
import javax.validation.constraints.Min;

import io.quarkus.arc.config.ConfigProperties;

@ConfigProperties(prefix = "greeting") ❶
public class GreetingConfiguration {
```

```
    public String message;  ❷
    public String suffix = "!";  ❸
}
```

❶ Sets this as a configuration POJO with a common prefix

❷ Maps the `greeting.message` property

❸ The default value for `greeting.suffix` in case the property is not set

One of the important things to notice in the preceding code is that the `prefix` attribute is not mandatory. If it is not set, then the prefix to be used will be determined by the class name (removing the suffix part `Configuration`). In this case, the `prefix` attribute could be auto-resolved to `greeting`.

Then you can inject this configuration POJO to start consuming the configuration values.

You can modify the `org.acme.quickstart.GreetingResource.java` class to inject this class:

```
@Inject  ❶
GreetingConfiguration greetingConfiguration;

@GET
@Path("/configurations")
@Produces(MediaType.TEXT_PLAIN)
public String helloConfigurations() {
    return greetingConfiguration.message + greetingConfiguration.suffix;
}
```

❶ The configuration is injected with the CDI `@Inject` annotation

And in a terminal window make a request to `/hello/configurations` to see that the configuration values are populated inside Java, for instance:

```
curl http://localhost:8080/hello/configurations

Hello World!!, How are you???
```

As you can now see, you don't need to annotate every field by using `@ConfigProperty` —you just leverage the class definition to get the property name or the default value.

Discussion

Furthermore, Quarkus supports nested object configuration so that you can also map subcategories by using inner classes.

Suppose we add a new property named `greeting.output.recipients` in *application.properties*:

```
greeting.output.recipients=Ada,Alexandra
```

You could use an inner class to map it into the configuration object. Modify the class
`org.acme.quickstart.GreetingConfiguration.java`. Then add a new inner class
representing the subcategory `output` and register it as a field:

```
public OutputConfiguration output; ❶

public static class OutputConfiguration {
    public List<String> recipients;
}
```

❶ Name of the subcategory is the field name (`output`)

Then you can access the `greetingConfiguration.output.recipients` field to get
the value. You can also annotate the fields with Bean Validation annotations to validate at start-up time that all configuration values are valid. If they are not valid, the
application will fail to start and will indicate the validation errors in the log.

4.12 Validating Configuration Values

Problem

You want to validate that configuration values are correct.

Solution

Use the Bean Validation specification to validate that a property value is valid when it
is injected using the `@ConfigProperty` annotation on a class.

The Bean Validation spec allows you to set constraints on objects using annotations.
Quarkus integrates the Eclipse MicroProfile Configuration spec with the Bean Validation spec so you can use them together to validate that a configuration value meets
certain criteria. This verification is executed at boot time, and if there is any violation,
an error message is shown in the console and the boot process is aborted.

The first thing you need to do is to register the *Quarkus Bean Validation* dependency.
You can do it manually by editing your *pom.xml* or by running the next Maven command from the root directory of the project:

```
./mvnw quarkus:add-extension -Dextensions="quarkus-hibernate-validator"
```

After that, you will need to create a configuration object, which you learned about in
the previous recipe. In the next example, a constraint on the `greeting.repeat` configuration property is set so that repetitions outside of the range 1–3 inclusive cannot
be set.

To validate integer range, the following Bean Validation annotations are used: `javax.validation.constraints.Max` and `javax.validation.constraints.Min`. Open `org.acme.quickstart.GreetingConfiguration.java` and add Bean Validation annotations:

```
@Min(1) ❶
@Max(3) ❷
public Integer repeat;
```

❶ Min value accepted

❷ Max value accepted

Open *src/main/resources/application.properties* file and set the `greeting.repeat` configuration property to 7:

```
greeting.repeat=7
```

Start the application, and you'll see an error message notifying that a configuration value is violating one of the defined constraints:

```
./mvnw compile quarkus:dev
```

Discussion

In this example, you've seen a brief introduction to Bean Validation specification, as well as some annotations you can use to validate fields. However, more constraints are supported by Hibernate Validation and the Bean Validation implementation used, such as `@Digits`, `@Email`, `@NotNull`, and `@NotBlank`.

CHAPTER 5

Programming Model

In this chapter, you'll learn about topics related to the programming model of Quarkus. Quarkus is unique in the programming model it follows. Unlike some other frameworks, Quarkus allows you to mix and match both an imperative model, using CDI, and a reactive model, using SmallRye Mutiny. Chapter 15 is dedicated to using the reactive approach. At times, you may find yourself needing both approaches, so it is good to know how to utilize each.

In this chapter, we're focusing on the imperative model, so you'll learn the following:

- How to marshal/unmarshal JSON and XML documents
- How to validate request parameters
- How to use the CDI spec as a context and dependency injection solution
- How to write tests for a Quarkus service

5.1 Marshalling/Unmarshalling JSON

Problem

You want to marshall/unmarshall JSON documents to/from Java objects.

Solution

Use the JSON-B specification or Jackson project to marshall and unmarshall JSON documents from/to Java objects.

When you are creating a REST API, you *usually* use JSON as a data format to exchange information. So far, you've seen examples of returning only simple plain-text responses; but in this recipe, you'll learn how to start using JSON as the data format for the body of the request and as a response.

The first thing you need to do is register the *JSON-B* extension in the *pom.xml*. Open a terminal window, and from the root directory of the project run the following:

```
./mvnw quarkus:add-extension -Dextensions="quarkus-resteasy-jsonb"

[INFO] --- quarkus-maven-plugin:1.4.1.Final:add-extension (default-cli)
        @ custom-config ---
✓ Adding extension io.quarkus:quarkus-resteasy-jsonb
```

This effectively adds io.quarkus:quarkus-resteasy-jsonb into the build tool.

> In Gradle, you can use ./gradlew addExtension
> --extensions="quarkus-resteasy-jsonb" to add the extension.

The next step is to create a developer class that will be marshalled and unmarshalled in the endpoint. Create a new class named org.acme.quickstart.Developer.java:

```
package org.acme.quickstart;

public class Developer {

    private String name;
    private String favoriteLanguage;
    private int age;

    public String getName() {
        return name;
    }

    public void setName(String name) {
        this.name = name;
    }

    public String getFavoriteLanguage() {
        return favoriteLanguage;
    }

    public void setFavoriteLanguage(String favoriteLanguage) {
        this.favoriteLanguage = favoriteLanguage;
    }

    public int getAge() {
        return age;
    }
```

```
    public void setAge(int age) {
        this.age = age;
    }

}
```

Finally, you can create a Rest API endpoint for implementing developer operations. Create a new class named org.acme.quickstart.DeveloperResource.java:

```java
package org.acme.quickstart;

import java.util.ArrayList;
import java.util.List;

import javax.ws.rs.Consumes;
import javax.ws.rs.GET;
import javax.ws.rs.POST;
import javax.ws.rs.Path;
import javax.ws.rs.Produces;
import javax.ws.rs.core.MediaType;
import javax.ws.rs.core.Response;

@Path("/developer")
public class DeveloperResource {

    private static final List<Developer> developers = new ArrayList<>();

    @POST
    @Consumes(MediaType.APPLICATION_JSON)
    public Response addDeveloper(Developer developer) {
        developers.add(developer);
        return Response.ok().build();
    }

    @GET
    @Produces(MediaType.APPLICATION_JSON)
    public List<Developer> getDevelopers() {
        return developers;
    }
}
```

Try it by opening a new terminal window, starting the Quarkus application, and sending requests for POST and GET methods:

```
./mvnw clean compile quarkus:dev

curl -d '{"name":"Alex","age":39, "favoriteLanguage":"java"}' \
  -H "Content-Type: application/json" -X POST http://localhost:8080/developer

curl localhost:8080/developer
[{"age":39,"favoriteLanguage":"java","name":"Alex"}]
```

Notice that each Java field is mapped directly to a JSON field. If you want to change that, you can use the `javax.json.bind.annotation.JsonbProperty` annotation to set a different mapping name:

```
@JsonbProperty("favorite-language")
String favoriteLanguage;
```

Discussion

You can use the Jackson project to marshall/unmarshall JSON documents to/from Java objects instead of JSON-B as well. You need to register the `Jackson-Extension` to use it as a JSON solution:

```
./mvnw quarkus:add-extension -Dextensions="quarkus-resteasy-jackson"
```

By default, a `com.fasterxml.jackson.databind.ObjectMapper` is provided, but you can provide a custom `ObjectMapper` using CDI:

```
package org.acme.quickstart;

import com.fasterxml.jackson.databind.ObjectMapper;
import io.quarkus.jackson.ObjectMapperCustomizer;
import javax.inject.Singleton;

@Singleton
public class RegisterCustomModuleCustomizer
    implements ObjectMapperCustomizer {

    public void customize(ObjectMapper mapper) {
        objectMapper.configure(
            DeserializationFeature.FAIL_ON_NULL_FOR_PRIMITIVES, false);
    }
}
```

See Also

You can learn more about JSON-B and Jackson at the following web pages:

- Jakarta JSON Binding (JSON-B) (*http://json-b.net*)
- Jackson Project Home @GitHub (*https://oreil.ly/U3hwH*)

5.2 Marshalling/Unmarshalling XML

Problem

You want to marshall/unmarshall XML documents to/from Java objects.

Solution

Use the JAX-B specification to marshall and unmarshall XML documents from/to Java objects.

When you are creating a REST API, you might want to use XML as a data format to exchange information. So far, you've seen how to do it in JSON format, but in this section, you'll learn how to start using XML as the data format for the body of the request and as a response.

The first thing you need to do is register the JAX-B extension in the *pom.xml*. Open a terminal window, and from the root directory of the project run the following:

```
./mvnw quarkus:add-extension -Dextensions="quarkus-resteasy-jaxb"

[INFO] --- quarkus-maven-plugin:1.4.1.Final:add-extension (default-cli)
    @ custom-config ---
✔ Adding extension io.quarkus:quarkus-resteasy-jaxb
```

This effectively adds `io.quarkus:quarkus-resteasy-jaxb` into the build tool.

> In Gradle, you can use `./gradlew addExtension --extensions="quarkus-resteasy-jaxb"` to add the extension.

The next step is to create a `computer` class that will be marshalled and unmarshalled in the endpoint. Create a new class named `org.acme.quickstart.Computer.java`:

```java
package org.acme.quickstart;

import javax.xml.bind.annotation.XmlRootElement;

@XmlRootElement ❶
public class Computer {

    private String brand;
    private String serialNumber;

    public String getBrand() {
        return brand;
    }

    public void setBrand(String brand) {
        this.brand = brand;
    }

    public String getSerialNumber() {
        return serialNumber;
    }
}
```

```
    public void setSerialNumber(String serialNumber) {
        this.serialNumber = serialNumber;
    }

}
```

❶ XmlRootElement sets this as XML document

Finally, you can create a REST API endpoint for implementing computer operations. Create a new class named org.acme.quickstart.ComputerResource.java:

```
package org.acme.quickstart;

import java.util.ArrayList;
import java.util.List;

import javax.ws.rs.Consumes;
import javax.ws.rs.GET;
import javax.ws.rs.POST;
import javax.ws.rs.Path;
import javax.ws.rs.Produces;
import javax.ws.rs.core.MediaType;
import javax.ws.rs.core.Response;

@Path("/computer")
public class ComputerResource {

    private static final List<Computer> computers = new ArrayList<>();

    @POST
    @Consumes(MediaType.APPLICATION_XML)
    public Response addComputer(Computer computer) {
        computers.add(computer);
        return Response.ok().build();
    }

    @GET
    @Produces(MediaType.APPLICATION_XML)
    public List<Computer> getComputers() {
        return computers;
    }

}
```

Try it by opening a new terminal window, starting the Quarkus application, and sending requests for POST and GET methods:

```
./mvnw clean compile quarkus:dev

curl \
    -d '<computer><brand>iMac</brand>
```

```
        <serialNumber>111-111-111</serialNumber></computer>'
    -H "Content-Type: application/xml" -X POST http://localhost:8080/computer

curl localhost:8080/computer
<?xml version="1.0" encoding="UTF-8" standalone="yes"?><collection><computer>
<brand>iMac</brand><serialNumber>111-111-111</serialNumber>
</computer></collection>
```

Discussion

Apart from @XmlRootElement, there are other important annotations in the JAX-B spec:

@XmlRootElement
Sets the root XML document. You can also use it to set the name of the element or the namespace.

@XmlType
Defines the order in which the fields are written.

@XmlElement
Defines the actual XML element name among other attributes like namespace, nillable, or required.

@XmlAttribute
Defines the field to be mapped as an attribute instead of as an element.

@XmlTransient
Indicates fields not to be included in XML.

See Also

You can learn more about JAX-B at the following web page:

- Oracle: Lesson: Introduction to JAXB (The Java Tutorials) (*https://oreil.ly/r9FKb*)

5.3 Validating Input and Output Values

Problem

You want to validate the input and output values of your REST and business services.

Solution

Use the Bean Validation specification to add validations to your model.

Usually, your model might contain some constraints, whether or not the model is semantically valid—for example, that a `name` is not null, or an `email` is a valid email. Quarkus integrates with Bean Validation to express constraints on object models via annotations.

The first thing you need to do is register the Bean Validation extension in the *pom.xml*. Open a terminal window, and from the root directory of the project run the following:

```
./mvnw quarkus:add-extension -Dextensions="quarkus-hibernate-validator"

[INFO] --- quarkus-maven-plugin:1.4.1.Final:add-extension (default-cli)
    @ custom-config ---
✔ Adding extension io.quarkus:quarkus-resteasy-jsonb
```

This effectively adds `io.quarkus:quarkus-hibernate-validator` into the build tool.

 In Gradle, you can use `./gradlew addExtension --extensions="quarkus-hibernate-validator"` to add the extension.

The next step is to update the `developer` class and annotate it with some constraints. Open the `org.acme.quickstart.Developer.java` class and annotate some of the fields:

```
@Size(min = 4) ❶
private String name;

@NotBlank ❷
private String favoriteLanguage;
```

❶ The minimum size of the string is 4

❷ The field is mandatory

 Either of the available packages is sufficient, but if you want to use only the spec APIs, use the `javax` packages.

Finally, you need to annotate with `javax.validation.Valid` that a parameter must be verified. Open the `org.acme.quickstart.DeveloperResource.java` class and annotate the `developer` parameter:

```
@POST
@Consumes(MediaType.APPLICATION_JSON)
public Response addDeveloper(@Valid Developer developer) { ❶
    developers.add(developer);
    return Response.ok().build();
}
```

❶ @Valid is mandatory to validate the object

Try it by opening a new terminal window, starting the Quarkus application, and executing requests for the POST method:

```
./mvnw clean compile quarkus:dev

curl -d '{"name":"Ada","age":7, "favoriteLanguage":"java"}' \
    -H "Content-Type: application/json" \
    -X POST http://localhost:8080/developer -v

< HTTP/1.1 400 Bad Request
< Content-Length: 89
< validation-exception: true
< Content-Type: text/plain;charset=UTF-8

curl -d '{"name":"Alexandra","age":5, "favoriteLanguage":"java"}' \
    -H "Content-Type: application/json" \
    -X POST http://localhost:8080/developer -v

< HTTP/1.1 200 OK
< Content-Length: 0
```

It is important to note that in the first request, the name has an incorrect size, hence a 400 Bad Request HTTP code is returned. In the second request, because the request body is correct, the method works as expected.

But notice that if there is an error, the response does not contain any information about what has failed. That's fine because it is important to show the internals not directly, but in a controlled way.

Discussion

If you want to provide a better response message, you can provide an implementation of ExceptionMapper.

Create a new class named org.acme.quickstart.BeanValidationExceptionMapper.java:

```
package org.acme.quickstart;

import javax.json.Json;
import javax.json.JsonArray;
import javax.json.JsonArrayBuilder;
```

```
import javax.validation.ConstraintViolation;
import javax.validation.ConstraintViolationException;
import javax.ws.rs.core.MediaType;
import javax.ws.rs.core.Response;
import javax.ws.rs.ext.ExceptionMapper;
import javax.ws.rs.ext.Provider;

@Provider ❶
public class BeanValidationExceptionMapper
  implements ExceptionMapper<ConstraintViolationException> { ❷

    @Override
    public Response toResponse(ConstraintViolationException exception) {
      return Response.status(Response.Status.BAD_REQUEST)
        .entity(createErrorMessage(exception))
        .type(MediaType.APPLICATION_JSON)
        .build();
    }

    private JsonArray createErrorMessage(ConstraintViolationException exc) {
      JsonArrayBuilder errors = Json.createArrayBuilder(); ❸
      for (ConstraintViolation<?> violation : exc.getConstraintViolations()) { ❹
        errors.add(
            Json.createObjectBuilder() ❺
            .add("path", violation.getPropertyPath().toString())
            .add("message", violation.getMessage())
            );
      }
      return errors.build();
    }
}
```

❶ @Provider set an implementation of an extension interface discoverable by the JAX-RS runtime

❷ javax.ws.rs.ext.ExceptionMapper is used to transform an exception into a javax.ws.rs.core.Response

❸ Creates an array of constraint violations

❹ Iterates over each of the constraint violations

❺ Creates a JSON object

Now you can send a request for the POST method again:

```
curl -d '{"name":"Ada","age":7, "favoriteLanguage":"java"}' \
    -H "Content-Type: application/json" \
    -X POST http://localhost:8080/developer -v

< HTTP/1.1 400 Bad Request
```

```
< Content-Length: 90
< Content-Type: application/json

[{"path":"addDeveloper.developer.name",
  "message":"size must be between 4 and 2147483647"}]%
```

The output is now slightly different. The error code is still the same, a 400 Bad Request, but now the body content of the response contains the JSON document that we created in the exception mapper.

You can also validate the output parameters (the parameters you send back to the caller) by adding @Valid annotation in the return type:

```
@GET
@Produces(MediaType.APPLICATION_JSON)
public @Valid List<Developer> getDevelopers() {
    return developers;
}
```

Moreover, sometimes you don't want to add validation rules at the endpoint but at the business service layer. Bean Validation can be used in your business service if you're using CDI. See the following example:

```
@ApplicationScoped
public class DeveloperService {
    public void promoteDeveloper(@Valid Developer developer) {
    }
}
```

See Also

If you want to learn more about Bean Validations and what constraints are implemented by default (i.e., @Min, @Max, @AssertTrue, @Email, and so on), you can find the information at the following website:

- Jakarta Bean Validation (*https://oreil.ly/YHR_X*)

5.4 Creating Custom Validations

Problem

You want to create custom validations.

Solution

Use the Bean Validation extension model by implementing the javax.validation.ConstraintValidator interface.

Sometimes the default constraints provided by the Bean Validation specification are not enough, and you will want to implement constraints that more closely align with your business model. Bean Validation allows you to do that by creating a class that implements the `javax.validation.ConstraintValidator` interface and the annotation for annotating the field to be validated.

Let's validate that your favorite language can only be a JVM-based language. First of all, you need to create the annotation. Create a new class named `org.acme.quick start.JvmLanguage.java`:

```
package org.acme.quickstart;

import java.lang.annotation.Documented;
import java.lang.annotation.ElementType;
import java.lang.annotation.Retention;
import java.lang.annotation.RetentionPolicy;
import java.lang.annotation.Target;

import javax.validation.Constraint;
import javax.validation.Payload;

@Target({ ElementType.METHOD, ElementType.FIELD, ElementType.ANNOTATION_TYPE,
        ElementType.CONSTRUCTOR, ElementType.PARAMETER, ElementType.TYPE_USE })
@Retention(RetentionPolicy.RUNTIME)
@Documented
@Constraint(validatedBy = { JvmLanguageValidator.class}) ❶
public @interface JvmLanguage {
    String message() default "You need to provide a Jvm based-language";
    Class<?>[] groups() default { };
    Class<? extends Payload>[] payload() default { };
}
```

❶ Raises the constraint as a normal compilation error

Then you need to create the logic to detect any constraint violation. This new class must implement the `javax.validation.ConstraintValidator` interface.

Next, create a class named `org.acme.quickstart.JvmLanguageValidator.java`:

```
package org.acme.quickstart;

import java.util.Arrays;
import java.util.List;

import javax.validation.ConstraintValidator;
import javax.validation.ConstraintValidatorContext;

public class JvmLanguageValidator
    implements ConstraintValidator<JvmLanguage, String> { ❶ ❷

        private List<String> favoriteLanguages = Arrays.asList("java",
```

```
        @Override
        public boolean isValid(String value, ConstraintValidatorContext context) {
            return favoriteLanguages.stream()
                .anyMatch(l -> l.equalsIgnoreCase(value)); ❸
        }
    }
```

❶ The annotation defined in previous step

❷ The type of object that the validation applies

❸ Checks if the provided favorite language (value) is a JVM-based language

Finally, you need to annotate the favoriteLanguage field from org.acme.quick start.Developer class:

```
@JvmLanguage
@NotBlank
private String favoriteLanguage;
```

Try it by opening a new terminal window, starting the Quarkus application, and sending some requests to the POST method:

```
./mvnw clean compile quarkus:dev

curl -d '{"name":"Alexadra","age":7, "favoriteLanguage":"python"}' \
    -H "Content-Type: application/json" \
    -X POST http://localhost:8080/developer -v

< HTTP/1.1 400 Bad Request
< Content-Length: 89
< validation-exception: true
< Content-Type: text/plain;charset=UTF-8

curl -d '{"name":"Alexandra","age":5, "favoriteLanguage":"java"}' \
    -H "Content-Type: application/json" \
    -X POST http://localhost:8080/developer -v

< HTTP/1.1 200 OK
< Content-Length: 106
< Content-Type: application/json
<

[{"path":"addDeveloper.developer.favoriteLanguage",
  "message":"You need to provide a Jvm based-language"}]
```

Discussion

Any validations following the Bean Validation specification on your REST endpoints, services methods, and ultimately any CDI-scoped object will be automatically executed during the run of your application. If you need something with more control, see the next recipe, Recipe 5.5, for additional means of validating objects.

It is also good to know that, by default, constraint violation messages will be returned using the system locale. If you would like to change this, you can do so in the *application.properties* file by setting the `quarkus.default-locale` setting:

```
quarkus.default-locale=es-ES
```

For REST endpoints, the locale will be based on the `Accept-Language` HTTP header. You can specify a list of supported locales in the *application.properties* file:

```
quarkus.locales=en-US, es-ES
```

See Also

For more information, visit the following websites:

- Jakarta Bean Validation (*https://oreil.ly/R6L4d*)
- Hibernate Validator (*https://oreil.ly/O7BNR*)

5.5 Validating Objects Programmatically

Problem

You want to validate objects programmatically.

Solution

Use the Bean Validation `javax.validation.Validator` class.

In some circumstances (for example, in non-CDI beans) you want to control when the validation process is executed. For this reason, `javax.validation.Validator` class is provided.

Let's create an endpoint that validates the input using `javax.validation.Validator` instead of using a declarative way with `@Valid` annotations. Open the `org.acme.quickstart.DeveloperResource.java` class and inject `Validator` instance:

```
@Inject
Validator validator; ❶

@POST
@Path("/programmaticvalidation")
@Consumes(MediaType.APPLICATION_JSON)
@Produces(MediaType.APPLICATION_JSON)
```

```
public Response addProgrammaticValidation(Developer developer) { ❷
    Set<ConstraintViolation<Developer>> violations =
        validator.validate(developer); ❸

    if (violations.isEmpty()) { ❹
        developers.add(developer);
        return Response.ok().build();
    } else {
        JsonArrayBuilder errors = Json.createArrayBuilder();
        for (ConstraintViolation<Developer> violation : violations) { ❺
            errors.add(
                Json.createObjectBuilder()
                .add("path", violation.getPropertyPath().toString())
                .add("message", violation.getMessage())
                );
        }

        return Response.status(Response.Status.BAD_REQUEST)
                    .entity(errors.build())
                    .build();
    }
}
```

❶ Inject `Validator` class from Bean Validation spec

❷ `@Valid` is not required

❸ Validate the object programmatically

❹ If there are no errors, proceed

❺ If there are errors, then build the output

Try it by opening a new terminal window, starting the Quarkus application, and sending a request for the new POST method:

```
./mvnw clean compile quarkus:dev

curl -d '{"name":"Ada","age":7, "favoriteLanguage":"java"}' \
    -H "Content-Type: application/json" \
    -X POST http://localhost:8080/developer/programmaticvalidation -v

< HTTP/1.1 400 Bad Request
< Content-Length: 89
< validation-exception: true
< Content-Type: text/plain;charset=UTF-8
```

Discussion

Quarkus will automatically create an instance of the `javax.validation.Validator` `Factory`. You can tweak this a little by creating your own replacement beans. An instance of the following types in your application will automatically be injected into the `ValidatorFactory`:

- `javax.validation.ClockProvider`
- `javax.validation.ConstraintValidator`
- `javax.validation.ConstraintValidatorFactory`
- `javax.validation.MessageInterpolator`
- `javax.validation.ParameterNameProvider`
- `javax.validation.TraversableResolver`
- `org.hibernate.validator.spi.properties.GetterPropertySelectionStrategy`
- `org.hibernate.validator.spi.scripting.ScriptEvaluatorFactory`

You may have only one instance of a particular type in the preceding list, and classes should be declared as `@ApplicationScoped`.

5.6 Injecting Dependencies

Problem

You want to inject dependencies into your classes.

Solution

Use Contexts and Dependency Injection (CDI).

Discussion

Dependency injection (DI) in Quarkus, which is based on the Contexts and Dependency Injection 2.0 specification (*https://oreil.ly/VcDnN*), is pretty standard, with only a few modifications needed for the basic use case.

Quarkus implements most of the specification, except for some corner cases that should not affect your code. The Quarkus website maintains a list of supported features and limitations, including more advanced features that are not covered here in the book. You can find those lists in the Quarkus CDI Reference Guide (*https://oreil.ly/-LPAd*).

Injection happens just as you would expect in any other application using CDI:

```
package org.acme.quickstart;

import javax.inject.Inject;
import javax.ws.rs.GET;
import javax.ws.rs.Path;
import javax.ws.rs.Produces;
import javax.ws.rs.core.MediaType;

@Path("/hello")
public class GreetingResource {
    @Inject                            ❶
    GreetingService service;           ❷
    @GET
    @Produces(MediaType.TEXT_PLAIN)
    public String hello() {
        return service.getGreeting();
    }
}
```

❶ Use of the @Inject annotation is required

❷ Due to restrictions on reflection, package-private injection fields are preferred

The injected service is pretty standard and without any surprises:

```
package org.acme.quickstart;

import java.util.Locale;

import javax.enterprise.context.ApplicationScoped;
import javax.inject.Inject;
import javax.inject.Named;

@ApplicationScoped                     ❶
public class GreetingService {
    public String getGreeting() {
        return "Hello";
    }
}
```

❶ As mentioned in the following, you should include a bean-defining annotation that allows classes to be found

Bean discovery in Quarkus follows a simplified process from standard CDI. In short, if your application classes do not have a bean-defining annotation (*https://oreil.ly/ jm4QF*), they will not be picked up by Quarkus.

See Also

To learn more, see the following web pages:

- JBoss: JSR 365: Contexts and Dependency Injection for Java 2.0 (*https://oreil.ly/ clOD4*)
- GitHub: GraalVM Native Image Compatibility and Optimization Guide (*https:// oreil.ly/7sgPm*)

5.7 Creating Factories

Problem

You want to create a factory for an object.

Solution

Use the `javax.enterise.inject.Produces` concept from CDI.

CDI has a concept called *producers* that allows you to do any sort of object creation necessary to add a new bean or class to the list of resolvable instances, like this:

```
package org.acme.quickstart;

import java.util.Locale;

import javax.enterprise.context.ApplicationScoped;
import javax.enterprise.inject.Produces;
import javax.inject.Named;

@ApplicationScoped
public class LocaleProducer {
    @Produces
    public Locale getDefaultLocale() {
        return Locale.getDefault();
    }
}
```

Discussion

Quarkus takes the producers concept a little further. Quarkus does so by adding the `@io.quarkus.arc.DefaultBean` annotation. In terms of CDI, this is like an enabled default alternative. Because Quarkus does not allow for alternatives, a class annotated with `DefaultBean` gives you a way to create a default instance of a bean. The following code is an example pulled from the Quarkus website:

```
@Dependent
public class TracerConfiguration {

    @Produces
    public Tracer tracer(Reporter reporter, Configuration configuration) {
        return new Tracer(reporter, configuration);
    }

    @Produces
    @DefaultBean
    public Configuration configuration() {
        // create a Configuration
    }

    @Produces
    @DefaultBean
    public Reporter reporter(){
        // create a Reporter
    }
}
```

The following excerpt allows your application or library to inject a tracer wherever necessary. It also allows for customization by creating a new producer:

```
@Dependent
public class CustomTracerConfiguration {

    @Produces
    public Reporter reporter(){
        // create a custom Reporter
    }
}
```

With this code in your application, the `Reporter` created from the `CustomTracerConfiguration` class will be used instead of the default.

See Also

To learn more, visit the following web page:

- JBoss: JSR 365: Contexts and Dependency Injection for Java 2.0 (*https://oreil.ly/4-OrV*)

5.8 Executing Object Life Cycle Events

Problem

You want to execute logic before and/or after objection creation/destruction.

Solution

CDI makes use of the @javax.annotation.PostConstruct and @javax.annota
tion.PreDestroy annotations for life cycle management. The methods annotated
with those annotations will be called after object creation for PostConstruct and
before the object is destroyed for PreDestroy:

```
package org.acme.quickstart;

import java.util.Arrays;
import java.util.List;

import javax.annotation.PostConstruct;
import javax.annotation.PreDestroy;
import javax.enterprise.context.ApplicationScoped;

@ApplicationScoped
public class RecommendationService {
    List<String> products;

    @PostConstruct
    public void init() {
        products = Arrays.asList("Orange", "Apple", "Mango");
        System.out.println("Products initialized");
    }

    @PreDestroy
    public void cleanup() {
        products = null;
        System.out.println("Products cleaned up");
    }

    public List<String> getProducts() {
        return products;
    }
}
```

Discussion

If there is logic that needs to happen after the constructor is called and after all the
injections happen, it should go into a method annotated with the @PostConstruct
annotation. This is guaranteed to be called only once in the lifetime of an object
instance.

Similarly, if logic needs to be executed before the object is destroyed, place it in a method annotated with the `@PreDestroy` annotation. Ideas for this would include closing connections, cleaning up resources, and finalizing logging.

See Also

To learn more, see the following pages on GitHub:

- Common Annotations API: PostConstruct.java (*https://oreil.ly/UxdG2*)
- Common Annotations API: PreDestroy.java (*https://oreil.ly/qsZUC*)

5.9 Executing Application Life Cycle Events

Problem

You want to execute logic at application startup and/or after application shutdown.

Solution

Observe the `io.quarkus.runtime.StartupEvent` and the `io.quarkus.runtime.Shut downEvent`. During application startup, Quarkus will fire the `StartupEvent`; and during shutdown, the `ShutdownEvent`, like this:

```
package org.acme.quickstart;

import javax.enterprise.context.ApplicationScoped;
import javax.enterprise.event.Observes;
import io.quarkus.runtime.ShutdownEvent;
import io.quarkus.runtime.StartupEvent;
import org.slf4j.Logger;
import org.slf4j.LoggerFactory;

@ApplicationScoped                                        ❶
public class ApplicationEventListener {
    private static final Logger LOGGER =
            LoggerFactory.getLogger(ApplicationEventListener.class);

    void onStart(@Observes StartupEvent event) {          ❷
        LOGGER.info("Application starting...");
    }

    void onStop(@Observes ShutdownEvent event) {          ❸
        LOGGER.info("Application shutting down...");
    }

}
```

❶ You must add a bean-defining annotation

❷ The startup event that is fired

❸ The shutdown event that Quarkus fires

Neither of these event objects carry any additional information, so there is not anything else to cover.

Discussion

Event observation is a very powerful way in Quarkus (and in other CDI frameworks) to decouple concerns with minimal overhead.

See Also

For more, see Recipe 5.8.

5.10 Using a Named Qualifier

Problem

You want to qualify an injection with a name.

Solution

Use the `@javax.inject.Named` annotation.

In CDI, a *qualifier* is any annotation defined as `@Retention(RUNTIME)` and annotated with `@javax.inject.Qualifier`. Qualifiers are typically defined so that they can be used everywhere you need them as `@Target({METHOD, FIELD, PARAMETER, TYPE})`.

CDI comes with a useful qualifier: `@javax.inject.Named`. The value isn't required, but it doesn't make sense to use `@Named` without an actual name. When resolving an injection point, CDI will look for any beans of the correct type that also contain the same qualifier. In the case of `@Named`, the value part of the annotation must match as well.

This is very useful if you have multiple instances of a type, but they are not the same object. CDI doesn't take into consideration the actual instance of the object because that isn't known until it is created and will be different each time anyway. To get around this problem, CDI uses qualifiers:

```
@Inject
@Named("en_US")
Locale en_US;
```

```
@Inject
@Named("es_ES")
Locale es_ES;

public String getGreeting(String locale) {
    if (locale.startsWith("en"))
        return "Hello from " + en_US.getDisplayCountry();

    if (locale.startsWith("es"))
        return "Hola desde " + es_ES.getDisplayCountry();

    return "Unknown locale";
}
```

Discussion

For completeness, this is a way to produce named beans:

```
package org.acme.quickstart;

import java.util.Locale;

import javax.enterprise.context.ApplicationScoped;
import javax.enterprise.inject.Produces;
import javax.inject.Named;

@ApplicationScoped
public class LocaleProducer {
    @Produces
    public Locale getDefaultLocale() {
        return Locale.getDefault();
    }
    @Produces
    @Named("en_US")
    public Locale getEnUSLocale() {
        return Locale.US;
    }

    @Produces
    @Named("es_ES")
    public Locale getEsESLocale() {
        return new Locale("es", "ES");
    }
}
```

@Named qualification, though weak—which is one of the things CDI tries to avoid—can be a useful trick during integrations. We recommend using strongly typed annotations where possible.

See Also

For more information, visit the following web page:

- JBoss: qualifier @Named at injection points (*https://oreil.ly/5NydQ*)

5.11 Using Custom Qualifiers

Problem

You want to qualify an injection with some other qualifier annotation.

Solution

Develop and use qualifier annotations.

In Recipe 5.10, you were introduced to the idea of a qualifier:

```
package org.acme.quickstart;

import java.lang.annotation.Retention;
import java.lang.annotation.RetentionPolicy;
import java.lang.annotation.Target;

import javax.inject.Qualifier;

import static java.lang.annotation.ElementType.FIELD;
import static java.lang.annotation.ElementType.METHOD;
import static java.lang.annotation.ElementType.PARAMETER;
import static java.lang.annotation.ElementType.TYPE;

@Qualifier
@Retention(RetentionPolicy.RUNTIME)
@Target({METHOD, FIELD, PARAMETER, TYPE})
public @interface SpainLocale {
}
```

Producing the bean is exactly as you would expect:

```
@Produces
@SpainLocale
public Locale getSpainLocale() {
    return new Locale("es", "ES");
}
```

Then, of course, injecting the newly qualified instance is just as easy:

```
@Inject
@SpainLocale
Locale spain;
```

Discussion

Using qualifier annotations is the preferred way to use qualified CDI injections both in a normal CDI application and in Quarkus.

See Also

For more information, visit the following web page:

- JBoss: Qualifiers (*https://oreil.ly/MOfwa*)

5.12 Qualifying and Configuring Annotations

Problem

You want to qualify and configure a dependency using annotations.

Solution

Using a combination of `InjectionPoint` in a producer and nonbinding attributes on the qualifier annotation, it is possible to both qualify and configure a bean.

This is an interesting, albeit atypical, use case for qualifiers and producers. Take a look at the following code to see it in action:

```
package org.acme.quickstart;

import java.lang.annotation.Retention;
import java.lang.annotation.Target;

import javax.enterprise.util.Nonbinding;
import javax.inject.Qualifier;

import static java.lang.annotation.ElementType.TYPE;
import static java.lang.annotation.ElementType.FIELD;
import static java.lang.annotation.ElementType.METHOD;
import static java.lang.annotation.ElementType.PARAMETER;
import static java.lang.annotation.RetentionPolicy.RUNTIME;

@Qualifier
@Retention(RUNTIME)
@Target({TYPE, METHOD, FIELD, PARAMETER})
public @interface Quote {
    @Nonbinding String msg() default "";        ❶
    @Nonbinding String source() default "";
}
```

❶ The attributes are listed as nonbinding, so injections actually work.

Normally, the attributes of a qualifier are considered for injections, so if the attributes don't match, the qualified object will not be injected:

```
@Produces
@Quote                                                              ❶
Message getQuote(InjectionPoint msg) {
    Quote q = msg.getAnnotated().getAnnotation(Quote.class);        ❷
    return new Message(q.msg(), q.source());                        ❸
}
```

❶ Only the default attributes on the producer

❷ Get the instance of the qualifier to pull configuration from the attributes

❸ Return the newly configured object

Usage is exactly the same as any other qualifier:

```
@Quote(msg = "Good-bye and hello, as always.", source = "Roger Zelazny")
Message myQuote;
```

See Also

For more information, visit the following web page:

• JBoss: Injection point metadata (*https://oreil.ly/BVmV2*)

5.13 Creating Interceptors

Problem

You want to implement cross-cutting concerns.

Solution

A *cross-cutting concern* is an aspect that affects other concerns of a program. The textbook example of this is *transaction control*. It is an action that affects the use of data in your program and must always be addressed, often in the same or similar manner.

Create @javax.inject.AroundInvoke and @javax.inject.AroundConstruct interceptors with the corresponding interceptor bindings. You are also able to create CDI stereotypes to better compose concerns into a single annotation.

To start, create an annotation with the @javax.interceptor.InterceptorBinding annotation. This will be used to link up the actual interceptor code and to annotate any of the methods or classes you wish to be intercepted:

```
package org.acme.quickstart;

import java.lang.annotation.Inherited;
import java.lang.annotation.Retention;
import java.lang.annotation.Target;

import javax.interceptor.InterceptorBinding;

import static java.lang.annotation.ElementType.METHOD;
import static java.lang.annotation.ElementType.TYPE;
import static java.lang.annotation.RetentionPolicy.RUNTIME;

@Inherited
@InterceptorBinding
@Retention(RUNTIME)
@Target({METHOD, TYPE})
public @interface LogEvent {
}
```

Nothing special going on there. Next, you need to create the interceptor:

```
package org.acme.quickstart;

import java.util.ArrayList;
import java.util.Arrays;
import java.util.List;

import javax.interceptor.AroundInvoke;
import javax.interceptor.Interceptor;
import javax.interceptor.InvocationContext;

@LogEvent
@Interceptor
public class LogEventInterceptor {
    static List<Event> events = new ArrayList<>();

    @AroundInvoke
    public Object logEvent(InvocationContext ctx) throws Exception {
        events.add(new Event(ctx.getMethod().getName(),
                             Arrays.deepToString(ctx.getParameters())));
        return ctx.proceed();
    }
}
```

This is a pretty contrived example, but it is easy to understand what is happening. Lastly, you simply need to annotate a method or class with the binding annotation:

```
@LogEvent
public void executeOrder(Order order) {
    // ...
}
```

Every time the `executeOrder` method is called, the method in the interceptor that is annotated with `@javax.interceptor.AroundInvoke`, `logEvent` in this case, will be called before the actual `executeOrder` method is called.

Discussion

Interceptors are very easy to implement in Quarkus using the standard CDI mechanism. This provides a simple way to define and utilize cross-cutting actions in your application.

Aspect-oriented programming (AOP) has been around for quite some time, since 1997 to be exact. A team at Xerox PARC lead by Gregor Kiczales created and termed cross-cutting and aspect-oriented programming. Some claim the Microsoft Transaction Server was the first widely adopted instance of AOP. Eventually, Enterprise JavaBeans developed AOP aspects. There's also Spring and AspectJ in the Java ecosystem.

However, we are talking about CDI and Quarkus. Quarkus ArC (the dependency injection flavor in Quarkus), the name of which is a play on arc welding, makes use of the same concepts.

See Also

For more information, check out the following:

- *Essential.NET, Volume 1: The Common Language Runtime* by Don Box and Chris Sells (Addison-Wesley Professional)
- JBoss: Interceptor bindings (*https://oreil.ly/QlAGP*)
- Stack Overflow: What does ArC mean? (*https://oreil.ly/0BpNz*)

5.14 Writing Behavioral Tests

Problem

You want to write behavioral tests to verify the correctness of service without verifying its internals.

Solution

Quarkus's testing solution is based on JUnit 5 (*https://oreil.ly/bh494*), the de facto testing tool in the Java ecosystem, and provides tight integration with REST-Assured (*http://rest-assured.io*) testing framework for validating RESTful Web APIs.

Using REST-Assured is not mandatory; it is just a recommendation or best practice, so you can use any other framework that you prefer for testing endpoints.

The most important part of the Quarkus testing framework is an annotation called `QuarkusTest`. When you annotate a test class with this annotation, you are effectively marking that test to be executed within the Quarkus test framework, which instructs the test to follow the following life cycle:

1. The Quarkus application is automatically started once. When the application has been booted up and is ready to start serving requests, the test execution is started.

2. Each test is executed against this running instance.

3. The Quarkus application is stopped.

To minimize the impact of running tests in terms of performance, the Quarkus application is started only once, and then all test classes defined in the testing plan are executed against this running instance, so the application is not restarted for each test class execution.

Open the `org.acme.quickstart.GreetingResourceTest.java` class located at *src/test/java* directory:

```java
package org.acme.quickstart;

import io.quarkus.test.junit.QuarkusTest;
import org.junit.jupiter.api.Test;
import static io.restassured.RestAssured.given;
import static org.hamcrest.CoreMatchers.is;

@QuarkusTest ❶
public class GreetingResourceTest {

    @Test
    public void testHelloEndpoint() {
        given() ❷
          .when()
          .get("/hello") ❸
          .then() ❹
            .statusCode(200)
            .body(is("hello"));
    }
}
```

❶ Sets this test as a Quarkus test

❷ REST-Assured static method to start the validation

❸ Sends a request using GET HTTP method to /hello path

❹ Starts the assertion section

You can run the test from your IDE as well, as shown in Figure 5-1.

```java
2
3    import io.quarkus.test.junit.QuarkusTest;
4    import org.junit.jupiter.api.Test;
5
6    import static io.restassured.RestAssured.given;
7    import static org.hamcrest.CoreMatchers.is;
8
9    @QuarkusTest
     Run Test | Debug Test | ✓
10   public class HelloResourceTest {
11
12       @Test
         Run Test | Debug Test | ✓
13       public void testHelloEndpoint() {
14           given()
15              .when().get("/hello")
16              .then()
17                 .statusCode(200)
18                 .body(is("hello"));
19       }
20
21   }
```

Figure 5-1. Visual Studio Code with Java integration

Or if you want to run the test in a terminal window, run the following:

```
./mvnw clean compile test

[INFO] ------------------------------------------------------------
[INFO]  T E S T S
[INFO] ------------------------------------------------------------
[INFO] Running org.acme.quickstart.GreetingResourceTest
   INFO  [io.qua.dep.QuarkusAugmentor] (main) Beginning quarkus augmentation
   INFO  [io.qua.resteasy] (build-13) Resteasy running without servlet container.
```

```
INFO  [io.qua.resteasy] (build-13) - Add quarkus-undertow to run Resteasy
                                within a servlet container
INFO  [io.qua.dep.QuarkusAugmentor] (main) Quarkus augmentation completed
                                in 803ms
INFO  [io.quarkus] (main) Quarkus 1.4.1.Final started in 0.427s.
                    Listening on: http://0.0.0.0:8081 ❶
INFO  [io.quarkus] (main) Profile test activated. ❷
INFO  [io.quarkus] (main) Installed features: [cdi, resteasy]
[INFO] Tests run: 1, Failures: 0, Errors: 0, Skipped: 0, Time elapsed: 3.586 s
    - in org.acme.quickstart.GreetingResourceTest
2019-11-06 13:02:43,431 INFO  [io.quarkus] (main) Quarkus stopped in 0.053s
[INFO]
[INFO] Results:
[INFO]
[INFO] Tests run: 1, Failures: 0, Errors: 0, Skipped: 0
```

❶   Quarkus listens on port 8081 when running tests

❷   The test profile is activated

As you've seen in the previous example, port 8081 is the default port used when tests
are executed.

Discussion

You can change the port used by tests by setting the quarkus.http.test-port property to a different value:

```
quarkus.http.test-port=8083
```

Because Quarkus offers nice integration with REST-Assured, it automatically updates
the port used, so no additional configuration is required in that part.

In some scenarios, you might want to run tests in a random port
instead of a specific one. This is also supported by Quarkus; the
only thing you need to set is the quarkus.http.test-port property to zero (0):

```
quarkus.http.test-port=0

./mvnw clean compile test

INFO  [io.quarkus] (main) Quarkus 1.4.1.Final started in 0.442s.
                    Listening on: http://0.0.0.0:49661
INFO  [io.quarkus] (main) Profile test activated.
INFO  [io.quarkus] (main) Installed features: [cdi, resteasy]
```

Quarkus supports writing behavioral tests, which are tests that validate the functionality of a service without knowing or verifying the internals of the service. Figure 5-2
shows the nature of behavioral testing.

In the case of REST APIs and microservices in general, you can understand a behavioral test as a form of test that follows the schema of sending a request to a running instance of the service and validating that the response is the expected one.

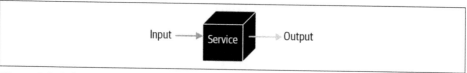

Figure 5-2. Behavioral testing

If you have scaffolded the project using any of the methods explained in Chapter 1, you should already have a completed behavioral test, including the required dependencies registered at your build tool script.

See Also

If you want to learn more about the underlying technologies used by the Quarkus testing framework, you can visit the following websites:

- JBoss: JUnit 5 User Guide (*https://oreil.ly/oahZK*)
- REST-Assured (*http://rest-assured.io*)

5.15 Writing Unit Tests

Problem

You want to write unit tests to verify the correctness of the internals of the service.

Solution

Use the Quarkus testing solution based on JUnit 5 (*https://oreil.ly/oahZK*) and its integration with CDI.

Quarkus allows you to inject CDI beans into your tests via the @Inject annotation. In fact, under the covers, a test in Quarkus is just a CDI bean, so everything that it is valid in a bean is also valid in a test.

Let's create a Greeting Service bean that uses Bean Validation to verify its input parameters. Remember to add the quarkus-hibernate-validator extension. Create a new class org.acme.quickstart.GreetingService.java:

```
package org.acme.quickstart;

import javax.enterprise.context.ApplicationScoped;
import javax.validation.constraints.Min;
```

```
@ApplicationScoped ❶
public class GreetingService {

    public String greetingMessage(@Min(value = 16) int age) { ❷
        if (age < 19) {
            return "Hey boys and girls";
        } else {
            return "Hey ladies and gentlemen";
        }
    }

}
```

❶ Sets service as CDI bean

❷ Adds validation in the method

Now, you want to test that Greeting Service works as expected in the next three cases:

- When the user age is less than 16, an exception is thrown.
- When the user age is between 16 and 18, the teenager's message is returned.
- When the user age is greater than 18, return the message for adults.

We recommend that you use the AssertJ (*https://oreil.ly/d5tI2*) project to write readable assertions. To use it, you need to register the AssertJ dependency in the build script:

```
<dependency>
  <groupId>org.assertj</groupId>
  <artifactId>assertj-core</artifactId>
  <version>3.14.0</version>
  <scope>test</scope>
</dependency>
```

Create a new class `org.acme.quickstart.GreetingService.java` at *src/test/java* directory:

```
package org.acme.quickstart;

import javax.inject.Inject;
import javax.validation.ConstraintViolationException;

import org.assertj.core.api.Assertions;
import org.junit.jupiter.api.Test;

import io.quarkus.test.junit.QuarkusTest;

@QuarkusTest ❶
public class GreetingServiceTest {
```

```
@Inject ❷
GreetingService greetingService;

@Test ❸
public void testGreetingServiceForYoungers() {

  Assertions.assertThatExceptionOfType(ConstraintViolationException.class) ❹
    .isThrownBy(() -> greetingService.greetingMessage(15));
}

@Test
public void testGreetingServiceForTeenagers() {
  String message = greetingService.greetingMessage(18);
  Assertions.assertThat(message).isEqualTo("Hey boys and girls");
}

@Test
public void testGreetingServiceForAdult() {
  String message = greetingService.greetingMessage(21);
  Assertions.assertThat(message).isEqualTo("Hey female and male");
}

}
```

❶ Sets this test as a Quarkus test

❷ Injects `GreetingService` instance

❸ Executes tests using the Greeting Service instance created by CDI container

❹ Uses AssertJ assertions

Try it by opening a new terminal window and running tests:

```
./mvnw clean compile test

[INFO] Running org.acme.quickstart.GreetingResourceTest
 INFO  [io.qua.dep.QuarkusAugmentor] (main) Beginning quarkus augmentation
 INFO  [io.qua.resteasy] (build-3) Resteasy running without servlet container.
 INFO  [io.qua.resteasy] (build-3) - Add quarkus-undertow to run Resteasy
                                    within a servlet container
 INFO  [io.qua.dep.QuarkusAugmentor] (main) Quarkus augmentation completed
                                    in 813ms
 INFO  [io.quarkus] (main) Quarkus 1.4.1.Final started in 0.715s.
                    Listening on: http://0.0.0.0:51581
 INFO  [io.quarkus] (main) Profile test activated.
 INFO  [io.quarkus] (main) Installed features:
                          [cdi, hibernate-validator, resteasy]
[INFO] Tests run: 1, Failures: 0, Errors: 0, Skipped: 0, Time elapsed: 3.614 s
           - in org.acme.quickstart.GreetingResourceTest
[INFO] Running org.acme.quickstart.GreetingServiceTest
```

```
[INFO] Tests run: 3, Failures: 0, Errors: 0, Skipped: 0, Time elapsed: 0.086 s
        - in org.acme.quickstart.GreetingServiceTest
2019-11-06 16:16:11,503 INFO  [io.quarkus] (main) Quarkus stopped in 0.029s
```

Notice that the Quarkus application is started once but both test classes are executed.

Discussion

In the Recipe 5.14 recipe, you learned how to write tests using a behavioral approach in which you care only about requests and responses of the service. However, more often than not, you want to validate what's happening inside the service, or you want to validate how some pieces are behaving inside a running instance without having to mock the environment. This is typically required when you want to validate that a business object works as expected, which includes its integration with the features provided by Quarkus (Bean Validation, CDI, etc.).

See Also

To learn more about AssertJ, visit the following web page:

- AssertJ: fluent assertions java library (*https://oreil.ly/d5tI2*)

5.16 Creating Mock Objects

Problem

You want to test classes that require extra processing time or need to communicate with external systems.

Solution

Use mock support in Quarkus to provide CDI objects that mimic the behavior of real objects by replacing the default ones.

Mock objects are simulated objects that simulate the behavior of real objects by providing some canned answer to a method call.

Let's mock the Greeting Service that was created in the Recipe 5.15 recipe.

Create a new class `org.acme.quickstart.MockedGreetingService.java` at *src/test/java* directory:

```
package org.acme.quickstart;

import io.quarkus.test.Mock;

@Mock ❶
```

```
public class MockedGreetingService
    extends GreetingService { ❷

        @Override
        public String greetingMessage(int age) {
            return "Hello World"; ❸
        }

}
```

❶ Mark POJO as a mocked class (alternative class) in CDI

❷ The class must extend or implement the base service

❸ Canned answer

Discussion

Creating mocks is not only a great way to bypass external services and longer running processes, but also a simple way of testing particular scenarios. In the previous solution, there could be two tests: one using the mock and the other using the actual object. One would demonstrate the expected behavior by the service, and the other could demonstrate an expected failure. This technique is especially useful for testing external service failures.

5.17 Creating Mock Objects with Mockito

Problem

Using Mockito, you want to test classes that require extra processing time or need to communicate with external systems.

Solution

Use the Mockito library to provide CDI objects that mimic the behavior of real objects by replacing the default ones.

Using Mockito, let's mock the Greeting Service that was created in the Recipe 5.15 recipe.

The first thing to do is add the Quarkus Mockito extension:

```
<dependency>
  <groupId>io.quarkus</groupId>
  <artifactId>quarkus-junit5-mockito</artifactId>
  <scope>test</scope>
</dependency>
```

Create a new class `org.acme.quickstart.GreetingResourceTest.java` at *src/main/ java* directory:

```
import io.quarkus.test.junit.mockito.InjectMock;
import org.junit.jupiter.api.BeforeEach;
import static org.mockito.Mockito.when;

@QuarkusTest
public class GreetingResourceTest {

    @InjectMock  ❶
    GreetingService greetingService;

    @BeforeEach  ❷
    public void prepareMocks() {
        when(greetingService.message())
                .thenReturn("Aloha from Mockito");
    }

    @Test
    public void testHelloEndpoint() {
        given()
          .when().get("/greeting")
          .then()
            .statusCode(200)
            .body(is("Aloha from Mockito"));  ❸
    }

}
```

❶ InjectMock makes this field a Mockito mock

❷ Before each test execution, the mock expectations are recorded

❸ The message that is returned is the mocked one

5.18 Grouping Several Annotations into One with a Meta-Annotation

Problem

You want to avoid the population of annotations in your application.

Solution

Use meta-annotations to group several annotations into one.

You can develop a meta-annotation that contains all the annotations required by the tests or other portions of your application. For example, you could create a TransactionalQuarkusTest annotation that contains both @QuarkusTest and @Transactional annotations, making a Quarkus test transactional by default if this newly created annotation is used.

Create a new class called org.acme.quickstart.TransactionalQuarkusTest.java in the *src/test/java* directory:

```
package org.acme.quickstart;

import java.lang.annotation.ElementType;
import java.lang.annotation.Retention;
import java.lang.annotation.RetentionPolicy;
import java.lang.annotation.Target;

import javax.enterprise.inject.Stereotype;
import javax.transaction.Transactional;

import io.quarkus.test.junit.QuarkusTest;

@QuarkusTest ❶
@Transactional
@Stereotype ❷
@Retention(RetentionPolicy.RUNTIME)
@Target(ElementType.TYPE)
public @interface TransactionalQuarkusTest {
}
```

❶ Adds the annotations that this meta-annotation might "inherit"

❷ Sets the annotation as a stereotype (meta-annotation)

If you then apply this annotation to a class, it will be like you had applied both the @QuarkusTest and the @Transactional annotations:

```
@TransactionalQuarkusTest
public class DeveloperDAO {
}
```

Notice that now the test is more readable and the annotations are reusable.

Discussion

Quarkus tests are CDI beans, and for this reason, you can apply CDI interceptors. For example, you could make your test become transactional by using the transactional interceptor. This interceptor is enabled by annotating the test class with @javax.transaction.Transactional. So, a transactional test might look like the following:

```
@QuarkusTest
@Transactional
public class DeveloperDAO {
}
```

Of course, this is perfectly valid, but there are two scenarios in which multiple annotations on the class might impact the readability of your test:

1. Your test requires more annotations—for example, JUnit 5 annotations like `@TestMethodOrder` to define the order execution of tests, or you need to enable other interceptors for the test. In these cases, you can end up setting more annotations than code.

2. You have a lot of tests that require the same annotations, so you continuously annotate, in most of the cases, all tests with the same annotations.

5.19 Executing Code Before or After a Test

Problem

You want to execute some logic before/after the test suite to start/stop/configure a resource for the test.

Solution

Use the *Quarkus Test Resource* extension mechanism to define the required resources to execute the tests.

Quarkus provides an extension mechanism that allows you to execute Java code before the test suite is started and after the test suite has finished. Furthermore, it allows you to create/override configuration properties programmatically so that any parameter required by the resource can be set in the test resource class instead of having to modify the *application.properties* file.

Let's write a simple Quarkus Test Resource that just prints some messages.

Create a new class named `org.acme.quickstart.HelloWorldQuarkusTestResource LifecycleManager` implementing `io.quarkus.test.common.QuarkusTestResource LifecycleManager` interface at *src/test/java* directory:

```
package org.acme.quickstart;

import java.util.Collections;
import java.util.Map;

import io.quarkus.test.common.QuarkusTestResourceLifecycleManager;
```

```
public class HelloWorldQuarkusTestResourceLifecycleManager
    implements QuarkusTestResourceLifecycleManager { ❶

    @Override
    public Map<String, String> start() { ❷
        System.out.println("Start Test Suite execution");
        return Collections.emptyMap(); ❸
    }

    @Override
    public void stop() { ❹
        System.out.println("Stop Test Suite execution");
    }

    @Override
    public void inject(Object testInstance) { ❺
        System.out.println("Executing " + testInstance.getClass().getName());
    }

    @Override
    public int order() { ❻
        return 0;
    }

}
```

❶ Must implement QuarkusTestResourceLifecycleManager

❷ The method that is executed before the test suite

❸ Map object with system properties to be used

❹ The method that is executed after the test suite

❺ For each test class execution, this method is invoked, passing the test instance so that you can inject specific fields

❻ Sets the order of execution in case multiple resources are defined

Finally, you need to register this extension to be executed during the test suite execution. To do that, you need to use the QuarkusTestResource annotation in any class placed within the *src/test/java* directory and set the test resource to be started. Although it could be any test class responsible for registering the resource, we recommend you create a specific empty class that registers the test resource.

Create a new class org.acme.quickstart.HelloWorldTestResource in *src/test/java* with the following content:

```
package org.acme.quickstart;

import io.quarkus.test.common.QuarkusTestResource;

@QuarkusTestResource(HelloWorldQuarkusTestResourceLifecycleManager.class) ❶
public class HelloWorldTestResource {
}
```

❶ Registers the test resource

Then run the tests in a terminal, and you'll see something similar as terminal output:

```
./mvnw clean compile test

INFO] --------------------------------------------------------
[INFO]  T E S T S
[INFO] --------------------------------------------------------
[INFO] Running org.acme.quickstart.GreetingResourceTest
Start Test Suite execution ❶
 INFO  [io.qua.dep.QuarkusAugmentor] (main) Beginning quarkus augmentation
 INFO  [io.qua.dep.QuarkusAugmentor] (main) Quarkus augmentation completed
                                     in 756ms
 INFO  [io.quarkus] (main) Quarkus 1.4.1.Final started in 0.381s.
                     Listening on: http://0.0.0.0:8081
 INFO  [io.quarkus] (main) Profile test activated.
 INFO  [io.quarkus] (main) Installed features: [cdi, resteasy]
Executing org.acme.quickstart.GreetingResourceTest ❷
[INFO] Tests run: 1, Failures: 0, Errors: 0, Skipped: 0, Time elapsed: 3.058 s
        - in org.acme.quickstart.GreetingResourceTest
Stop Test Suite execution ❸
2019-11-08 16:57:01,020 INFO  [io.quarkus] (main) Quarkus stopped in 0.027s
```

❶ `start` method is invoked before Quarkus is started

❷ `inject` method is invoked before `GreetingResourceTest` is run

❸ `stop` method is invoked after all tests have been executed

This example is not very usable; however, it is simple to understand the test life cycle, but nothing more.

Discussion

As you move forward, the complexity of your tests (integration tests, end-to-end tests, etc.) and the required dependencies to run them increases. For example, the tests might require a database instance, a Kafka broker, a JMS queue, or an identity provider like Keycloak.

With this background, let's write a more interesting test resource that uses Docker to boot up a MariaDB Docker container.

For this example, you are going to use the Testcontainers (*https://oreil.ly/aEeAV*) test framework; at the time of writing, the latest version is 1.14.3.

About Test Containers

Testcontainers is a Java library that supports JUnit tests, providing lightweight, throwaway instances of Docker containers. Testcontainers manages the life cycle of each of these containers, so you can start and stop them programmatically.

You might use Docker containers in tests in the following circumstances:

- Data access layer integration tests in which you containerize the database servers (i.e., PostgreSQL, MySQL, or Oracle)

- Application integration tests requiring some external dependencies such as webservers or messaging systems like Kafka

- UI/Acceptance tests where you containerize the web browsers so every test runs in a fresh instance of the browser

---

Before running tests, you need to have Docker installed in your machine so Testcontainers can boot up the MariaDB container locally.

The first step in developing the Testcontainers Quarkus Test Resource is registering the Testcontainers dependency in your build tool for using the MariaDB Docker container in your test:

```
<dependency>
  <groupId>org.testcontainers</groupId>
  <artifactId>mariadb</artifactId>
  <version>${testcontainers.version}</version>
  <scope>test</scope>
</dependency>
<dependency>
  <groupId>io.quarkus</groupId>
  <artifactId>quarkus-jdbc-mariadb</artifactId>
</dependency>
```

The implementation of `QuarkusTestResourceLifecycleManager` is as follows:

```
package org.acme.quickstart;

import java.util.HashMap;
import java.util.Map;

import org.acme.quickstart.MariaDbTestResource.Initializer;
import org.testcontainers.containers.MariaDBContainer;

import io.quarkus.test.common.QuarkusTestResource;
import io.quarkus.test.common.QuarkusTestResourceLifecycleManager;
```

```java
@QuarkusTestResource(Initializer.class) ❶
public class MariaDbTestResource {

    public static class Initializer
        implements QuarkusTestResourceLifecycleManager { ❷

        private MariaDBContainer mariaDBContainer; ❸

        @Override
        public Map<String, String> start() {

            this.mariaDBContainer = new MariaDBContainer<>("mariadb:10.4.4"); ❹
            this.mariaDBContainer.start();❺

            return getConfigurationParameters();
        }

        private Map<String, String> getConfigurationParameters() { ❻
            final Map<String, String> conf = new HashMap<>();

            conf.put("quarkus.datasource.url", this.mariaDBContainer.getJdbcUrl());
            conf.put("quarkus.datsource.username", this.mariaDBContainer
                                                    .getUsername());
            conf.put("quarkus.datasource.password", this.mariaDBContainer
                                                    .getPassword());
            conf.put("quarkus.datasource.driver", this.mariaDBContainer
                                                    .getDriverClassName());

            return conf;
        }

        @Override
        public void stop() {
            if (this.mariaDBContainer != null) {
                this.mariaDBContainer.close(); ❼
            }
        }
    }
}
```

❶ Registers the test resource

❷ Defines the test resource interface

❸ Sets MariaDB container object

❹ Instantiate MariaDB container with required Docker image

❺ Starts the container and waits until the container is accepting connections

❻ Overrides Quarkus's configuration to point database connection to the container one

❼ Stops the container

Finally, run the tests in a terminal. You'll see something like this in the terminal output:

```
./mvnw clean test

[INFO] -------------------------------------------------------
[INFO]  T E S T S
[INFO] -------------------------------------------------------
[INFO] Running org.acme.quickstart.GreetingResourceTest
        i Checking the system...
        ✓ Docker version should be at least 1.6.0
        ✓ Docker environment should have more than 2GB free disk space
Start Test Suite execution
  INFO  [org.tes.doc.DockerClientProviderStrategy] (main)
        Loaded org.testcontainers.dockerclient
                      .UnixSocketClientProviderStrategy
        from ~/.testcontainers.properties, will try it first
...
  INFO  [▢▢ 4.4]] (main) Creating container for image: mariadb:10.4.4 ❶
  INFO  [▢▢ 4.4]] (main) Starting container with ID:
        0d07d45111b1103fd7e64ac2050320ee329ca14eb46a72d525f61bc5e433dc69
  INFO  [▢▢ 4.4]] (main) Container mariadb:10.4.4 is starting:
        0d07d45111b1103fd7e64ac2050320ee329ca14eb46a72d525f61bc5e433dc69
  INFO  [▢▢ 4.4]] (main) Waiting for database connection to become available at
        jdbc:mariadb://localhost:32773/test using query 'SELECT 1'
  INFO  [▢▢ 4.4]] (main) Container is started
        (JDBC URL: jdbc:mariadb://localhost:32773/test)
  INFO  [▢▢ 4.4]] (main) Container mariadb:10.4.4 started ❷
  INFO  [io.qua.dep.QuarkusAugmentor] (main) Beginning quarkus augmentation
  INFO  [io.qua.dep.QuarkusAugmentor] (main) Quarkus augmentation completed
                                  in 1461ms
  INFO  [io.quarkus] (main) Quarkus 1.4.1.Final started in 0.909s.
                        Listening on: http://0.0.0.0:8081
  INFO  [io.quarkus] (main) Profile test activated.
  INFO  [io.quarkus] (main) Installed features: [cdi, jdbc-mariadb, resteasy]
Executing org.acme.quickstart.GreetingResourceTest
[INFO] Tests run: 1, Failures: 0, Errors: 0, Skipped: 0, Time elapsed: 32.666 s
        - in org.acme.quickstart.GreetingResourceTest
Stop Test Suite execution
2019-11-12 11:57:27,758 INFO  [io.quarkus] (main) Quarkus stopped in 0.043s
```

❶ MariaDB Docker container is created

❷ Container is up and running and ready to receive incoming requests

You can develop Quarkus Test Resources in a separate project and package them as an external JAR library. You can then reuse them in as many projects as required.

Quarkus provides the following default Quarkus Test Resource implementations:

H2DatabaseTestResource
> For starting/stopping H2 database in server mode

DerbyDatabaseTestResource
> For starting/stopping Derby database in server mode

InfinispanEmbeddedTestResource
> For starting/stopping Infinispan in embedded mode

InfinispanServerTestResource
> For starting/stopping Infinispan in server mode

KeycloakTestResource
> For starting/stopping Keycloak identity provider

ArtemisTestResource
> For starting/stopping Embedded ActiveMQ

KafkaTestResource
> For starting/stopping a Kafka cluster using Debezium classes

KubernetesMockServerTestResource
> For starting/stopping Kubernetes Mock server

See Also

You can learn more about how to install Docker in your local machine and find more examples about Testcontainers test framework at the following:

- Docker: Get Docker (*https://oreil.ly/WrfY8*)
- Testcontainers (*https://oreil.ly/aEeAV*)

5.20 Testing the Native Executable

Problem

You want to test that the native executable is correct.

Solution

Use `NativeImageTest` annotation to start the application from the native file instead of using the JVM.

If you plan to produce a native executable of your application, it is always a good idea to write some behavioral tests against the application running in the native executable.

Quarkus provides the `NativeImageTest` annotation to start the application from the native file instead of using the JVM. It is important to note that you must generate the native executable before running the tests or using the `quarkus.package.type` system property to generate the native executable before running the tests. You can learn more about how to generate a native executable in the Recipe 6.4 recipe.

If the project is scaffolded using any of the methods explained before, a native executable test is already provided.

 It is not possible to mix JVM and native image tests in the same test suite. The JVM tests must be run in a different cycle than the native tests (e.g., in Maven, this would be `surefire` for JVM tests and `failsafe` for native tests).

This configuration is provided by default when a project is scaffolded by any of the methods explained earlier:

```
<profile>
  <id>native</id>
  <activation>
    <property>
      <name>native</name>
    </property>
  </activation>
  <build>
    <plugins>
      <plugin>
        <artifactId>maven-failsafe-plugin</artifactId>
        <version>${surefire-plugin.version}</version>
        <executions>
          <execution>
            <goals>
              <goal>integration-test</goal>
              <goal>verify</goal> ❶
            </goals>
            <configuration>
              <systemProperties>
                <native.image.path>
                  ${project.build.directory}/
                  ${project.build.finalName}-runner
```

```
            </native.image.path> ❷
          </systemProperties>
        </configuration>
      </execution>
    </executions>
  </plugin>
</plugins>
</build>
<properties>
  <quarkus.package.type>
      native
  </quarkus.package.type> ❸
</properties>
</profile>
```

❶ Native tests are run in `verify` goal (`./mvnw verify`)

❷ The location of the produced native executable (the line should not be split in the pom)

❸ Produces a native executable before running tests

Open the `org.acme.quickstart.NativeGreetingResourceIT.java` class located at *src/test/java* directory:

```
package org.acme.quickstart;

import io.quarkus.test.junit.NativeImageTest;

@NativeImageTest ❶
public class NativeGreetingResourceIT
    extends GreetingResourceTest { ❷

    // Execute the same tests but in native mode.
}
```

❶ Starts the native executable located at `native.image.path`.

❷ Extends JVM tests to make them run against native executable. This is not mandatory; you can write your tests, but remember to annotate them with @QuarkusTest. This will run the same test but against the native executable.

 All testing features showed in this section are valid except injecting into tests.

Discussion

There are some things that you need to take into consideration when writing native tests:

1. Quarkus waits for 60 seconds for the native image to start before automatically failing the native tests. This duration can be changed using the `quarkus.test.native-image-wait-time` property (i.e., `./mvnw verify -Pnative -Dquarkus.test.native-image-wait-time=200`).

2. Native tests run on `prod` profile; if you want to change that, you can use the `quarkus.test.native-image-profile` property to set an alternative profile.

3. You can disable certain test methods (or classes) to be able to run them in native tests by annotating them with the `io.quarkus.test.junit.DisabledOnNativeImage` annotation (i.e., `@DisabledOnNativeImage @Test public void nonNativeTest(){}`).

CHAPTER 6

Packaging Quarkus Applications

In this chapter, you will learn about packaging a Quarkus service into a JVM or a native format so that it can be distributed and deployed. Today, when containers are becoming the standard way to distribute applications, you need to know how to containerize them.

We'll cover the following topics:

- How to package a Quarkus application for running in the JVM
- How to package a Quarkus application in a native executable
- How to containerize a Quarkus application

6.1 Running in Command Mode

Problem

You want to create a CLI application.

Solution

With Quarkus, you can also write applications that run and then optionally exit.

To enable command mode in Quarkus, you need to create a class that implements the `io.quarkus.runtime.QuarkusApplication` interface:

```
package org.acme.quickstart;

import io.quarkus.runtime.Quarkus;
import io.quarkus.runtime.QuarkusApplication;
```

```
public class GreetingMain implements QuarkusApplication { ❶

    @Override
    public int run(String... args) throws Exception { ❷
        System.out.println("Hello World");
        Quarkus.waitForExit(); ❸
        return 0;
    }

}
```

❶ Interface to set Quarkus in command mode

❷ The method executed when the `main` is called

❸ Do not exit but wait until Quarkus process is stopped

Then you can implement the well-known Java `main` method. One of the requirements is that the class with the `main` method must be annotated with the `@io.quarkus.run time.annotations.QuarkusMain`:

```
package org.acme.quickstart;

import io.quarkus.runtime.Quarkus;
import io.quarkus.runtime.annotations.QuarkusMain;

@QuarkusMain ❶
public class JavaMain {

    public static void main(String... args) {
        Quarkus.run(GreetingMain.class, args); ❷
    }

}
```

❶ Sets the class as `main`

❷ Starts the process

If you want to access the command arguments, you can inject them using the `@io.quarkus.runtime.annotations.CommandLineArguments` annotation:

```
package org.acme.quickstart;

import javax.ws.rs.GET;
import javax.ws.rs.Path;
import javax.ws.rs.Produces;
import javax.ws.rs.core.MediaType;

import io.quarkus.runtime.annotations.CommandLineArguments;
```

```
@Path("/hello")
public class GreetingResource {

    @CommandLineArguments ❶
    String[] args;

    @GET
    @Produces(MediaType.TEXT_PLAIN)
    public String hello() {
        return args[0];
    }
}
```

❶ Injects the command-line arguments

Finally, you can build the project and run it:

```
./mvnw clean package -DskipTests

java -jar target/greeting-started-cli-1.0-SNAPSHOT-runner.jar Aloha

curl localhost:8080/hello
Aloha
```

Discussion

Two different methods can be used to implement applications that exit. We explained the first method in the previous section; the second method is by annotating the class that is implementing the `io.quarkus.runtime.QuarkusApplication` interface with `@io.quarkus.runtime.annotations.QuarkusMain` annotation.

The drawback of the second solution is that you cannot run it from the IDE, and this is the reason we suggest you use the former approach.

As you've seen in the example, if you want to run some logic on startup and then run it like a normal application (i.e., not exit), then you should call `Quarkus.waitForExit` from the main thread. If you don't call this method, then the Quarkus application is started and then terminated, so your application effectively behaves like any other CLI program.

6.2 Creating a Runnable JAR File

Problem

You want to create a runnable JAR file to be distributed/containerized into a machine with a JVM installed.

Solution

Use the *Quarkus Maven plug-in* to create a runnable JAR.

The Quarkus Maven plug-in is installed by default if you have scaffolded the project using any of the starters mentioned in previous recipes:

```
<plugin>
  <groupId>io.quarkus</groupId>
  <artifactId>quarkus-maven-plugin</artifactId>
  <version>${quarkus.version}</version>
  <executions>
    <execution>
      <goals>
        <goal>build</goal>
      </goals>
    </execution>
  </executions>
</plugin>
```

Then run `package` goal to build the JAR file:

```
./mvnw clean package
```

The `target` directory contains the following contents:

```
target
├── classes
├── generated-sources
├── generated-test-sources
├── getting-started-1.0-SNAPSHOT-runner.jar  ❶
├── getting-started-1.0-SNAPSHOT.jar  ❷
├── lib  ❸
├── maven-archiver
├── maven-status
├── test-classes
├── transformed-classes
└── wiring-classes
```

❶ An executable JAR (not über-JAR)

❷ Location of dependencies

❸ Lib folder with application dependencies

If you want to deploy the application, it is important to copy together the *executable JAR* with the `lib` directory.

You can run the application by running the next command:

```
java -jar target/getting-started-1.0-SNAPSHOT-runner.jar
```

Running Quarkus in this way is known as running Quarkus in the *JVM mode*. This means that you are not producing a native compilation but are running your application inside the JVM.

 If you want to package a Quarkus application in JVM mode into a container, we recommend using this approach because the layers created during the container build stage are cached to be reused later. Libraries are something that do not usually change, so this dependency layer might be reused several times in future executions, speeding up the container build time.

Discussion

To create a runnable JAR file with Gradle, you can run the `quarkusBuild` task:

```
./gradlew quarkusBuild
```

See Also

If you are interested in how to create an über-JAR or how to containerize a Quarkus application, see Recipe 6.3.

6.3 Über-JAR Packaging

Problem

You want to create an über-JAR of your Quarkus application.

Solution

Quarkus Maven plug-in supports the generation of über-JARs by specifying an `uber Jar` configuration option in your *pom.xml*.

To create an über-JAR, a JAR that contains your code `runnable classes` and all required dependencies, you need to configure Quarkus accordingly in the *application.properties* file by setting `quarkus.package.uber-jar` to `true`:

```
quarkus.package.uber-jar=true
```

6.4 Building a Native Executable

Problem

You want to build your Quarkus application as a native executable file.

Solution

Use Quarkus and GraalVM to build a native runnable file that is ideal for containers and serverless loads.

Native executables make Quarkus applications ideal for containers and serverless workloads. Quarkus relies on GraalVM (*https://www.graalvm.org*) to build a Java application as a native executable.

Before building a native executable, make sure to have the GRAALVM_HOME environment variable set to the GraalVM 19.3.1 or 20.0.0 installation directory.

 If you are using macOS, the variable should point to the *Home* sub-directory: export GRAALVM_HOME=<installation_dir>/Develop ment/graalvm/Contents/Home/.

When a Quarkus project is generated using any of the methods explained before, it registers a default Maven profile with the name native that can be used to build a Quarkus native executable application:

```
<profile>
  <id>native</id>
  <activation>
    <property>
      <name>native</name>
    </property>
  </activation>
  <build>
    <plugins>
      <plugin>
        <artifactId>maven-failsafe-plugin</artifactId>
        <version>${surefire-plugin.version}</version>
        <executions>
          <execution>
            <goals>
              <goal>integration-test</goal>
              <goal>verify</goal>
            </goals>
            <configuration>
              <systemProperties>
                <native.image.path>
                  ${project.build.directory}/${project.build.finalName}-runner
                </native.image.path>
              </systemProperties>
            </configuration>
          </execution>
        </executions>
      </plugin>
```

```
      </plugins>
    </build>
    <properties>
      <quarkus.package.type>native</quarkus.package.type>
    </properties>
  </profile>
```

Then you need to build the project with the native profile enabled:

```
./mvnw package -Pnative
```

After a few minutes, a native executable will be present in target directory:

```
[INFO] --- quarkus-maven-plugin:1.4.1.Final:native-image (default) @
       getting-started ---
[INFO] [io.quarkus.creator.phase.nativeimage.NativeImagePhase] Running Quarkus
       native-image plugin on Java HotSpot(TM) 64-Bit Server VM
...
[getting-started-1.0-SNAPSHOT-runner:19]   classlist:  13,614.07 ms
[getting-started-1.0-SNAPSHOT-runner:19]      (cap):   2,306.78 ms
[getting-started-1.0-SNAPSHOT-runner:19]      setup:   4,793.43 ms
...
Printing list of used packages to
  /project/reports/used_packages_getting-started-1.0-SNAPSHOT-
                              runner_20190927_134032.txt
[getting-started-1.0-SNAPSHOT-runner:19]   (compile):  42,452.12 ms
[getting-started-1.0-SNAPSHOT-runner:19]    compile:  62,356.07 ms
[getting-started-1.0-SNAPSHOT-runner:19]      image:   2,939.16 ms
[getting-started-1.0-SNAPSHOT-runner:19]      write:     696.65 ms
[getting-started-1.0-SNAPSHOT-runner:19]    [total]: 151,743.29 ms

target/getting-started-1.0-SNAPSHOT-runner
```

Discussion

To build a native executable in Gradle, you can use the buildNative task:

```
./gradlew buildNative
```

6.5 Building a Docker Container for JAR File

Problem

You want to build a container with the JAR built in the Recipe 6.2 recipe.

Solution

Use the *Dockerfile.jvm* file provided to build the container.

When a Quarkus project is generated using any of the methods explained before, two Dockerfiles are created in *src/main/docker*: one for generating a Docker container using Quarkus in the JVM mode and another one for the native executable.

To generate a container for running Quarkus inside the JVM (no native), you can use the *Dockerfile.jvm* file to build the container. This Dockerfile adds the *lib* directory and the runnable JAR and exposes JMX.

To build the Docker image, you need to package the project as shown in Recipe 6.2 and then build the container:

```
./mvnw clean package
```

```
docker build -f src/main/docker/Dockerfile.jvm -t example/greetings-app .
```

The container can be started by running the following:

```
docker run -it --rm -p 8080:8080 example/greetings-app
```

6.6 Building a Docker Container for Native File

Problem

You want to build a native executable container image.

Solution

To generate a container for running a Quarkus native executable, you can use the *Dockerfile.native* file to build the container.

To build the Docker image, you need to create a native file that can be run in a Docker container. For this reason, don't use local GraalVM to build the native executable because the result file will be specific to your operating system and will not be able to run inside a container.

To create an executable that will run in a container, use the following command in your terminal:

```
./mvnw clean package -Pnative -Dquarkus.native.container-build=true
```

This command creates a Docker image that contains GraalVM installed to produce a 64-bit Linux executable from your code.

> You need to have native profile defined in your *pom.xml*, as explained in the Recipe 6.4 recipe.

The last step is to build the Docker image with the native executable that was generated in the previous step:

```
docker build -f src/main/docker/Dockerfile.native -t example/greetings-app .
```

Then the container can be started by running the following:

```
docker run -it --rm -p 8080:8080 example/greetings-app
```

Discussion

By default, Quarkus uses docker to build the container. The container runtime can be changed by using the `quarkus.native.container-runtime` property. At the time of writing the book, docker and podman are the supported options:

```
./mvnw package -Pnative -Dquarkus.native.container-build=true \
            -Dquarkus.native.container-runtime=podman
```

6.7 Build and Dockerize a Native SSL Application

Problem

When building a native executable, you want to secure connections to prevent an attacker from stealing sensitive information.

Solution

Enable Quarkus to use SSL to secure connections in a native executable.

If you are running the Quarkus application in JVM mode, SSL is supported without any problem, just as any other JVM application. But SSL is not supported out of the box in the case of native executables, and some extra steps (especially when Dockerizing the application) must be executed to enable SSL support.

Let's enable SSL support for native executables in Quarkus by adding the `quarkus.ssl.native` configuration property at *application.properties*:

```
quarkus.ssl.native=true
```

Enabling this property allows the Graal VM `native-image` process to enable SSL. Create a native executable using the next command:

```
./mvnw clean package -Pnative -DskipTests -Dquarkus.native.container-build=true

...

docker run -v \
  gretting-started/target/gretting-started-1.0-SNAPSHOT-native-image-source-jar: \
  /project:z
```

The following are the important flags that are added automatically by the process to enable SSL:

```
-H:EnableURLProtocols=http,https --enable-all-security-services -H:+JNI
```

To Dockerize this native executable, the Docker-related scripts need to be modified slightly to support SSL.

Open .dockeringnore and add the keystore.jks file as a nonignorable file to be added into the resulted container. This is necessary because the keystore file needs to be copied together with the executable:

```
*
!target/classes/keystore.jks
!target/*-runner
!target/*-runner.jar
!target/lib/*
```

The *src/main/docker/Dockerfile.native* file must also be adapted to package the following elements:

- The SunEC library
- The collection of trusted certificate authority files needed to verify certificates used in the application.

```
FROM quay.io/quarkus/ubi-quarkus-native-image:19.2.1 as nativebuilder  ❶
FROM quay.io/quarkus/ubi-quarkus-native-image:19.3.1-java11 as nativebuilder
RUN mkdir -p /tmp/ssl \
    && cp /opt/graalvm/lib/security/cacerts /tmp/ssl/

FROM registry.access.redhat.com/ubi8/ubi-minimal
WORKDIR /work/
COPY --from=nativebuilder /tmp/ssl/ /work/  ❷
COPY target/*-runner /work/application
RUN chmod 775 /work /work/application \  ❸
    && chown -R 1001 /work \
    && chmod -R "g+rwX" /work \
    && chown -R 1001:root /work
EXPOSE 8080 8443  ❹
USER 1001
CMD ["./application",
"-Dquarkus.http.host=0.0.0.0",
"-Djavax.net.ssl.trustStore=/work/cacerts"]  ❺
```

❶ Gets SunEC library and cacerts from GraalVM Docker image

❷ Copies custom keystore.jks at root working directory

❸ Sets up permissions

❹ Exposes HTTPS port

❺ Loads SunEC and `cacerts` when running the application

The container image can be built by running the next command:

```
docker build -f src/main/docker/Dockerfile.native -t greeting-ssl .
```

Discussion

Security and SSL are common now, and it is good practice to always have all your services communicate using SSL. For this reason, Quarkus enables SSL support automatically when any of the following extensions are registered:

- Agroal connection pooling
- Amazon DynamoDB
- Hibernate Search Elasticsearch
- Infinispan Client
- Jaeger
- JGit
- Keycloak
- Kubernetes client
- Mailer
- MongoDB
- Neo4j
- OAuth2
- REST client

As long as you have one of those extensions in your project, the `quarkus.native.ssl` property is set to `true` by default.

CHAPTER 7

Persistence

The underlying persistence strategies used by Quarkus should already be familiar to you. Transactions, datasources, Java Persistence API (JPA), and so on are all standards that have existed for many years. Quarkus uses these and, in some cases, builds on top of them to make working with persistent stores easier. In this chapter, you will learn about working with persistent stores in Quarkus. We cover both traditional relational database management systems (RDBMS) and NoSQL databases.

Quarkus has some additional gems if you're using a traditional RDBMS or MongoDB in the form a Panache, an opinionated, entity or active record type API. Panache simplifies much of the standard JPA syntax, making your application easier to read and maintain—again, helping you to be more productive!

In this chapter, you'll learn how to accomplish the following tasks:

- Configure datasources
- Deal with transactions
- Manage database schema migrations
- Make use of the Panache API
- Interact with NoSQL data stores

7.1 Defining a Datasource

Problem

You want to define and use a datasource.

Solution

Use the Agroal extension and *application.properties.*

Discussion

Agroal is the preferred datasource and connection pooling implementation in Quarkus. The Agroal extension has integrations with security, transaction management, and health metrics. While it does have its own extension, if you are using Hibernate ORM or Panache, the Agroal extension is pulled in transitively. You will also need a database driver extension. Currently, H2, PostgreSQL, MariaDB, MySQL, Microsoft SQL Server, and Derby all have supported extensions. You can add the correct database driver with the Maven `add-extension`:

```
./mvnw quarkus:add-extension -Dextensions="jdbc-mariadb"
```

Configuration for the datasource, just like all the other configurations for Quarkus, is done in the *src/main/resources/application.properties* file:

```
quarkus.datasource.url=jdbc::mariadb://localhost:3306/test
quarkus.datasource.driver=org.mariadb.jdbc.Driver
quarkus.datasource.username=username-default
quarkus.datasource.min-size=3
quarkus.datasource.max-size=13
```

> Sensitive data can be passed via system properties, environment properties, Kubernetes Secrets, or Vault, as you will see in later chapters.

Should you need access to the datasource, you can inject it as follows:

```
@Inject
DataSource defaultDataSource;
```

> You can also use the `AgroalDataSource` type, which is a subtype of `DataSource`.

7.2 Using Multiple Datasources

Problem

You want to use multiple datasources when more than one datasource is necessary for your application.

Solution

Use named datasources.

Agroal allows for multiple datasources. They are configured exactly the same as the default, with one noteable exception—a name:

```
quarkus.datasource.driver=org.h2.Driver
quarkus.datasource.url=jdbc:h2:tcp://localhost/mem:default
quarkus.datasource.username=username-default
quarkus.datasource.min-size=3
quarkus.datasource.max-size=13

quarkus.datasource.users.driver=org.h2.Driver
quarkus.datasource.users.url=jdbc:h2:tcp://localhost/mem:users
quarkus.datasource.users.username=username1
quarkus.datasource.users.min-size=1
quarkus.datasource.users.max-size=11

quarkus.datasource.inventory.driver=org.h2.Driver
quarkus.datasource.inventory.url=jdbc:h2:tcp://localhost/mem:inventory
quarkus.datasource.inventory.username=username2
quarkus.datasource.inventory.min-size=2
quarkus.datasource.inventory.max-size=12
```

The format is as follows: quarkus.*datasource.*[*optional name.*][*datasource property*].

Discussion

Injection works identically; however, you will need a qualifier (please see Recipe 5.10 for more information about qualifiers):

```
@Inject
AgroalDataSource defaultDataSource;

@Inject
@DataSource("users")
AgroalDataSource dataSource1;

@Inject
@DataSource("inventory")
AgroalDataSource dataSource2;
```

7.3 Adding Datasource Health Check

Problem

You want to add a health check entry for the datasource(s).

Solution

Use both the `quarkus-agroal` and `quarkus-smallrye-health` extensions.

Discussion

The health check for datasources is automatically added when the `quarkus-smallrye-health` extension is in use. It can be disabled, if desired, with the `quarkus.datasource.health.enabled` (default to `true`) property in *application.properties*. To view the status, access the */health/ready* endpoint of your application. That endpoint is created from the `quarkus-smallrye-health` extension.

See Also

For more information, visit the following page on GitHub:

- MicroProfile Health (*https://oreil.ly/CDLOd*)

7.4 Defining Transaction Boundaries Declaratively

Problem

You want to define a transaction boundary using annotations.

Solution

Use the `@javax.transaction.Transactional` annotation from the `quarkus-narayana-jta` extension.

Discussion

The `quarkus-narayana-jta` extension adds in the `@javax.transaction.Transactional` annotations, as well as the `TransactionManager` and `UserTransaction` classes. This extension is automatically added by any persistence extensions. Of course, this can be added manually if needed.

The `@Transactional` annotation can be added to any CDI bean at the method or class level to make those methods transactional—this also includes REST endpoints:

```
package org.acme.transaction;

import javax.inject.Inject;
import javax.transaction.Transactional;
import javax.ws.rs.GET;
import javax.ws.rs.Path;
```

```
import javax.ws.rs.Produces;
import javax.ws.rs.core.MediaType;

@Path("/tx")
@Transactional
public class Transact {
}
```

7.5 Setting a Transaction Context

Problem

You want a different transaction context.

Solution

The `value` attribute on `@Transactional` allows the scope to be set for the transaction.

Discussion

The transaction context specified is propagated to all nested calls within the method that has been annotated. Unless a runtime exception is thrown in the stack, the transaction will commit at the end of the method call:

```
package org.acme.transaction;

import javax.inject.Inject;
import javax.transaction.Transactional;
import javax.ws.rs.GET;
import javax.ws.rs.Path;
import javax.ws.rs.Produces;
import javax.ws.rs.core.MediaType;

@Path("/tx")
@Transactional
public class Transact {
    @Inject
    NoTransact noTx;

    @GET
    @Path("/no")
    @Produces(MediaType.TEXT_PLAIN)
    public String hi() {
        return noTx.word();
    }
}

package org.acme.transaction;

import javax.enterprise.context.ApplicationScoped;
```

```
import javax.transaction.Transactional;

import static javax.transaction.Transactional.TxType.NEVER;

@ApplicationScoped
public class NoTransact {
    @Transactional(NEVER)
    public String word() {
        return "Hi";
    }
}
```

This is overridable with the dontRollbackOn or rollbackOn attributes of @Trans
actional. You can also inject the TransactionManager if you need to manually roll
back a transaction.

Here is a list of available transactional contexts:

@Transactional(REQUIRED) *(default)*
> Starts a transaction if none was started; otherwise, stays with the existing one

@Transactional(REQUIRES_NEW)
> Starts a transaction if none was started; if an existing one was started, suspends it
> and starts a new one for the boundary of that method

@Transactional(MANDATORY)
> Fails if no transaction was started; otherwise, works within the existing transac-
> tion

@Transactional(SUPPORTS)
> If a transaction was started, joins it; otherwise, works with no transaction

@Transactional(NOT_SUPPORTED)
> If a transaction was started, suspends it and works with no transaction for the
> boundary of the method; otherwise, works with no transaction

@Transactional(NEVER)
> If a transaction was started, raises an exception; otherwise, works with no
> transaction

7.6 Programmatic Transaction Control

Problem

You want more fine-grained control over transactions.

Solution

Inject the `UserTransaction` and use the methods of that class.

The `UserTransaction` class has a very simple API:

- `begin()`
- `commit()`
- `rollback()`
- `setRollbackOnly()`
- `getStatus()`
- `setTransactionTimeout(int)`

The first three methods will be the main methods used. `getStatus()` is useful in determining where the transaction is in its life cycle. Lastly, you are able to set the timeout for a transaction.

 If needed, you can also use the `javax.transaction.Transaction Manager` by injecting it.

See Also

For more information, visit the following web page:

- Jakarta EE 8 Specification APIs: Interface UserTransaction (*https://oreil.ly/lmjR_*)

7.7 Setting and Modifying a Transaction Timeout

Problem

You want a transaction to time out and roll back after a certain amount of time.

Solution

Use the `@io.quarkus.narayana.jta.runtime.TransactionConfiguration` annotation if using declarative transactions; otherwise, the transaction API can be used for programmatic transaction control. You can also change the global timeout for transactions with the `quarkus.transaction-manager.default-transaction-timeout` property, specified as a `java.time.Duration`.

Modifying the timeout of a transaction for a one-off is very easy with the `@Transac tionConfiguration` annotation. Use the `timeout` attribute to set the number of seconds for the timeout.

Discussion

Should every transaction in the application need a longer or shorter time, use the `quarkus.transaction-manager.default-transaction-timeout` property in *application.properties*. That property takes a `java.time.Duration`, which can be specified as a string parsable via `Duration#parse()`. You may also start the duration with an integer. Quarkus will then automatically prepend `PT` to the value to create the correct formatting.

See Also

For more information, visit the following website:

- Oracle: Java Platform, Standard Edition 8 API Specification: `parse` (*https:// oreil.ly/8gvMZ*)

7.8 Setup with Persistence.xml

Problem

You want to use JPA with a *persistence.xml* file.

Solution

Use JPA like you normally would; just set up the datasource in *application.properties*.

Discussion

JPA in Quarkus works exactly as it does in other settings, so there no changes are necessary.

 You cannot use the `quarkus.hibernate-orm.*` properties if you are using *persistence.xml*. If you are, only the persistence units defined in the *persistence.xml* file will be available.

7.9 Setup Without persistence.xml

Problem

You want to use JPA, but without a *persistence.xml* file.

Solution

Add the `quarkus-hibernate-orm` extension, the JDBC driver for your RDBMS, configuration via *application.properties*, and finally annotate your entities with `@Entity`.

Discussion

There isn't anything special to set up using Quarkus and JPA beyond database connectivity. Quarkus will make some opinionated choices, but don't worry—they're probably the choices you would have made anyway—and continue on with your entities. You will be able to inject and utilize an `EntityManager` just as your normally would.

In a nutshell, you continue as you usually would with standard JPA, but without all the additional configuration of a *persistence.xml*. This is the preferred way to use JPA in Quarkus.

7.10 Using Entities from a Different JAR

Problem

You want to include entities from a different jar.

Solution

Include an empty *META-INF/beans.xml* file in the jar containing the entities.

Discussion

Quarkus relies on compile-type bytecode enhancements to entities. If these entities are defined in the same project (jar) as the rest of the application, everything works as it should.

However, if other classes such as entities or other CDI beans are defined in an external library, that library must contain an empty *META-INF/beans.xml* file to be properly indexed and enhanced.

7.11 Persisting Data with Panache

Problem

You want to persist data with Hibernate and Panache.

Solution

Call the `persist` method on a `PanacheEntity`.

Naturally, you'll need to add the `quarkus-hibernate-orm-panache` extension, and the corresponding JDBC extension for your data store. Next, you'll need to define an entity. All that entails is creating a class, annotating it with `@javax.persis tence.Entity`, and extending from `PanacheEntity`.

Discussion

Panache is an opinionated API built on top of a traditional JPA. It follows more of an active record approach to data entities; however, under the hood, it is done using traditional JPA.

As you will find throughout the exploration of Panache, much of the functionality is passed on to your entities through the `PanacheEntity` or `PanacheEntityBase` parent class—persist is no exception to this. `PanacheEntityBase` contains both the `per sist()` and `persistAndFlush()` methods. While the flush option will immediately send the data to the database, it is not the recommended way of persisting the data.

Persisting is very simple, as you can see in the following:

```
@POST
public Response newLibrary(Library library) {
    library.persist();
    return Response.created(URI.create("/library/" + library.encodedName()))
            .entity(library).build();
}
```

For completion, here is the `Library` entity:

```
package org.acme.panache;

import java.io.UnsupportedEncodingException;
import java.net.URLEncoder;
import java.util.List;

import javax.persistence.CascadeType;
import javax.persistence.Entity;
import javax.persistence.OneToMany;

import io.quarkus.hibernate.orm.panache.PanacheEntity;
```

```
import io.quarkus.panache.common.Parameters;

@Entity
public class Library extends PanacheEntity {
    public String name;

    @OneToMany(cascade = CascadeType.ALL, orphanRemoval = true,
            mappedBy = "library")
    public List<Inventory> inventory;
    public String encodedName() {
        String result;

        try {
            result = URLEncoder.encode(name, "UTF-8")
                    .replaceAll("\\+", "%20")
                    .replaceAll("\\%21", "!")
                    .replaceAll("\\%27", "'")
                    .replaceAll("\\%28", "(")
                    .replaceAll("\\%29", ")")
                    .replaceAll("\\%7E", "~");
        } catch (UnsupportedEncodingException e) {
            result = name;
        }

        return result;
    }
}
```

7.12 Finding All Entity Instances with Panache listAll Method

Problem

You want to find all entries of an entity.

Solution

Use the listAll() method from the PanacheEntityBase class.

Just like the persist() method covered in the previous recipe, listAll() is a method from the PanacheEntityBase class. There isn't anything special about it; it queries the database for all the entries of the given entity. It returns those entities in a List:

```
@GET
public List<Book> getAllBooks() {
    return Book.listAll();
}
```

This method is actually a shortcut for the `findAll().list()` chain. More info can be found in the `hibernate-orm-panache` code base.

7.13 Finding Individual Entities with Panache findById Method

Problem

I want to find and load an entity from the database based on its ID.

Solution

Use `PanacheEntityBase.findById(Object)`.

Panache simplifies finding an entity by using the `findById(Object)` method. All you need to do is pass the ID of the object and you will be returned the correct instance from the database:

```
@GET
@Path("/byId/{id}")
public Book getBookById(@PathParam(value = "id") Long id) {
    Book b = Book.findById(id);
    return b;
}
```

7.14 Finding Entities Using Panache Find and List Methods

Problem

You want to query the database for a specific entity based on its properties.

Solution

Use the various instances of the `find` and `list` methods from `PanacheEntityBase`.

Depending on how you need the result returned, you will use either `list` or `find` from the `PanacheEntityBase`. Internally, `list` uses `find`, so they are essentially the same:

```
public static Book findByTitle(String title) {
    return find("title", title).firstResult();
}
```

```
public static List<Book> findByAuthor(String author) {
    return list("author", author);
}

public static List<Book> findByIsbn(String isbn) {
    return list("isbn", isbn);
}
```

There are multiple overrides for both methods—they change based on the necessity of sorting and how you wish to send parameters. The following code is an example of using Hibernate Query Language (HQL) (or Java Persistence Query Language [JPQL]) and using the Parameters class:

```
public static Library findByName(String name) {
    return Library
            .find("SELECT l FROM Library l " +
                "LEFT JOIN fetch l.inventory " +
                "WHERE l.name = :name ",
                Parameters.with("name", name)).firstResult();
}
```

The Parameters class override is available for both find and list methods. Consult the API for more information.

 You may be wondering, Why the full JPQL query? Put simply, it is to avoid serialization issues with the list. Using the left join, we are able to fetch the library and all the inventory for that library.

7.15 Obtaining a Count of Entities Using the Panache count Method

Problem

You want to get a count of items for a resource.

Solution

Use the various count methods from PanacheEntityBase.

Just like the find methods discussed earlier, Panache has various count method overrides available to obtain the number of entities of a given type in the database:

```
Book.count()
Book.count("WHERE title = ?", )
```

7.16 Paginating Through Entity Lists Using the Panache page Method

Problem

You want to use pagination.

Solution

Quarkus, specifically Panache, has pagination built in. There are a number of methods on the PanacheQuery object that support pagination.

Discussion

Pagination is very easy to get going. The first step is to get an instance of a Panache Query. This is as easy as using the find methods:

```
PanacheQuery<Book> authors = Book.find("author", author);
authors.page(Page.of(3, 25)).list();                        ❶

authors.page(Page.sizeOf(10)).list();
```

❶ Pages of 25 items, starting on page 3

There are, of course, other methods such as firstPage(), lastPage(), nextPage(), and previousPage(). Boolean supporting methods exist as well: hasNextPage(), hasPreviousPage(), and pageCount().

See Also

For more information, see the following pages on GitHub:

- Page object (*https://oreil.ly/KYlsJ*)
- PanacheQuery interface (*https://oreil.ly/BtgHK*)

7.17 Streaming Results via the Panache Stream Method

Problem

You want to use streams for data.

Solution

All `list` methods have corresponding `stream` methods when using Panache. Below you will see how these are used, which isn't any different than how `list` methods are used:

```
Book.streamAll();
...
Book.stream("author", "Alex Soto");
```

Each of the `stream` and `streamAll` methods return a `java.util.Stream` instance.

 `stream` methods require a transaction to work correctly.

See Also

For more information, visit the following website:

- io.quarkus: `PanacheEntityBase` (*https://oreil.ly/OW2fV*)

7.18 Testing Panache Entities

Problem

You want to use an embedded database for testing.

Solution

Quarkus comes with helpers for the in-memory databases H2 and Derby to properly boot the database as a separate process.

Be sure to add either the `io.quarkus:quarkus-test-h2:1.4.1.Final` or the `io.quarkus:quarkus-test-derby:1.4.1.Final` artifacts to your build file.

The next step is to annotate any test using the embedded database with `@QuarkusTestResource(H2DatabaseTestResource.class)` or `@QuarkusTestResource(DerbyDatabaseTestResource.class)`. Lastly, be sure to set the correct database URL and driver for the chosen database in *src/test/resources/META-INF/application.properties*.

The following is an example for H2:

```
package my.app.integrationtests.db;

import io.quarkus.test.common.QuarkusTestResource;
import io.quarkus.test.h2.H2DatabaseTestResource;

@QuarkusTestResource(H2DatabaseTestResource.class)
public class TestResources {
}

quarkus.datasource.url=jdbc:h2:tcp://localhost/mem:test
quarkus.datasource.driver=org.h2.Driver
```

 This helper does not add the database into the native image, only the client code. However, feel free to use this for tests against your application in JVM mode or native image mode.

See Also

For more information, visit the following websites:

- H2 Database Engine (*https://oreil.ly/_MMus*)
- Apache Derby (*https://oreil.ly/FUFeH*)

7.19 Using a Data Access Object (DAO) or Repository Pattern

Problem

You want to use the DAO or the repository pattern.

Solution

Quarkus doesn't limit with Panache; you can use the Entity pattern as previously described, a DAO, or a repository pattern.

The two interfaces you'll need to understand to use a repository are PanacheReposi tory and PanacheRepositoryBase. The base interface is necessary only if you have a primary key that isn't a Long. All of the same operations available on PanacheEntity are available on PanacheRepository. A repository is a CDI bean, so it must be injected when it is being used. Here are some basic examples:

```
package org.acme.panache;

import java.util.Collections;

import javax.enterprise.context.ApplicationScoped;

import io.quarkus.hibernate.orm.panache.PanacheQuery;
import io.quarkus.hibernate.orm.panache.PanacheRepository;
import io.quarkus.panache.common.Parameters;
import io.quarkus.panache.common.Sort;

@ApplicationScoped
public class LibraryRepository implements PanacheRepository<Library> {
    public Library findByName(String name) {
        return find("SELECT l FROM Library l " +
                    "left join fetch l.inventory where l.name = :name ",
                Parameters.with("name", name)).firstResult();
    }

    @Override
    public PanacheQuery<Library> findAll() {
        return find("from Library l left join fetch l.inventory");
    }

    @Override
    public PanacheQuery<Library> findAll(Sort sort) {
        return find("from Library l left join fetch l.inventory",
                sort, Collections.emptyMap());
    }
}
```

A DAO would work exactly as you would expect. You would need to inject an `Entity Manager` and query as normal. There are a myriad of solutions and examples for using a DAO with Java that are available both online and in other books. Those examples will all function the same with Quarkus.

See Also

For more information, visit the following website:

- io.quarkus: `PanacheRepositoryBase` (*https://oreil.ly/H6kTU*)

7.20 Using Amazon DynamoDB

Problem

You want to use DynamoDB with a Quarkus application.

Solution

Use the DynamoDB extension and setup configuration. The DynamoDB extension allows both sync and async clients to make use of the Apache Amazon Web Service Software Development Kit (AWS SDK) client. There are a few things necessary to set up and enable in your project to get this running. The first is, of course, the dependency:

```
<dependency>
    <groupId>software.amazon.awssdk</groupId>
    <artifactId>url-connection-client</artifactId>
</dependency>
```

 There is no Quarkus extension for the AWS connection client.

The extension uses the URLConnection HTTP client by default. You need to add the correct client (URLConnection, Apache, or Netty NIO) to your build script:

```
<dependency>
    <groupId>software.amazon.awssdk</groupId>
    <artifactId>apache-client</artifactId>
    <exclusions>        ❶
        <exclusion>
            <groupId>commons-logging</groupId>
            <artifactId>commons-logging</artifactId>
        </exclusion>
    </exclusions>
</dependency>
```

❶ You must exclude commons-logging to force the client to use the Quarkus logger

If you are using the Apache client, you will also need to make an adjustment to the *application.properties* file because url is the default:

```
quarkus.dynamodb.sync-client.type=apache
```

There are also configurations for the client in *application.properties* (please see the properties references (*https://oreil.ly/HZ4A-*) for more):

```
quarkus.dynamodb.endpoint-override=http://localhost:8000       ❶
quarkus.dynamodb.aws.region=eu-central-1                       ❷
quarkus.dynamodb.aws.credentials.type=static                   ❸
quarkus.dynamodb.aws.credentials.static-provider.access-key-id=test-key
quarkus.dynamodb.aws.credentials.static-provider.secret-access-key=test-secret
```

❶ Useful if using a nonstandard endpoint, such as a local DynamoDB instance

❷ Correct, and valid, region

❸ `static` or `default`

The `default` credential type will look for credentials in order:

- System properties `aws.accessKeyId` and `aws.secretKey`
- Environment variables `AWS_ACCESS_KEY_ID` and `AWS_SECRET_ACCESS_KEY`
- Credential profiles at the default location (*$HOME/.aws/credentials*)
- Credentials delivered through the Amazon EC2 container service
- Instance profile credentials delivered through Amazon EC2 metadata service

Discussion

The following example is from Recipe 7.11, but with DynamoDB as the persistence store.

Here are the two classes used to talk to DynamoDB and create an injectable service to be used in the REST endpoint:

```
package org.acme.dynamodb;

import java.util.List;
import java.util.stream.Collectors;

import javax.enterprise.context.ApplicationScoped;
import javax.inject.Inject;

import software.amazon.awssdk.services.dynamodb.DynamoDbClient;

@ApplicationScoped
public class BookSyncService extends AbstractBookService {
    @Inject
    DynamoDbClient dynamoDbClient;

    public List<Book> findAll() {
        return dynamoDbClient.scanPaginator(scanRequest()).items().stream()
                .map(Book::from)
                .collect(Collectors.toList());
    }

    public List<Book> add(Book b) {
        dynamoDbClient.putItem(putRequest(b));
        return findAll();
    }

    public Book get(String isbn) {
```

```
        return Book.from(dynamoDbClient.getItem(getRequest(isbn)).item());
    }
}
```

The following abstract class contains boilerplate code needed to talk to DynamoDB
and persist and query Book instances:

```
package org.acme.dynamodb;

import java.util.HashMap;
import java.util.Map;

import software.amazon.awssdk.services.dynamodb.model.AttributeValue;
import software.amazon.awssdk.services.dynamodb.model.GetItemRequest;
import software.amazon.awssdk.services.dynamodb.model.PutItemRequest;
import software.amazon.awssdk.services.dynamodb.model.ScanRequest;

public abstract class AbstractBookService {

    public final static String BOOK_TITLE = "title";
    public final static String BOOK_ISBN = "isbn";
    public final static String BOOK_AUTHOR = "author";

    public String getTableName() {
        return "QuarkusBook";
    }

    protected ScanRequest scanRequest() {
        return ScanRequest.builder().tableName(getTableName()).build();
    }

    protected PutItemRequest putRequest(Book book) {
        Map<String, AttributeValue> item = new HashMap<>();
        item.put(BOOK_ISBN, AttributeValue.builder()
                            .s(book.getIsbn()).build());
        item.put(BOOK_AUTHOR, AttributeValue.builder()
                              .s(book.getAuthor()).build());
        item.put(BOOK_TITLE, AttributeValue.builder()
                             .s(book.getTitle()).build());

        return PutItemRequest.builder()
                .tableName(getTableName())
                .item(item)
                .build();
    }

    protected GetItemRequest getRequest(String isbn) {
        Map<String, AttributeValue> key = new HashMap<>();
        key.put(BOOK_ISBN, AttributeValue.builder().s(isbn).build());

        return GetItemRequest.builder()
                .tableName(getTableName())
                .key(key)
```

```
            .build();
    }
}
```

This last class is the class representing the Book entity:

```
package org.acme.dynamodb;

import java.util.Map;
import java.util.Objects;

import io.quarkus.runtime.annotations.RegisterForReflection;
import software.amazon.awssdk.services.dynamodb.model.AttributeValue;

@RegisterForReflection        ❶
public class Book {
    private String isbn;
    private String author;
    private String title;

    public Book() {           ❷
    }

    public static Book from(Map<String, AttributeValue> item) {
        Book b = new Book();
        if (item != null && !item.isEmpty()) {
            b.setAuthor(item.get(AbstractBookService.BOOK_AUTHOR).s());
            b.setIsbn(item.get(AbstractBookService.BOOK_ISBN).s());
            b.setTitle(item.get(AbstractBookService.BOOK_TITLE).s());
        }
        return b;
    }

    public String getIsbn() {
        return isbn;
    }

    public void setIsbn(String isbn) {
        this.isbn = isbn;
    }

    public String getAuthor() {
        return author;
    }

    public void setAuthor(String author) {
        this.author = author;
    }

    public String getTitle() {
        return title;
    }
```

```
        public void setTitle(String title) {
            this.title = title;
        }

        @Override
        public boolean equals(Object o) {
            if (this == o) return true;
            if (o == null || getClass() != o.getClass()) return false;
            Book book = (Book) o;
            return Objects.equals(isbn, book.isbn) &&
                    Objects.equals(author, book.author) &&
                    Objects.equals(title, book.title);
        }

        @Override
        public int hashCode() {
            return Objects.hash(isbn, author, title);
        }
    }
```

❶   Necessary to have reflection in a native application

❷   Required by DynamoDB client

Most of this is standard DynamoDB code, with the exception of the Quarkus annotation registering the Book class for reflection, which is necessary only if you are creating a native image.

As you can see, the skills you have already acquired while working previously with DynamoDB are still usable without much modification when working with Quarkus, which helps you be more productive.

7.21 Working with MongoDB

Problem

You want to use MongoDB as a persistent store.

Solution

The Quarkus MongoDB extension makes use of the MongoDB Driver and Client.

Discussion

By now you should be familiar with the basics of a RESTful resource and Quarkus configuration. Here we'll show the code and example configuration used to talk to a local MongoDB instance.

Naturally, you'll need to add the connection information to your application:

```
quarkus.mongodb.connection-string = mongodb://localhost:27017
```

The Book class is a representation of the document within MongoDB:

```java
package org.acme.mongodb;

import java.util.HashSet;
import java.util.Objects;
import java.util.Set;

import org.bson.Document;

public class Book {
    public String id;
    public String title;
    public String isbn;
    public Set<String> authors;

    // Needed for JSON-B
    public Book() {}

    public Book(String title) {
        this.title = title;
    }

    public Book(String title, String isbn) {
        this.title = title;
        this.isbn = isbn;
    }

    public Book(String title, String isbn, Set<String> authors) {
        this.title = title;
        this.isbn = isbn;
        this.authors = authors;
    }

    public Book(String id, String title, String isbn, Set<String> authors) {
        this.id = id;
        this.title = title;
        this.isbn = isbn;
        this.authors = authors;
    }

    public static Book from(Document doc) {
        return new Book(doc.getString("id"),
                        doc.getString("title"),
                        doc.getString("isbn"),
                        new HashSet<>(doc.getList("authors", String.class)));
    }

    @Override
```

```
    public boolean equals(Object o) {
        if (this == o) return true;
        if (o == null || getClass() != o.getClass()) return false;
        Book book = (Book) o;
        return Objects.equals(id, book.id) &&
                Objects.equals(title, book.title) &&
                Objects.equals(isbn, book.isbn) &&
                Objects.equals(authors, book.authors);
    }

    @Override
    public int hashCode() {
        return Objects.hash(id, title, isbn, authors);
    }
}
```

This service class acts as a DAO, a way into the MongoDB instance:

```
package org.acme.mongodb;

import java.util.ArrayList;
import java.util.List;
import java.util.Objects;

import javax.enterprise.context.ApplicationScoped;
import javax.inject.Inject;

import com.mongodb.client.MongoClient;
import com.mongodb.client.MongoCollection;
import com.mongodb.client.MongoCursor;
import com.mongodb.client.model.Filters;
import org.bson.Document;

@ApplicationScoped
public class BookService {

    @Inject
    MongoClient mongoClient;

    public List<Book> list() {
        List<Book> list = new ArrayList<>();

        try (MongoCursor<Document> cursor = getCollection()
                                    .find()
                                    .iterator()) {
            cursor.forEachRemaining(doc -> list.add(Book.from(doc)));
        }

        return list;
    }

    public Book findSingle(String isbn) {
        Document document = Objects.requireNonNull(getCollection()
```

```
                .find(Filters.eq("isbn", isbn))
                .limit(1).first());
        return Book.from(document);
    }

    public void add(Book b) {
        Document doc = new Document()
                .append("isbn", b.isbn)
                .append("title", b.title)
                .append("authors", b.authors);
        getCollection().insertOne(doc);
    }

    private MongoCollection<Document> getCollection() {
        return mongoClient.getDatabase("book").getCollection("book");
    }
}
```

Lastly, a RESTful resource makes use of the previous two classes:

```
package org.acme.mongodb;

import java.util.List;

import javax.inject.Inject;
import javax.ws.rs.Consumes;
import javax.ws.rs.GET;
import javax.ws.rs.POST;
import javax.ws.rs.Path;
import javax.ws.rs.PathParam;
import javax.ws.rs.Produces;
import javax.ws.rs.core.MediaType;
import javax.ws.rs.core.Response;

@Path("/book")
@Produces(MediaType.APPLICATION_JSON)
@Consumes(MediaType.APPLICATION_JSON)
public class BookResource {
    @Inject
    BookService service;

    @GET
    public List<Book> getAll() {
        return service.list();
    }

    @GET
    @Path("{isbn}")
    public Book getSingle(@PathParam("isbn") String isbn) {
        return service.findSingle(isbn);
    }

    @POST
```

```
    public Response add(Book b) {
        service.add(b);
        return Response.status(Response.Status.CREATED)
                .entity(service.list()).build();
    }
}
```

We'll leave it as an exercise for the reader to create and use a BSON Codec. One of the other handy features of the MongoDB extension is an automatic health check that runs when using the `quarkus-smallrye-health` extension. The `quarkus-smallrye-health` extension will automatically create a readiness health check for your MongoDB connection. The readiness check, of course, is configurable.

The Quarkus MongoDB extension also includes a reactive client, which will be detailed in Recipe 15.12.

7.22 Using Panache with MongoDB

Problem

You want to use Panache with MongoDB.

Solution

Add the `mongodb-panache` extension and use all the Panache abilities with `Panache MongoEntity`.

Panache for MongoDB works the same as Panache for Hibernate, which we saw in recipes 7.7 through 7.17. It significantly simplifies your entity code:

```
package org.acme.mongodb.panache;

import java.time.LocalDate;
import java.util.List;

import io.quarkus.mongodb.panache.MongoEntity;
import io.quarkus.mongodb.panache.PanacheMongoEntity;
import org.bson.codecs.pojo.annotations.BsonProperty;

@MongoEntity(collection = "book", database = "book")        ❶
public class Book extends PanacheMongoEntity {              ❷
    public String title;
    public String isbn;
    public List<String> authors;

    @BsonProperty("pubDate")                                ❸
    public LocalDate publishDate;

    public static Book findByIsbn(String isbn) {
```

```
        return find("isbn", isbn).firstResult(); ❹
    }

    public static List<Book> findPublishedOn(LocalDate date) {
        return list("pubDate", date);
    }

}
```

❶ The optional @MongoEntity annotation allows you to customize the database and/or collection used

❷ The required part—add your fields as public fields

❸ Customize the serialized field name with @BsonProperty

❹ Query using PanacheQL (subset of JPQL), just like with JPA

Discussion

The Panache MongoDB extension uses the `PojoCodecProvider` to map entites to a MongoDB `Document`. Besides `@BsonProperty`, you can also ignore fields with `@BsonIgnore`. You are also able to set up custom IDs with `@BsonId` and extend `PanacheMongoEntityBase`.

Of course, if you need to write accessor methods, Panache doesn't stop you from doing that; in fact, at build time all the field calls are replaced with the corresponding accessor/mutator calls. Just like Panache for Hibernate, the MongoDB version supports pagination, sorting, streams, and the rest of the Panache API.

The PanacheQL query you see in the previous example is easy to use and understand; but if you prefer to use regular MongoDB queries, those are also supported, provided that the query starts with {.

A slight difference between the Hibernate and MongoDB Panache varieties is MongoDB's ability to use Query Projection on the return of a `find()` method. This allows you to restrict which fields are returned from the database. Here is a very basic example with our Book entity:

```
import io.quarkus.mongodb.panache.ProjectionFor;

@ProjectionFor(Book.class)
public class BookTitle {
    public String title;
}

PanacheQuery<BookTitle> query = Book.find("isbn", "978-1-492-06265-3")
                                    .project(BookTitle.class);
```

If you have a hierarchy of projection classes, the parent class(es) will also need to be annotated with @ProjectionFor.

7.23 Using Neo4j with Quarkus

Problem

You want to connect to and use Neo4j.

Solution

Use the Quarkus Neo4j extension based on the Neo4j Java Driver.

The following examples make use of the asynchronous programming model (based on JDK's completable futures). The driver also makes use of a blocking model, similar to JDBC, and a reactive model. The reactive model is available only to Neo4j 4+ versions.

By now you've seen how to add additional extensions to your project, so we won't cover that here. The following example also manages books, like others before it:

```java
package org.acme.neo4j;

import java.util.HashSet;
import java.util.Set;
import java.util.StringJoiner;

import org.neo4j.driver.Values;
import org.neo4j.driver.types.Node;

public class Book {
  public Long id;
  public String title;
  public String isbn;
  public Set<String> authors;

  // Needed for JSON-B
  public Book() {}

  public Book(String title) {
    this.title = title;
  }

  public Book(String title, String isbn) {
    this.title = title;
    this.isbn = isbn;
  }

  public Book(String title, String isbn, Set<String> authors) {
    this.title = title;
```

```java
    this.isbn = isbn;
    this.authors = authors;
  }

  public Book(Long id, String title, String isbn, Set<String> authors) {
    this.id = id;
    this.title = title;
    this.isbn = isbn;
    this.authors = authors;
  }

  public static Book from(Node node) {
    return new Book(node.id(),
        node.get("title").asString(),
        node.get("isbn").asString(),
        new HashSet<>(
          node.get("authors")
          .asList(Values.ofString())
          )
        );
  }

  public String toJson() {
    final StringJoiner authorString =
      new StringJoiner("\",\"", "[\"", "\"]");

    authors.forEach(authorString::add);

    return "{" +
      "\"title\":\"" + this.title + "\"," +
      "\"isbn\":\"" + this.isbn + "\"," +
      "\"authors\":" + authorString.toString() +
      "}";
  }
}
```

Naturally, you will need to configure the client. This can be as easy as setting the `quarkus.neo4j.uri`, `quarkus.neo4j.authentication.username`, and `quarkus .neo4j.authentication.password` properties. You can consult the extension for more properties.

The first thing you will need to configure the client is the Neo4j Driver. The extension provides an injectable instance:

```java
@Inject
Driver driver;
```

Next, create a new REST resource and add the Driver injection point, then add the basic CRUD operations:

```java
@GET
public CompletionStage<Response> getAll() {
```

```
        AsyncSession session = driver.asyncSession();    ❶

        return session
                .runAsync("MATCH (b:Book) RETURN b ORDER BY b.title")    ❷
                .thenCompose(cursor -> cursor.listAsync(record ->
                        Book.from(record.get("b").asNode()))) ❸
                .thenCompose(books -> session.
                        closeAsync().thenApply(signal -> books)) ❹
                .thenApply(Response::ok)    ❺
                .thenApply(Response.ResponseBuilder::build);
    }
```

❶ Gets an `AsyncSession` from the driver

❷ Executes Cypher (Neo4j's query language) to fetch the data

❸ Retrieves a cursor, creating `Book` instances from the nodes

❹ Closes the session once we're done

❺ Builds a JAX-RS response

The rest of the class/code follow the same pattern:

```
    @POST
    public CompletionStage<Response> create(Book b) {
        AsyncSession session = driver.asyncSession();
        return session
                .writeTransactionAsync(tx ->
                        {
                            String query = "CREATE (b:Book " +
                            "{title: $title, isbn: $isbn, authors: $authors})" +
                            " RETURN b";
                            return tx.runAsync(query,
                                    Values.parameters("title", b.title,
                                            "isbn", b.isbn,
                                            "authors", b.authors))
                                    .thenCompose(ResultCursor::singleAsync);
                        }
                )
                .thenApply(record -> Book.from(record.get("b").asNode()))
                .thenCompose(persistedBook -> session.closeAsync()
                        .thenApply(signal -> persistedBook))
                .thenApply(persistedBook -> Response.created(
                        URI.create("/book/" + persistedBook.id)).build());
    }

    @DELETE
    @Path("{id}")
    public CompletionStage<Response> delete(@PathParam("id") Long id) {
        AsyncSession session = driver.asyncSession();
        return session
```

```
            .writeTransactionAsync(tx -> tx
                    .runAsync("MATCH (b:Book) WHERE id(b) = $id DELETE b",
                            Values.parameters("id", id))
                    .thenCompose(ResultCursor::consumeAsync))
            .thenCompose(resp -> session.closeAsync())
            .thenApply(signal -> Response.noContent().build());
    }
```

This last one is a little different, in that it handles errors:

```
@GET
@Path("{id}")
public CompletionStage<Response> getById(@PathParam("id") Long id) {
    AsyncSession session = driver.asyncSession();
    return session.readTransactionAsync(tx ->
            tx.runAsync("MATCH (b:Book) WHERE id(b) = $id RETURN b",
                            Values.parameters("id", id))
                    .thenCompose(ResultCursor::singleAsync))
            .handle(((record, err) -> {
                if (err != null) {
                    Throwable source = err;
                    if (err instanceof CompletionException)
                        source = ((CompletionException) err).getCause();
                    Response.Status status = Response.Status.
                                                INTERNAL_SERVER_ERROR;
                    if (source instanceof NoSuchRecordException)
                        status = Response.Status.NOT_FOUND;

                    return Response.status(status).build();
                } else {
                    return Response.ok(Book.from(record.get("b")
                                        .asNode())).build();
                }
            }))
            .thenCompose(response -> session.closeAsync()
                                    .thenApply(signal -> response));
    }
```

See Also

The Neo4j Cypher Manual (*https://oreil.ly/ITHPx*) will come in handy as you learn and try new things with Cypher.

7.24 Flyway at Startup

Problem

You want to use Flyway to migrate my database schema.

Solution

Use the `quarkus-flyway` integration extension.

Discussion

Quarkus has first-class support for schema migrations using Flyway. There are five things you need to do to use Flyway with Quarkus at application start:

1. Add the Flyway extension.
2. Add the JDBC driver for your database.
3. Setup the datasource(s).
4. Add migrations to *src/main/resources/db/migration*.
5. Set the `quarkus.flyway.migrate-at-start` to `true`.

The default naming schema for Flyway migrations is `V.<version>__<descrip tion>.sql`. Everything else is taken care of.

You can also use Flyway with multiple datasources. Any settings that need to be configured for each datasource are named with the same schema as datasource names: `quarkus.flyway.datasource name.setting`. For example, it might be `quarkus.flyway.users.migrate-at-start`.

7.25 Using Flyway Programmatically

Problem

You want to use Flyway programmatically. There may be times when you want to control when the schema is migrated instead of doing it at application startup.

Solution

Use the `quarkus-flyway` extension and inject the `Flyway` instance:

```
@Inject
Flyway flyway
```

Discussion

This will inject the default `org.flywaydb.core.Flyway` instance configured against the default datasource. If you have multiple datasources and Flyway instances, you can inject specific ones using either the `@FlywayDataSource` or `@Named` annotation. When using `@FlywayDataSource`, the value is the name of the datasource. If instead you use @Named, the value should be the name of the datasource with the flyway_ prefix:

```
@Inject
@FlywayDataSource("books")
Flyway flywayBooks;

@Inject
@Named("flyway_users")
Flyway flywayUsers;
```

Naturally, you will be able to run all the standard Flyway operations such as clean, migrate, validate, info, baseline, and repair.

CHAPTER 8

Fault Tolerance

In this chapter, you'll learn why you need to embrace failures in microservice architectures because this is something that will happen more often than not. One of the reasons this happens is because microservices architecture heavily relies on the network to function, and the network is a critical part that might not always be available (network down, saturation of the wire, change on the topology, update of the downstream service, etc.).

For this reason, it is important to build services that are fault-tolerant to any kind of problem and to provide graceful solutions instead of just propagating the error.

This chapter will include recipes for the following tasks:

- Implement different resilient strategies
- Provide some fallback logic in case there is an error
- Correctly configure fault-tolerance parameters

8.1 Implementing Automatic Retries

Problem

If there are errors, you want to execute automatic retries in order to try to recover from the failure.

Solution

MicroProfile Fault Tolerance specification provides a way to implement automatic retries on any CDI element, including CDI beans and the MicroProfile REST Client.

One can implement several strategies to protect against failures and, in the worst cases, provide some default logic instead of a failure. Suppose you have a service that suggests books depending on reader preference. If this service is down, instead of failing, you could cache a list of best-selling books so that at least you could provide the list and not a failure. So one of the important parts to define as a fault-tolerance strategy is a fallback logic to execute in case there is no possible recovery.

MicroProfile Fault Tolerance focuses on several strategies to make your code fault-tolerant. Let's look at the first strategy, which is as simple as executing automatic retries.

You need to add extensions for using a MicroProfile Fault Tolerance specification:

```
./mvnw quarkus:add-extension -Dextensions="quarkus-smallrye-fault-tolerance"
```

One of the easiest and sometimes most effective ways to recover from a network failure is to do a retry of the same operation. If it was an intermittent error, then the error could be fixed with some retries.

The classes or methods annotated with `@org.eclipse.microprofile.faulttoler ance.Retry` execute automatic retries if an exception is thrown. You can set different parameters, like max retries, max duration, or jitter; or you can specify the kind of exceptions for which the retries should be executed.

Moreover, you can implement fallback logic by annotating the methods with `@org.eclipse.microprofile.faulttolerance.Fallback`. The logic to execute as a fallback can be implemented as a class implementing the `org.eclipse.micropro file.faulttolerance.FallbackHandler` interface:

```
@Retry(maxRetries = 3, ❶
        delay = 1000) ❷
@Fallback(RecoverHelloMessageFallback.class) ❸
public String getHelloWithFallback() {
    failureSimulator.failAlways();
    return "hello";
}

public static class RecoverHelloMessageFallback
    implements FallbackHandler<String> { ❹

    @Override
    public String handle(ExecutionContext executionContext) {
        return "good bye";
    }

}
```

❶ Sets the maximum retries to 3

❷ There is a delay of 1 second between retries

❸ Adds fallback logic if after 3 retries the problem still persists

❹ `FallbackHandler` template must be the same type as the return type of the recovering method

Discussion

You can override any of these properties via the configuration file. The configuration key follows the followings format: *fully_qualified_class_name/method_name/fault_tolerant_annotation/parameter.*

For example, you can set the parameters specific to a method or a class, or globally:

```
org.acme.quickstart.ServiceInvoker/getHelloWithFallback/Retry/maxDuration=30 ❶
org.acme.quickstart.ServiceInvoker/Retry/maxDuration=3000 ❷
Retry/maxDuration=3000 ❸
```

❶ Overrides at the method level

❷ Overrides at the class level

❸ Overrides globally

See Also

For more information, visit the following pages on the Eclipse MicroProfile website:

- Fault Tolerance (*https://oreil.ly/WzhhA*)
- Fault Tolerance: Retry Policy (*https://oreil.ly/Kjhzj*)

8.2 Implementing Timeouts

Problem

You want to prevent an execution from waiting forever.

Solution

MicroProfile Fault Tolerance specification provides a way to implement timeouts to operations and prevent the execution from waiting forever.

When there is an invocation to an external service, it is good practice to ensure that this operation has a timeout associated with it. This way, if there are network delays or failures, the process doesn't wait for a long time and end up with a failure, but fails fast so you can react to the problem sooner than later.

The classes or methods annotated with @org.eclipse.microprofile.faulttoler ance.Timeout define a timeout. If there is a timeout, then the org.eclipse.micropro file.faulttolerance.exceptions.TimeoutException exception is thrown:

```
@Timeout(value = 2000) ❶
public String getHelloWithTimeout() {
    failureSimulator.longMethod();
    return "hello";
}
```

❶ Sets timeout to 2 seconds

You can override any of these properties via the configuration file, like so:

```
org.acme.quickstart.ServiceInvoker/getHelloWithTimeout/Timeout/value=3000 ❶
org.acme.quickstart.ServiceInvoker/Timeout/value=3000 ❷
Timeout/value=3000 ❸
```

❶ Overrides at the method level

❷ Overrides at the class level

❸ Overrides globally

You can mix the @Timeout annotation with @Fallback to implement some recovery logic in case of a timeout or use @Retry to execute an automatic retry if a timeout exception occurs (@Retry(retryOn=TimeoutException.class)).

See Also

To learn more about the timeout pattern in MicroProfile Fault Tolerance, see the following page on GitHub:

- Timeout (*https://oreil.ly/af9DD*)

8.3 Avoiding Overloads with the Bulkhead Pattern

Problem

You want to limit the number of accepted requests to a service.

Solution

The MicroProfile Fault Tolerance specification provides a *bulkhead* pattern implementation.

The bulkhead pattern limits the operations that can be executed at the same time, keeping the new requests waiting, until the current execution requests can finish. If the waiting requests cannot be executed after a certain amount of time, they are discarded and an exception is thrown.

The classes or methods annotated with `@org.eclipse.microprofile.faulttoler` `ance.Bulkhead` apply a bulkhead limitation. If there are synchronous calls (you'll learn how the bulkhead limitation works with asynchronous calls in Chapter 15), the `org.eclipse.microprofile.faulttolerance.exceptions.BulkheadException` exception is thrown when the limit of concurrent executions is reached, instead of queuing the requests:

```
@Bulkhead(2) ❶
public String getHelloBulkhead() {
    failureSimulator.shortMethod();
    return "hello";
}
```

❶ Sets the limit to two concurrent executions

If you use the `siege` tool to simulate 4 concurrent requests, then the output will look like the following:

```
siege -r 1 -c 4 -v http://localhost:8080/hello/bulkhead

** SIEGE 4.0.4
** Preparing 4 concurrent users for battle.
The server is now under siege...
HTTP/1.1 500     0.47 secs:    2954 bytes ==> GET   /hello/bulkhead
HTTP/1.1 500     0.47 secs:    2954 bytes ==> GET   /hello/bulkhead
HTTP/1.1 200     2.46 secs:       5 bytes ==> GET   /hello/bulkhead
HTTP/1.1 200     2.46 secs:       5 bytes ==> GET   /hello/bulkhead

Transactions:               2 hits
Availability:               50.00 % ❶
```

❶ Only 2 requests are processed

Moreover, you can override any of these properties via the configuration file:

```
org.acme.quickstart.ServiceInvoker/getHelloBulkhead/Bulkhead/value=10 ❶
org.acme.quickstart.ServiceInvoker/Bulkhead/value=10 ❷
Bulkhead/value=10 ❸
```

❶ Overrides at the method level

❷ Overrides at the class level

❸ Overrides globally

Discussion

When you are dealing with (micro)services architecture, a problem can occur when another service is overloaded by more calls than it can consume at one time. If the overload continues, this service might be overwhelmed and stop processing requests in an acceptable amount of time.

You can mix @Bulkhead annotation with any other previously demonstrated fault tolerance annotations to implement a more resilient strategy—for example, a *bulkhead + retry* with delays.

See Also

To learn more about the bulkhead pattern in MicroProfile Fault Tolerance, see the following page on GitHub:

- Bulkhead (*https://oreil.ly/anYN5*)

8.4 Avoiding Unnecessary Calls with the Circuit Breaker Pattern

Problem

You want to prevent a service failure from propagating to other services and consuming several resources.

Solution

MicroProfile Fault Tolerance specification provides the *circuit breaker* pattern to avoid making unnecessary calls if there are errors.

Let's define a circuit breaker that is tripped after 3 errors in a window of 4 requests:

```
@CircuitBreaker(requestVolumeThreshold = 4, ❶
                failureRatio = 0.75, ❷
                delay = 2000) ❸
public String getHelloCircuitBreaker() {
    failureSimulator.fail4Consecutive();
    return "hello";
}
```

❶ Defines the rolling window

❷ Threshold to trip the circuit (4 × 0.75 = 3)

❸ Amount of time that the circuit is opened

You can override any of these properties via the configuration file:

```
org.acme.quickstart.ServiceInvoker/getHelloCircuitBreaker \
    /CircuitBreaker/failureRatio=0.75  ❶
org.acme.quickstart.ServiceInvoker/CircuitBreaker/failureRatio=3000  ❷
Timeout/value=3000  ❸
```

❶ Overrides at method level; this should be on the same line

❷ Overrides at class level

❸ Overrides globally

Discussion

When you are dealing with (micro)services architecture, a problem can occur when the communication to another service becomes impossible, either because the service is down or because of high latency. When this happens, expensive resources such as threads or file descriptors might be consumed on the caller while waiting for the other service to respond. If this continues, you could end up with resource exhaustion, which would mean that no more requests can be handled by this service, which would trigger a cascade of errors to other services throughout the application.

Figure 8-1 illustrates how a failure happening in a service, in the middle of the mesh, is propagated through all its callers. This is an example of a cascading failure.

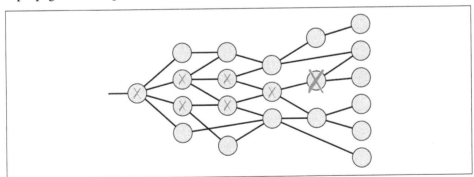

Figure 8-1. Cascading failure

The circuit breaker pattern fixes a cascading failure by detecting the number of consecutive failures inside a detection window. If the defined error threshold is overtaken, then the circuit is tripped, meaning that for a certain amount of time, all attempts to call this method will fail immediately without trying to execute it. Figure 8-2 illustrates the schema of circuit breaker calls.

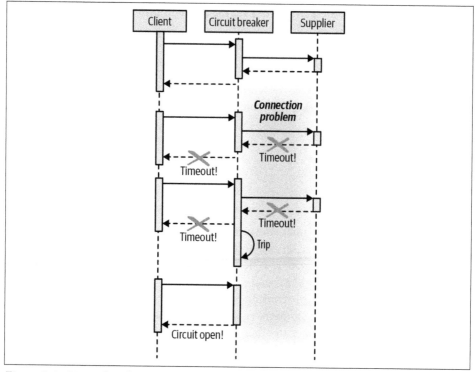

Figure 8-2. Circuit breaker calls

After some time, the circuit will become half-opened, which means that the next call will not fail immediately but will try again against the real system. If the call succeeds, then the circuit will be closed; otherwise, it will remain open. All possible states of a circuit breaker pattern are shown in Figure 8-3.

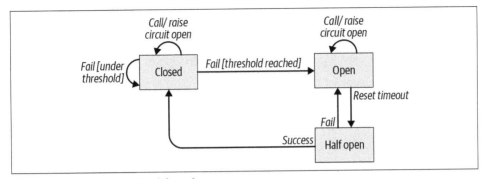

Figure 8-3. Circuit breaker life cycle

The classes or methods annotated with `@org.eclipse.microprofile.faulttoler` `ance.CircuitBreaker` define a circuit breaker for that specific operation. If the circuit is opened, then the `org.eclipse.microprofile.faulttolerance.excep` `tions.CircuitBreakerOpenException` exception is thrown.

You can also mix `@CircuitBreaker` with `@Timeout`, `@Fallback`, `@Bulkhead`, or `@Retry`, but the following must be taken into consideration:

- If `@Fallback` is used, the fallback logic is executed if a `CircuitBreakerOpenExcep` `tion` is thrown.

- If `@Retry` is used, each retry is processed by the circuit breaker and recorded as either a success or a failure.

- If `@Bulkhead` is used, the circuit breaker is checked before attempting to enter the bulkhead.

See Also

To learn more about the circuit breaker pattern in MicroProfile Fault Tolerance, see the following page on GitHub:

- Circuit Breaker (*https://oreil.ly/iOWuR*)

8.5 Disabling Fault Tolerance

Problem

You want to disable fault tolerance in some environments.

Solution

The MicroProfile Fault Tolerance specification provides a special parameter to enable or disable fault-tolerance logic either globally or individually.

There are some cases in which you might want to disable fault-tolerance logic. The MicroProfile Fault Tolerance specification defines a special parameter called `enabled` that can be used to enable or disable the logic from the configuration file either globally or individually:

```
org.acme.quickstart.ServiceInvoker/getHelloCircuitBreaker/\
    CircuitBreaker/enabled=false ❶
org.acme.quickstart.ServiceInvoker/CircuitBreaker/enabled=false ❷
CircuitBreaker/enabled=false ❸
MP_Fault_Tolerance_NonFallback_Enabled=false ❹
```

❶ Disable at the method level; this should be on the same line

❷ Disable at the class level

❸ Disable globally by type

❹ Disable all fault tolerance

CHAPTER 9

Observability

In this chapter, you'll learn about observability and why it is important to have in the microservices architecture. Observability answers the question of how your system is behaving by observing some parameters like error codes, performance, or any kind of business metric. Quarkus integrates with several technologies used for observability natively.

This chapter will include recipes for how to accomplish the following tasks:

- Define health checks
- Provide metrics to the monitoring system
- Configure distributed tracing to have an overview of a request inside the mesh

9.1 Using Automatic Health Checks

Problem

You want to check whether the service is up and running and able to handle requests correctly.

Solution

The MicroProfile Health specification provides an API to probe the state of a service from another machine (e.g., Kubernetes Controller).

To enable MicroProfile Health in a Quarkus application, you need to register only the `quarkus-smallrye-health` extension:

```
./mvnw quarkus:add-extension -Dextensions="quarkus-smallrye-health"
```

With the extension in the classpath, Quarkus automatically registers a default liveness and readiness probe, which both return UP when the service is up and running:

```
./mvnw compile quarkus:dev

curl localhost:8080/health/live ❶

{
    "status": "UP", ❷
    "checks": [ ❸
    ]
}


curl localhost:8080/health/ready ❹

{
    "status": "UP",
    "checks": [
    ]
}
```

❶ Liveness URL

❷ Status is UP

❸ No checks (just defaults)

❹ Readiness URL

Discussion

The MicroProfile Health specification provides two kinds of health checks:

Liveness
> Returns a 200 OK with result UP if the service has been started, 503 Service Unavailable with result DOWN if the service is not live, and 500 Server Error if the health check couldn't be calculated. The liveness probe endpoint is registered by default at the */health/live* endpoint.

Readiness
> Returns a 200 OK with result UP if the service is ready to process requests. This is different from the liveness probe because liveness simply means that the service is up but might not be able to process any request yet (e.g., because it is executing a database migration). A 503 Service Unavailable with result DOWN is returned if the service cannot yet accept any request, and a 500 Server Error is returned if the health check couldn't be calculated. The readiness probe endpoint is registered by default at the */health/ready* endpoint.

If you are configuring Quarkus to use an SQL database (JDBC), it will automatically register a readiness health check (in the `checks` section) that validates that the connection to the database is possible.

The following extensions provide automatic readiness/liveness probes:

Datasource
    A readiness probe to check database connection status.

Kafka
    A readiness probe to check Kafka connection status. It is disabled by default and needs to be enabled by setting `quarkus.kafka.health.enabled` property to `true`.

MongoDB
    A readiness probe to check MongoDB connection status.

Neo4j
    A readiness probe to check Neo4j connection status.

Artemis
    A readiness probe to check Artemis JMS connection status.

Kafka Streams
    Liveness (for stream state) and readiness (topics created) probes.

Vault
    A readiness probe to check Vault status.

The automatic generation of the probes can be disabled by setting the `quarkus.component.health.enabled` to `false`:

```
quarkus.kafka-streams.health.enabled=false
quarkus.mongodb.health.enabled=false
quarkus.neo4j.health.enabled=false
```

See Also

To learn more about the MicroProfile Health specification, see the following page on GitHub:

- MicroProfile Health (*https://oreil.ly/wZjHC*)

9.2 Creating Custom Health Checks

Problem

You want to customize how to check that a service is up and running and that it is able to handle requests correctly.

Solution

The MicroProfile Health specification enables you to create custom liveness and readiness health checks. In some circumstances, a custom health-check logic might be needed for either liveness or readiness probes.

The MicroProfile Health specification allows you to create custom health checks by creating a method annotated with @org.eclipse.microprofile.health.Liveness and @org.eclipse.microprofile.health.Readiness and returning an implementation of org.eclipse.microprofile.health.HealthCheck interface.

Create a new class at org.acme.quickstart.LivenessCheck.java to implement a custom liveness probe:

```
@ApplicationScoped ❶
@Liveness ❷
public class LivenessCheck implements HealthCheck { ❸

    @Override
    public HealthCheckResponse call() {
        HealthCheckResponseBuilder checkResponseBuilder = HealthCheckResponse
        .named("custom liveness"); ❹

        if(isUpAndRunning()) {
            return checkResponseBuilder.up().build(); ❺
        } else {
            return checkResponseBuilder.down()
                .withData("reason", "Failed connection")
                .build(); ❻
        }

    }
}
```

❶ Needs to be a CDI class

❷ Sets health check as liveness

❸ Implements HealthCheck as a requirement

❹ Sets health check name

❺ Sets result as up

❻ Sets result as down

Let's check that this liveness probe works as expected:

```
./mvnw compile quarkus:dev

curl localhost:8080/health/live

{
    "status": "UP",
    "checks": [
        {
            "name": "custom liveness",
            "status": "UP"
        }
    ]
}
```

Discussion

Because health checks are registered as CDI beans, you can also produce health checks in factory objects, as explained in Recipe 5.7.

Create a new factory class to contain the new health check—in this case, a readiness check:

```
@ApplicationScoped ❶
public class CustomHealthCheck {

    @Produces ❷
    @Readiness ❸
    public HealthCheck ready() {
        if (isReady()) {
            return io.smallrye.health.HealthStatus.up("Custom readiness"); ❹
        } else {
            return io.smallrye.health.HealthStatus.down("Custom readiness");
        }
    }
}
```

❶ Needs to be a CDI class

❷ The method produces a health check

❸ Readiness probe

❹ HealthStatus is a utility class that implements the HealthCheck interface for you

Let's check that this readiness probe works as expected:

```
./mvnw compile quarkus:dev

curl localhost:8080/health/ready

{
    "checks": [
        {
            "name": "Custom readiness",
            "status": "UP"
        }
    ],
    "status": "UP"
}
```

See Also

The MicroProfile Health specification is perfect for defining Kubernetes liveness and readiness probes. You can learn about them at the following website:

- Kubernetes: Configure Liveness, Readiness, and Startup Probes (*https://oreil.ly/ nTaaa*)

9.3 Exposing Metrics

Problem

You want to proactively check the current status of a service in production by exposing service metrics in order to detect any misbehavior as quickly as possible.

Solution

The MicroProfile Metrics specification provides a way to build and expose metrics from your application to a monitoring tool (e.g., Prometheus).

To enable MicroProfile Metrics in a Quarkus application, you need to register only the `quarkus-smallrye-metrics` extension:

```
./mvnw quarkus:add-extension -Dextensions="quarkus-smallrye-metrics"
```

With the extension in the classpath, Quarkus provides monitoring parameters by default, exposing them at the `/metrics` endpoint in Prometheus format:

```
./mvnw compile quarkus:dev

curl localhost:8080/metrics

base_cpu_processCpuLoad_percent 0.0
```

```
base_memory_maxHeap_bytes 4.294967296E9
base_cpu_systemLoadAverage 2.580078125
base_thread_daemon_count 6.0
...
vendor_memoryPool_usage_max_bytes{name="Compressed Class Space"} 3336768.0
vendor_memory_usedNonHeap_bytes 3.9182104E7
```

The output format can be changed to JSON by adding `application/json` type in the HTTP Accept header:

```
curl --header "Accept:application/json" localhost:8080/metrics

{
    "base": {
        "cpu.systemLoadAverage": 4.06201171875,
        "thread.count": 20,
        "classloader.loadedClasses.count": 4914,
        ...
    },
    "vendor": {
        "memoryPool.usage.max;name=G1 Survivor Space": 7340032,
        "memory.freePhysicalSize": 814391296,
        "memoryPool.usage.max;name=CodeHeap 'non-profiled nmethods'": 5773056,
        ...
    }
}
```

Discussion

Knowing how a service is behaving in microservices architectures is critical in anticipating any problem that might affect all your applications.

With monolith applications, monitoring service behavior was fairly easy because you had only three or four elements to monitor; but now with (micro)services architectures, you might have hundreds of elements to monitor.

There are many possible values to monitor, such as the following:

- Memory
- Disk space
- Network
- JVM resources
- Performance of critical methods
- Business metrics (e.g., the number of payments per second)
- Overall health of your cluster

If you look closely at the output, you'll see that the parameters are prefixed with either `base` or `vendor`. MicroProfile Metrics categorizes the metrics under three categories:

base

> The core information of the server. These metrics are always required because they are specified in the specification. Access them at */metrics/base*.

vendor

> Vendor-specific information. Each implementation might provide different ones. Access them at */metrics/vendor*.

application

> Custom information developed ad hoc for that service using the MicroProfile Metrics extension mechanism. Access them at */metrics/application*.

You can configure where metrics are exposed by setting the `quarkus.smallrye-metrics.path` property to the path where you want to expose them. By default, this property is set to `/metrics`.

See Also

To learn more about MicroProfile Metrics, visit the following page on GitHub:

* Metrics for Eclipse MicroProfile (*https://oreil.ly/Q875g*)

9.4 Creating Metrics

Problem

You want to monitor some custom metrics, such as performance metrics or business metrics.

Solution

The MicroProfile Metrics specification provides different annotations to register different kinds of monitoring parameters like counters, durations, and gauges. With these annotations, you can create custom metrics that might be related to business or performance parameters instead of physical values like memory, and CPU.

The following are the MicroProfile Metrics annotations:

Annotation	Description
org.eclipse.microprofile.met rics.annotation.Counted	Counts number of invocations.
org.eclipse.microprofile.met rics.annotation.Timed	Tracks the duration of invocations.
org.eclipse.microprofile.met rics.annotation.SimplyTimed	Tracks the duration of invocations without mean and distribution calculations. A simplified version of Timed.
org.eclipse.microprofile.met rics.annotation.Metered	Tracks the frequency of invocations.
org.eclipse.microprofile.met rics.annotation.Gauge	Samples a discrete value of an annotated field or method.
org.eclipse.microprofile.met rics.annotation.ConcurrentGauge	Gauge to count parallel invocations.
org.eclipse.microprofile.met rics.annotation.Metric	Used to inject a metric. Valid types are Meter, Timer, Counter and Histogram. Gauge with Metric can only be used in a CDI producer.

Let's look at how to use metrics annotations and how to create an histogram metric.

Counter

A *counter* increments invocations that are done to a method annotated with @Counted and can be used at method or class level.

In the following example, the number of invocations of a method is counted:

```
@Counted( ❶
        name = "number-of-transactions", ❷
        displayName = "Transactions", ❸
        description = "How many transactions have been processed" ❹
)
@POST
@Consumes(MediaType.APPLICATION_JSON)
public Response doTransaction(Transaction transaction) {
    return Response.ok().build();
}
```

❶ Registers the counter

❷ Name of the counter

❸ Sets a display name

❹ Description of the counter

Let's check the counter monitor:

```
./mvnw compile quarkus:dev

curl -d '{"from":"A", "to":"B", "amount":2000}' \
    -H "Content-Type: application/json" \
    -X POST http://localhost:8080/tx

curl localhost:8080/metrics/application

application_org_acme_TransactionResource_number_of_transactions_total 1.0
```

Gauge

A *gauge* is a simple value that you want to expose to be measured, similar to a gas gauge on a car. To register it, you need to annotate either a field or a method with @Gauge, and the value/return value will be exposed automatically:

```
private long highestTransaction = 0; ❶

@POST
@Consumes(MediaType.APPLICATION_JSON)
public Response doTransaction(Transaction transaction) {
    if (transaction.amount > highestTransaction) { ❷
        highestTransaction = transaction.amount;
    }
    return Response.ok().build();
}
@Gauge( ❸
        name = "highest-gross-transaction", ❹
        description = "Highest transaction so far.",
        unit= MetricUnits.NONE ❺
)
public long highestTransaction() {
    return highestTransaction;
}
```

❶ Field to store the highest transaction

❷ Updates the field if the current transaction is higher

❸ Sets return value as a gauge

❹ Name of the gauge

❺ Metrics of this gauge (e.g., seconds, percentage, per second, bytes, etc.)

Execute the following commands to run the application, seed some metrics data, and view the output:

```
./mvnw compile quarkus:dev

curl -d '{"from":"A", "to":"B", "amount":2000}' \
    -H "Content-Type: application/json" \
    -X POST http://localhost:8080/tx

curl localhost:8080/metrics/application

application_org_acme_TransactionResource_highest_gross_transaction 2000.0
```

Metered

A *metered* metric measures the rate at which a method is called. The @Metered annotation can be used at the method or class level:

```
@Metered( ❶
        name = "transactions",
        unit = MetricUnits.SECONDS, ❷
        description = "Rate of transactions"
)
```

❶ Registers the metered metric

❷ Sets units as seconds

Execute the following commands to run the application, seed some metrics data, and view the output:

```
./mvnw compile quarkus:dev

curl -d '{"from":"A", "to":"B", "amount":2000}' \
    -H "Content-Type: application/json" \
    -X POST http://localhost:8080/tx

curl localhost:8080/metrics/application

application_org_acme_TransactionResource_transactions \
  _rate_per_second  0.09766473618811813
application_org_acme_TransactionResource_transactions \
  _one_min_rate_per_second  0.015991117074135343
application_org_acme_TransactionResource_transactions \
  _five_min_rate_per_second  0.0033057092356765017
application_org_acme_TransactionResource_transactions \
  _fifteen_min_rate_per_second  0.0011080303990206543
```

Timed

A *timed* metric measures the duration of a call. The @Timed annotation can be used at method or class level:

```
@Timed( ❶
    name = "average-transaction",
    unit = MetricUnits.SECONDS,
    description = "Average duration of transaction"
)
```

❶ Registers the timed metric

Execute the following commands to run the application, seed some metrics data, and view the output:

```
./mvnw compile quarkus:dev

curl -d '{"from":"A", "to":"B", "amount":2000}' \
    -H "Content-Type: application/json" \
    -X POST http://localhost:8080/tx

curl localhost:8080/metrics/application

application_org_acme_TransactionResource_average_transaction \
  _rate_per_second 0.7080455375154214
application_org_acme_TransactionResource_average_transaction \
  _one_min_rate_per_second 0.0
application_org_acme_TransactionResource_average_transaction \
  _five_min_rate_per_second 0.0
application_org_acme_TransactionResource_average_transaction \
  _fifteen_min_rate_per_second 0.0
application_org_acme_TransactionResource_average_transaction \
  _min_seconds 1.0693E-5
application_org_acme_TransactionResource_average_transaction \
  _max_seconds 4.9597E-5
application_org_acme_TransactionResource_average_transaction \
  _mean_seconds 3.0145E-5
application_org_acme_TransactionResource_average_transaction \
  _stddev_seconds 1.9452E-5
application_org_acme_TransactionResource_average_transaction \
  _seconds_count 2.0
application_org_acme_TransactionResource_average_transaction \
  _seconds{quantile="0.5"} 4.9597E-5
application_org_acme_TransactionResource_average_transaction \
  _seconds{quantile="0.75"} 4.9597E-5
application_org_acme_TransactionResource_average_transaction \
  _seconds{quantile="0.95"} 4.9597E-5
application_org_acme_TransactionResource_average_transaction \
  _seconds{quantile="0.98"} 4.9597E-5
application_org_acme_TransactionResource_average_transaction \
  _seconds{quantile="0.99"} 4.9597E-5
application_org_acme_TransactionResource_average_transaction \
  _seconds{quantile="0.999"} 4.9597E-5
```

Histogram

A *histogram* measures the distribution of values across time; it measures things like min, max, standard deviation, or quantiles like the median or 95th. Histograms do not have a proper annotation, but the `org.eclipse.microprofile.metrics.Histogram` class is used to update the metric:

```
@Metric(name = "transaction-evolution") ❶
Histogram transactionHistogram;

@POST
@Consumes(MediaType.APPLICATION_JSON)
public Response doTransaction(Transaction transaction) {
    transactionHistogram.update(transaction.amount); ❷
    return Response.ok().build();
}
```

❶ Injects a histogram with given name

❷ Updates the histogram with a new value

Execute the following commands to run the application, seed some metrics data, and view the output:

```
./mvnw compile quarkus:dev

curl -d '{"from":"A", "to":"B", "amount":2000}' \
    -H "Content-Type: application/json" \
    -X POST http://localhost:8080/tx

curl localhost:8080/metrics/application

application_org_acme_TransactionResource_transaction_evolution_min 2000.0
application_org_acme_TransactionResource_transaction_evolution_max 2000.0
application_org_acme_TransactionResource_transaction_evolution_mean 2000.0
application_org_acme_TransactionResource_transaction_evolution_stddev 0.0
application_org_acme_TransactionResource_transaction_evolution_count 2.0
application_org_acme_TransactionResource_transaction_evolution \
   {quantile="0.5"}  2000.0
application_org_acme_TransactionResource_transaction_evolution \
   {quantile="0.75"}  2000.0
application_org_acme_TransactionResource_transaction_evolution \
   {quantile="0.95"}  2000.0
application_org_acme_TransactionResource_transaction_evolution \
   {quantile="0.98"}  2000.0
application_org_acme_TransactionResource_transaction_evolution \
   {quantile="0.99"}  2000.0
application_org_acme_TransactionResource_transaction_evolution \
   {quantile="0.999"}  2000.0
```

Discussion

You can get metadata information from any metric by querying into a specific endpoint using the OPTION HTTP method. The metadata is exposed at /metrics/*scope*/*metric_name*, where the *scope* is base, vendor, or application and the *metric_name* is the name of the metric (in case of application one, the one set in name attribute).

9.5 Using Distributed Tracing

Problem

You want to profile and monitor the whole application.

Solution

The MicroProfile OpenTracing specification uses the OpenTracing standard API (*https://opentracing.io*) for instrumenting microservices for distributed tracing. Quarkus integrates with the MicroProfile OpenTracing specification as a solution for distributed tracing.

Distributed tracing is a method used to profile and monitor your distributed systems. It can be used to detect failures in the communication between services, determine which points are performance problems, or perform a log record of all requests and responses that are happening within the network mesh.

There are five important concepts in OpenTracing that you must understand before proceeding with distributed tracing:

Span
A named operation representing a unit of work done (e.g., a service executed). A span can contain more spans in a child-parent form.

Span context
Trace information that is propagated from service to service (e.g., span ID).

Baggage items
Custom key/value pairs that are propagated from service to service.

Tags
Key/value pairs defined by the user that are set in spans so they can be queried and filtered (e.g., http.status_code).

Logs
Key/value pairs associated with a span that contains logging messages or other important information. Logs are used to identify a specific moment in the span; meanwhile, tags apply to the whole span independently of time.

For this example, the Jaeger (*https://www.jaegertracing.io*) server is used to collect all traces from your application and make them available to be consumed or queried. Figure 9-1 shows the interaction between services and Jaeger.

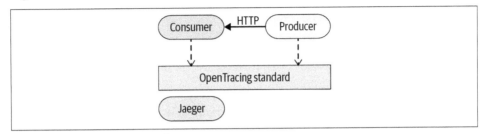

Figure 9-1. Microservices and Jaeger

The Jaeger concepts explained in the previous paragraph are illustrated in Figure 9-2.

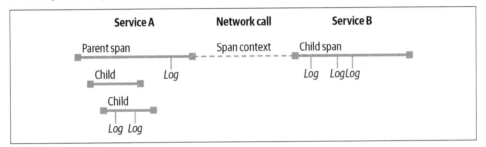

Figure 9-2. Jaeger concepts

The `jaegertracing/all-in-one` container image is used because it contains all of the Jaeger backend components and the UI in a single image. This is not meant to be used in production, but, for the sake of simplicity, this is the image used in Recipe 9.5:

```
docker run -e COLLECTOR_ZIPKIN_HTTP_PORT=9411 -p 5775:5775/udp \
    -p 6831:6831/udp -p 6832:6832/udp -p 5778:5778 -p 16686:16686 \
    -p 14268:14268 -p 9411:9411 jaegertracing/all-in-one:1.15.1
```

To enable MicroProfile OpenTracing in a Quarkus application, you need to register only the `quarkus-smallrye-opentracing` extension.

```
./mvnw quarkus:add-extension -Dextensions="quarkus-smallrye-opentracing"
```

With the extension in the classpath, Quarkus/MicroProfile OpenTracing sends default tracing information to the Jaeger server. The only thing you need to do is configure the Jaeger endpoint where all tracing information should be sent.

The default tracing information collected includes the following:

- Hardware metrics like CPU, memory, and available processors.
- JVM metrics like memory heap and thread pool.

MicroProfile OpenTracing creates a new span for every inbound request. The default name of this new span is *HTTP method:package name.class name.method name.*

Spans created for incoming requests will contain the following tags with correct values:

- `Tags.SPAN_KIND` = `Tags.SPAN_KIND_SERVER`
- `Tags.HTTP_METHOD` with the HTTP method used in the incoming request
- `Tags.HTTP_URL` with the URL of incoming endpoints
- `Tags.HTTP_STATUS` with the HTTP status result code
- `Tags.COMPONENT` = `"jaxrs"`
- `Tags.ERROR` to `true` if a server error (5XX error code) occurred; if an exception has a provided object, two logs are added, one with `event=error` and another one with `error.object=<error object instance>`

In cases of outbound requests, a new span is created that is a child of the current active span (if it exists). The default name of the new span is <HTTP method>. Spans created for outgoing requests will contain the following tags with correct values:

- `Tags.SPAN_KIND=Tags.SPAN_KIND_SCLIENT`
- `Tags.HTTP_METHOD` with the HTTP method used in outgoing request
- `Tags.HTTP_URL` with the URL of the outgoing endpoint
- `Tags.HTTP_STATUS` with the *HTTP* status result code
- `Tags.COMPONENT` = `"jaxrs"`
- `Tags.ERROR` to `true` if a client error (4XX error code) occurred; if an exception has a provided object, two logs are added, one with `event=error` and another one with `error.object=<error object instance>`

The last thing to do is configure the Jaeger parameters:

```
quarkus.jaeger.service-name=shopping-cart ❶
quarkus.jaeger.sampler-type=const ❷
quarkus.jaeger.sampler-param=1 ❸
quarkus.jaeger.endpoint=http://localhost:14268/api/traces ❹
```

❶ Service name to be identified inside Jaeger

❷ Set up a sampler

❸ Percentage of requests to sample in percentage (1 is sampling all)

❹ The Jaeger server location

Then start the application and send some requests to one of the endpoints defined in the service. After that, inspect all distributed tracings by accessing Jaeger UI. Open a browser, and visit *http://localhost:16686* (the Jaeger UI) to see the tracing information.

In the initial page, you can filter by several parameters, but one of them is used to select the service that will be used to view the completed requests.

The home page of Jaeger is shown in Figure 9-3.

Figure 9-3. Jaeger's home page

Push the Find Traces button to select all the traces that meet the given criteria, and you should see the image shown in Figure 9-4.

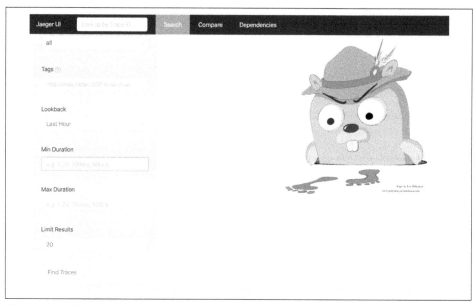

Figure 9-4. Find traces

You'll see all the requests that meet the criteria. In this case, the requests are all traces that are involved in the `shopping-cart` service, as seen in Figure 9-5.

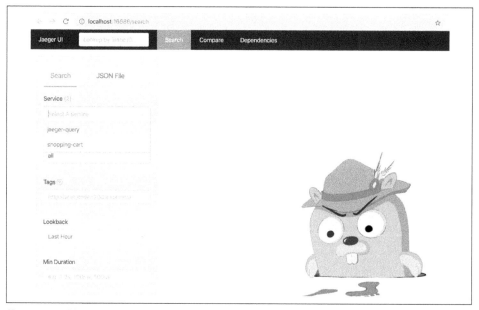

Figure 9-5. View traces

If you click on any of the requests, more detail of the specific request is shown, as shown in Figure 9-6.

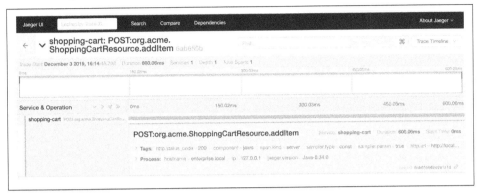

Figure 9-6. Detail of a request

In case of errors, a new log entry is added that sets the error message, as shown in Figure 9-7.

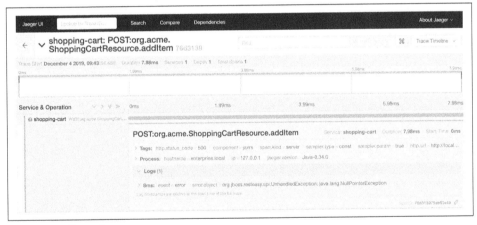

Figure 9-7. Error log message

Disabling Tracing

Any request (incoming or outgoing) is traced by default. Disable the tracing of a specific class or method by annotating it with `@org.eclipse.microprofile.opentracing.Traced`:

```
@Traced(false)
public class TransactionResource {}
```

Discussion

Configure OpenTracing by setting options in the *src/main/resources/application.properties* file or by using any other method discussed in Recipe 9.6. Some of the most important configuration properties are listed in Table 9-1.

Table 9-1. OpenTracing configuration properties

Property	Description
`quarkus.jaeger.enabled`	Defines if the Jaeger extension is enabled (default: `true`). It is a build property and cannot be modified at runtime.
`quarkus.jaeger.endpoint`	Traces server endpoint.
`quarkus.jaeger.auth-token`	Authentication token to the endpoint.
`quarkus.jaeger.user`	Username to send as part of authentication to the endpoint.
`quarkus.jaeger.password`	Password to send as part of authentication to the endpoint.
`quarkus.jaeger.sampler-type`	The sampler type (`const`, `probabilistic`, `ratelimiting`. or `remote`).
`quarkus.jaeger.sampler-param`	Percentage of traffic sampled (0.0-1.0).
`quarkus.jaeger.service-name`	The service name.
`quarkus.jaeger.tags`	A comma-separated list of key/value tags that are added to all spans. Environment variables are supported by using `${environment Var:default}`.
`quarkus.jaeger.propagation`	The format used to propagate the trace context (default is `jaeger`). Possible values are `jaeger` and `b3`.
`quarkus.jaeger.sender-factory`	The sender factory class name.

See Also

See Quarkus's guide to using OpenTracing (*https://oreil.ly/A2GJu*) for the full list of supported properties.

More information about MicroProfile OpenTracing specification can be found at the following page on GitHub:

- MicroProfile OpenTracing (*https://oreil.ly/v7kjr*)

9.6 Custom Distributed Tracing

Problem

You want to add custom information in the current tracing span.

Solution

The MicroProfile OpenTracing specification uses the `io.opentracing.Tracer` class to add new information in the current span.

In some situations, it is required to create a new child span or add information in the current span, like a new tag, logging information, or a baggage item. To add this information, MicroProfile OpenTracing produces an instance of the `io.opentracing.Tracer` class to manipulate the current span.

Suppose you want to tag all requests that are made by important customers. For this example, important customers are those whose ID starts with 1:

```
@Inject ❶
Tracer tracer;
@POST
@Path("/add/{customerId}")
@Transactional
@Consumes(MediaType.APPLICATION_JSON)
public Response addItem(@PathParam("customerId") String customerId, Item item) {

    if (customerId.startsWith("1")) {
        tracer.activeSpan().setTag("important.customer", true); ❷
    }
}
```

❶ Injects a `Tracer` instance

❷ Creates a new tag in the current span

Then any request for an important customer is tagged accordingly.

Custom tags are presented as shown in Figure 9-8.

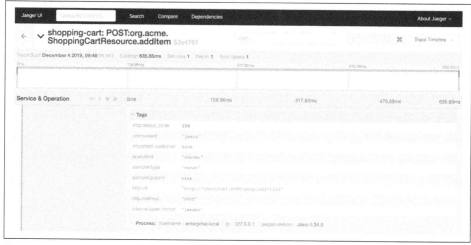

Figure 9-8. Custom tags

Discussion

Quarkus supports one of the OpenTracing customizations to instrument JDBC, so if you want to monitor SQL queries, you don't need to customize the current span yourself; you can use the integration provided in the form of dependency.

Register the `opentracing-jdbc` artifact into your build tool:

```
<dependency>
    <groupId>io.opentracing.contrib</groupId>
    <artifactId>opentracing-jdbc</artifactId>
</dependency>
```

Then activate tracing for JDBC connections. This is done by adding the word `trac ing` in the JDBC URL. Because Quarkus uses JPA, you also need to configure the datasource and Hibernate to use the dedicated tracing driver:

```
quarkus.datasource.url=jdbc:tracing:h2:mem:mydb ❶
quarkus.datasource.driver=io.opentracing.contrib.jdbc.TracingDriver ❷
quarkus.datasource.username=sa
quarkus.datasource.password=
quarkus.hibernate-orm.database.generation=update
quarkus.hibernate-orm.log.sql=true
quarkus.hibernate-orm.dialect=org.hibernate.dialect.H2Dialect ❸
```

❶ Updates JDBC URL with `tracing`

❷ Sets the `TracingDriver` instead of the database driver

❸ Configure dialect of the real database

All queries that are done in a request are also reflected in the Jaeger UI.

JDBC traces are presented as shown in Figure 9-9.

Figure 9-9. JDBC traces

If you look closely at the screenshot, you'll notice that there is a new tag, with the name db.statement, that reflects the query that has been traced. Also, notice that there is one *shopping-cart* span that at the same time contains six more spans, one for each query.

To ignore specific queries, you can set (multiple times) the ignoreForTracing property with the queries to ignore (e.g., jdbc:tracing:h2:mem:test?ignoreForTracing=SELECT * FROM \"TEST\").

CHAPTER 10

Integrating with Kubernetes

So far, you've been learning how to develop and run Quarkus applications on bare-metal, but where Quarkus really shines is when it is running in a Kubernetes cluster.

In this chapter, you'll learn about the integration between Quarkus and Kubernetes, and how several extensions can help develop and deploy a Quarkus service for Kubernetes.

Kubernetes is becoming the de facto platform to deploy applications; for this reason it is important to have a good understanding of Kubernetes and how to correctly develop and deploy applications on it.

In this chapter, you'll learn how to accomplish the following tasks:

- Build and push container images
- Generate Kubernetes resources
- Deploy a Quarkus service
- Develop a Kubernetes operator
- Deploy a service in Knative

10.1 Building and Pushing Container Images

Problem

You want to build and push container images.

Solution

The working unit in Kubernetes is a *pod*. A pod represents a group of containers that are running in the same host machine and share resources like IP and ports. To deploy a service to Kubernetes, you need to create a pod. Since a pod is composed by one or more containers, you need to build a container image of your service.

Quarkus provides extensions for building and optionally pushing container images. At the time of writing, the following container build strategies are supported:

Jib

Jib builds Docker and OCI container images for your Java applications without a Docker daemon (Dockerless). This makes it perfect for building Docker images when running the process inside a container because you avoid the hassle of the Docker-in-Docker (DinD) process. Further, using Jib with Quarkus caches all dependencies in a different layer than the actual application, making rebuilds fast and small. This improves push times as well as build times.

Docker

Using the Docker strategy builds container images using the `docker` binary, which is installed locally and by default uses `Dockerfiles` located under *src/main/docker* to build the images.

S2I

The Source-to-Image (S2I) strategy uses `s2i` binary builds to perform container builds inside an OpenShift cluster. S2I builds require creating a `BuildConfig` and two `ImageStream` resources. The creation of these resources is leveraged by the Quarkus Kubernetes extension.

In this recipe, we're going to build and push the container using Jib; the "Discussion" section of this recipe will address Docker and S2I.

To build and push a container image using Jib, first you need to add the Jib extension:

```
./mvnw quarkus:add-extensions -Dextensions="quarkus-container-image-jib"
```

Then you can customize the container image build process. You can set these properties in the *application.properties*, system properties, or environment variables, just as any other configuration parameter in Quarkus:

```
quarkus.container-image.group=lordofthejars ❶
quarkus.container-image.registry=quay.io ❷
quarkus.container-image.username=lordofthejars ❸
#quarkus.container-image.password= ❹
```

❶ Sets the group part of the image; by default this is `${user.name}`

❷ Registry where to push the image; by default, images are pushed to `docker.io`

❸ The username to log into the container registry

❹ The password to log into the container registry

To build and push the container image for the project, you need to set the `quarkus.container-image.push` parameter to `true`, and during the `package` stage, the container is created and pushed:

```
./mvnw clean package -Dquarkus.container-image.push=true

...
[INFO] --- maven-jar-plugin:2.4:jar (default-jar) @ greeting-jib ---
[INFO] Building jar: /greeting-jib/target/greeting-jib-1.0-SNAPSHOT.jar
[INFO]
[INFO] --- quarkus-maven-plugin:1.3.0.CR2:build (default) @ greeting-jib ---
[INFO] [org.jboss.threads] JBoss Threads version 3.0.1.Final
[INFO] [io.quarkus.deployment.pkg.steps.JarResultBuildStep] Building thin jar:
    greeting-jib/target/greeting-jib-1.0-SNAPSHOT-runner.jar
[INFO] [io.quarkus.container.image.jib.deployment.JibProcessor]
    Starting container image build ❶
[WARNING] [io.quarkus.container.image.jib.deployment.JibProcessor]
    Base image 'fabric8/java-alpine-openjdk8-jre' does not use a specific image
    digest - build may not be reproducible
[INFO] [io.quarkus.container.image.jib.deployment.JibProcessor] LogEvent
    [level=INFO, message=trying docker-credential-desktop for quay.io]
[INFO] [io.quarkus.container.image.jib.deployment.JibProcessor] LogEvent
    [level=LIFECYCLE, message=Using credentials from Docker config
    ($HOME/.docker/config.json) for
    quay.io/lordofthejars/greeting-jib:1.0-SNAPSHOT]
[INFO] [io.quarkus.container.image.jib.deployment.JibProcessor] The base image
    requires auth. Trying again for fabric8/java-alpine-openjdk8-jre...
[INFO] [io.quarkus.container.image.jib.deployment.JibProcessor] Using base
    image with digest:
    sha256:a5d31f17d618032812ae85d12426b112279f02951fa92a7ff8a9d69a6d3411b1
[INFO] [io.quarkus.container.image.jib.deployment.JibProcessor] Container
    entrypoint set to [java, -Dquarkus.http.host=0.0.0.0,
    -Djava.util.logging.manager=org.jboss.logmanager.LogManager,
    -cp, /app/resources:/app/classes:/app/libs/*,
        io.quarkus.runner.GeneratedMain]
[INFO] [io.quarkus.container.image.jib.deployment.JibProcessor] Pushed
container image quay.io/lordofthejars/greeting-jib:1.0-SNAPSHOT
(sha256:e173e0b49bd5ec1f500016f46f2cde03a055f558f72ca8ee1d6cb034a385a657)❷

[INFO] [io.quarkus.deployment.QuarkusAugmentor] Quarkus augmentation completed
    in 12980ms
```

❶ The container image is built

❷ The container image is pushed to quay.io

Discussion

Apart from Jib, there are two other options available to build a container image; to use them you simply need to register the extension:

Docker
```
quarkus-container-image-docker
```

S2I
```
quarkus-container-image-s2i
```

Each of the extensions provides specific configuration parameters to change the build process. These parameters let you change the base images used for building the container image and let you set environment variables, the arguments to pass to the executable, or the location of the Dockerfiles.

You can also build the image but not push it to a registry. To do this, you need to set the `quarkus.container-image.build` property to `true` and not set the `quarkus.container-image.push` property:

```
./mvnw clean package -Dquarkus.container-image.build=true
```

 If `Jib` is used and `push` is set to `false`, the extension creates a container image and registers it with the Docker daemon. This means that although Docker isn't used to build the image, it is still necessary.

The container image extensions can create a container from a JAR package (for use in JVM mode) and from a native executable, depending on what is found in the *build/ output* directory. If you want to create a native executable that can be run from a Linux container and then create a container image with the resulting native executable inside, you can run the following command:

```
./mvnw clean package -Dquarkus.container-image.push=true -Pnative \
    -Dquarkus.native.container-build=true
```

Setting the `quarkus.native.container-build` property to `true` creates the native executable inside a Docker container.

See Also

For more information, visit the following pages on GitHub:

- Google Container Tools: Jib (*https://oreil.ly/6vrh5*)
- Source-To-Image (*https://oreil.ly/8PEgn*)

10.2 Generating Kubernetes Resources

Problem

You want to generate Kubernetes resources automatically.

Solution

Quarkus has a Kubernetes extension that is able to generate Kubernetes resources automatically with sane defaults and optional user-supplied configuration. Currently, the extension can produce resources for Kubernetes and OpenShift.

To enable the generation of Kubernetes resources, you need to register the `quarkus-kubernetes` extension:

```
./mvnw quarkus:add-extension -Dextensions="quarkus-kubernetes"
```

To generate the Kubernetes resources, execute in a new terminal `./mvnw package`. Then among the usual files generated by the build tool in the `target` directory, two new files are created inside the *target/kubernetes* directory. These new files are named *kubernetes.json* and *kubernetes.yaml*, and they each contain the definition of both a `Deployment` and a `Service`:

```
{
  "apiVersion" : "v1",
  "kind" : "List",
  "items" : [ {
    "apiVersion" : "v1",
    "kind" : "Service",
    "metadata" : {
      "labels" : {
        "app" : "getting-started",      ❶
        "version" : "1.0-SNAPSHOT",     ❷
        "group" : "alex"                ❸
      },
      "name" : "getting-started"
    },
    "spec" : {
      "ports" : [ {
        "name" : "http",
        "port" : 8080,
        "targetPort" : 8080
      } ],
      "selector" : {
        "app" : "getting-started",
        "version" : "1.0-SNAPSHOT",
        "group" : "alex"
      },
      "type" : "ClusterIP"
    }
```

```
  }, {
    "apiVersion" : "apps/v1",
    "kind" : "Deployment",
    "metadata" : {
      "labels" : {
        "app" : "getting-started",
        "version" : "1.0-SNAPSHOT",
        "group" : "alex"
      },
      "name" : "getting-started"
    },
    "spec" : {
      "replicas" : 1,
      "selector" : {
        "matchLabels" : {
          "app" : "getting-started",
          "version" : "1.0-SNAPSHOT",
          "group" : "alex"
        }
      },
      "template" : {
        "metadata" : {
          "labels" : {
            "app" : "getting-started",
            "version" : "1.0-SNAPSHOT",
            "group" : "alex"
          }
        },
        "spec" : {
          "containers" : [ {
            "env" : [ {
              "name" : "KUBERNETES_NAMESPACE",
              "valueFrom" : {
                "fieldRef" : {
                  "fieldPath" : "metadata.namespace"
                }
              }
            } ],
            "image" : "alex/getting-started:1.0-SNAPSHOT",
            "imagePullPolicy" : "IfNotPresent",
            "name" : "getting-started",
            "ports" : [ {
              "containerPort" : 8080,
              "name" : "http",
              "protocol" : "TCP"
            } ]
          } ]
        }
      }
    }
  } ]
}
```

❶ Defaults to project name

❷ Defaults to version field

❸ Defaults to OS username

Discussion

You can customize the group and the name used in the generated manifest by adding these properties to *application.properties*:

```
quarkus.container-image.group=redhat
quarkus.application.name=message-app
```

The Kubernetes extension allows user customizations to be supplied to different parts of the manifest:

```
quarkus.kubernetes.replicas=3 ❶

quarkus.container-image.registry=http://my.docker-registry.net ❷
quarkus.kubernetes.labels.environment=prod ❸

quarkus.kubernetes.readiness-probe.initial-delay-seconds=10 ❹
quarkus.kubernetes.readiness-probe.period-seconds=30
```

❶ Sets the number of replicas

❷ Adds the Docker registry to pull images

❸ Adds new labels

❹ Sets readiness probe

You can generate different resources by setting the property as `quarkus.kubernetes.deployment-target` in the *application.properties* file or as a system property.

The default value of this property is kubernetes, but the following values are also supported at the time of writing: kubernetes, openshift, and knative.

See Also

The following web page provides a list of all Kubernetes configuration options to modify the generated file:

- Quarkus: Kubernetes Extension (*https://oreil.ly/oLxhT*)

10.3 Generating Kubernetes Resources with Health Checks

Problem

You want to automatically generate Kubernetes resources with liveness and readiness probes.

Solution

By default, health probes are not generated in the output file, but if the quarkus-smallrye-health extension is present (as explained in Recipe 9.1), then readiness and liveness probe sections are generated automatically:

```
"image" : "alex/getting-started:1.0-SNAPSHOT",
"imagePullPolicy" : "IfNotPresent",
"livenessProbe" : {  ❶
    "failureThreshold" : 3,
    "httpGet" : {
        "path" : "/health/live",  ❷
        "port" : 8080,
        "scheme" : "HTTP"
        },
    "initialDelaySeconds" : 0,
    "periodSeconds" : 30,
    "successThreshold" : 1,
    "timeoutSeconds" : 10
},
"name" : "getting-started",
"ports" : [ {
    "containerPort" : 8080,
    "name" : "http",
    "protocol" : "TCP"
    } ],
"readinessProbe" : {  ❸
    "failureThreshold" : 3,
    "httpGet" : {
        "path" : "/health/ready",  ❹
        "port" : 8080,
        "scheme" : "HTTP"
    },
    "initialDelaySeconds" : 0,
    "periodSeconds" : 30,
    "successThreshold" : 1,
    "timeoutSeconds" : 10
}
```

❶ Defines the liveness probe

---

❷ The path is the one defined by MicroProfile Health spec

❸ Defines the readiness probe

❹ The path is the one defined by MicroProfile Health spec

Discussion

Kubernetes uses probes to determine the health state of a service and take automatic actions to solve any problem.

Quarkus automatically generates two Kubernetes probes:

Liveness
>   Kubernetes uses a liveness probe to decide if a service must be restarted. If the application becomes unresponsive, perhaps because of a deadlock or memory problem, restarting the container might be a good solution to fix the problem.

Readiness
>   Kubernetes uses a readiness probe to decide if a service is available for accepting traffic. Sometimes a service might need to execute some operations before accepting requests. Examples include updating local caching system, populating a change to the database schema, applying a batch process, or connecting to an external service like Kafka Streams.

See Also

For more information, see the following website:

- Kubernetes: Configure Liveness, Readiness, and Startup Probes (*https://oreil.ly/ PWl_B*)

10.4 Deploying Services on Kubernetes

Problem

You want to deploy services on Kubernetes.

Solution

Use kubectl and all the features offered by Quarkus to create and deploy a service on Kubernetes.

Quarkus makes it really easy to create and deploy a Java application into Kubernetes by doing the following:

---

1. Generating a container native executable of your enterprise application, as explained in Recipe 6.6

2. Providing a *Dockerfile.native* file to build the Docker container

3. Generating a Kubernetes resources file by using `quarkus-kubernetes` extension, as explained in Recipe 10.2

It is time to see all these steps working together.

To create a native executable that can be run within a container:

```
./mvnw package -DskipTests -Pnative -Dquarkus.native.container-build=true ❶

docker build -f src/main/docker/Dockerfile.native \
    -t alex/geeting-started:1.0-SNAPSHOT . ❷
docker push docker build -f src/main/docker/Dockerfile.native \
    -t alex/getting-started:1.0-SNAPSHOT . ❸

kubectl apply -f target/kubernetes/kubernetes.json ❹

kubectl patch svc getting-started --type='json' \
    -p '[{"op":"replace","path":"/spec/type","value":"NodePort"}]' ❺

curl $(minikube service getting-started --url)/hello ❻
```

❶ Creates the native executable inside a Docker container

❷ Creates a Docker image with the native executable generated previously

❸ Pushes image to the Docker registry (in minikube, this is `eval $(minikube docker-env)`, so no push.)

❹ Deploys the application to Kubernetes

❺ Changes to `NodePort`

❻ Gets the URL to access the service

Notice that steps 5 and 6 are required only because the service is deployed in minikube. Depending on the Kubernetes platform you are using to deploy the service to, you might need to do different things.

Discussion

Steps 1 and 2 could be simplified into one if you use the multi-stage Docker build feature. In the first stage, the native executable is generated, and the second stage creates the runtime image:

```
FROM quay.io/quarkus/centos-quarkus-maven:19.2.1 AS build ❶
COPY src /usr/src/app/src
COPY pom.xml /usr/src/app
USER root
RUN chown -R quarkus /usr/src/app
USER quarkus
RUN mvn -f /usr/src/app/pom.xml -Pnative clean package

FROM registry.access.redhat.com/ubi8/ubi-minimal ❷
WORKDIR /work/
COPY --from=build /usr/src/app/target/*-runner /work/application
RUN chmod 775 /work
EXPOSE 8080
CMD ["./application", "-Dquarkus.http.host=0.0.0.0"]
```

❶ Generates the native executable

❷ Creates the runtime image from the output of the previous stage

Remove the *.dockerignore* file from the root directory of the project (rm .docker ignore). This is necessary because, by default, the *src* directory is ignored, and to build the native executable, the *src* directory is required:

```
docker build -f src/main/docker/Dockerfile.multistage -t docker \
    build -f src/main/docker/Dockerfile.multistage -t ❶
```

❶ Creates the runtime image with native executable bundled

10.5 Deploying Services on OpenShift

Problem

You want to deploy services on OpenShift.

Solution

OpenShift works perfectly with the resources generated in the previous recipe, so even though you are using OpenShift, you can still use everything provided previously. But if you want to use some of the capabilities offered by OpenShift, you can set the kubernetes.deployment.target property to openshift.

The two generated files are placed at *target/kubernetes/openshift.json* and *target/kubernetes/openshift.yaml*:

```
{
  "apiVersion" : "v1",
  "kind" : "List",
  "items" : [ {
    "apiVersion" : "v1",
```

```
  "kind" : "Service",
  "metadata" : {
    "labels" : {
      "app" : "getting-started",
      "version" : "1.0-SNAPSHOT",
      "group" : "alex"
    },
    "name" : "getting-started"
  },
  "spec" : {
    "ports" : [ {
      "name" : "http",
      "port" : 8080,
      "targetPort" : 8080
    } ],
    "selector" : {
      "app" : "getting-started",
      "version" : "1.0-SNAPSHOT",
      "group" : "alex"
    },
    "type" : "ClusterIP"
  }
}, {
  "apiVersion" : "image.openshift.io/v1",
  "kind" : "ImageStream",
  "metadata" : {
    "labels" : {
      "app" : "getting-started",
      "version" : "1.0-SNAPSHOT",
      "group" : "alex"
    },
    "name" : "getting-started"
  }
}, {
  "apiVersion" : "image.openshift.io/v1",
  "kind" : "ImageStream",
  "metadata" : {
    "labels" : {
      "app" : "getting-started",
      "version" : "1.0-SNAPSHOT",
      "group" : "alex"
    },
    "name" : "s2i-java"
  },
  "spec" : {
    "dockerImageRepository" : "fabric8/s2i-java"
  }
}, {
  "apiVersion" : "build.openshift.io/v1",
  "kind" : "BuildConfig",
  "metadata" : {
    "labels" : {
```

```
        "app" : "getting-started",
        "version" : "1.0-SNAPSHOT",
        "group" : "alex"
      },
      "name" : "getting-started"
    },
    "spec" : {
      "output" : {
        "to" : {
          "kind" : "ImageStreamTag",
          "name" : "getting-started:1.0-SNAPSHOT"
        }
      },
      "source" : {
        "binary" : { }
      },
      "strategy" : {
        "sourceStrategy" : {
          "from" : {
            "kind" : "ImageStreamTag",
            "name" : "s2i-java:2.3"
          }
        }
      }
    }
  }, {
    "apiVersion" : "apps.openshift.io/v1",
    "kind" : "DeploymentConfig",
    "metadata" : {
      "labels" : {
        "app" : "getting-started",
        "version" : "1.0-SNAPSHOT",
        "group" : "alex"
      },
      "name" : "getting-started"
    },
    "spec" : {
      "replicas" : 1,
      "selector" : {
        "app" : "getting-started",
        "version" : "1.0-SNAPSHOT",
        "group" : "alex"
      },
      "template" : {
        "metadata" : {
          "labels" : {
            "app" : "getting-started",
            "version" : "1.0-SNAPSHOT",
            "group" : "alex"
          }
        },
        "spec" : {
```

```
        "containers" : [ {
          "env" : [ {
            "name" : "KUBERNETES_NAMESPACE",
            "valueFrom" : {
              "fieldRef" : {
                "fieldPath" : "metadata.namespace"
              }
            }
          }, {
            "name" : "JAVA_APP_JAR",
            "value" : "/deployments/getting-started-1.0-SNAPSHOT.jar"
          } ],
          "image" : "",
          "imagePullPolicy" : "IfNotPresent",
          "name" : "getting-started",
          "ports" : [ {
            "containerPort" : 8080,
            "name" : "http",
            "protocol" : "TCP"
          } ],
        } ]
      }
    },
    "triggers" : [ {
      "imageChangeParams" : {
        "automatic" : true,
        "containerNames" : [ "getting-started" ],
        "from" : {
          "kind" : "ImageStreamTag",
          "name" : "getting-started:1.0-SNAPSHOT"
        }
      },
      "type" : "ImageChange"
    } ]
  }
 } ]
}
```

10.6 Building and Deploying a Container Image Automatically

Problem

You want to build, push, and deploy container images automatically.

Solution

Quarkus provides extensions for building and pushing container images with the `container-image` extensions and for deploying to Kubernetes using the `kubernetes` extension.

To build, push, and deploy a container image, you need to first add the required extensions:

```
./mvnw quarkus:add-extensions \
    -Dextensions="quarkus-container-image-jib, quarkus-kubernetes"
```

Then you can customize the container image build process. You can set these properties in the *application.properties*, system properties, or environment variables as any other configuration parameter in Quarkus:

```
quarkus.container-image.group=lordofthejars    ❶
quarkus.container-image.registry=quay.io    ❷
quarkus.container-image.username=lordofthejars    ❸
#quarkus.container-image.password=    ❹
```

❶ Sets the group part of the image; by default this is `${user.name}`

❷ Registry where to push the image; by default, images are pushed to `docker.io`

❸ The username to log into the container registry

❹ The password to log into the container registry

Finally, deploy to Kubernetes using the following command:

```
./mvnw clean package -Dquarkus.kubernetes.deploy=true
```

Discussion

Notice that setting `quarkus.kubernetes.deploy` to `true` implicitly sets the `quarkus.container-image.push` property to `true`, so you do not need to set it manually.

The Kubernetes extension uses the standard `kubectl` configuration file located at *~/.kube/config* to know where to deploy the application.

> You can also use `-Pnative` `-Dquarkus.native.container-build=true` flags to create and deploy a container image with native compilation.

10.7 Configuring an Application from Kubernetes

Problem

You want to configure your application through (or via) Kubernetes instead of the configuration file.

Solution

Use `ConfigMaps` to configure the applications running inside a pod.

In this example, you are going to configure a service using a `ConfigMap` and Kubernetes extension. To enable the generation of Kubernetes resources with the Config Map injection in the Pod, you need to register the `quarkus-kubernetes` extension:

```
./mvnw quarkus:add-extension -Dextensions="quarkus-kubernetes"
```

The service returns the `greeting.message` configuration value when the `/hello` endpoint is called:

```
@ConfigProperty(name = "greeting.message")
String message;

@GET
@Produces(MediaType.TEXT_PLAIN)
public String hello() {
    return "hello " + message;
}
```

Create the `ConfigMap` resource with the key-value pairs:

```
apiVersion: v1
kind: ConfigMap ❶
metadata:
    name: greeting-config
data:
    greeting: "Kubernetes" ❷
```

❶ Defines the `ConfigMap` type

❷ For the key `greeting` defines the value `Kubernetes`

Then the resource must be applied to the Kubernetes cluster by running the next command in a terminal window:

```
kubectl apply -f src/main/kubernetes/config-greeting.yaml
```

Finally, set the Kubernetes extension properties in the *application.properties* so that the generated Kubernetes deployment file contains the segments to inject the config map as an environment variable:

```
greeting.message=local
quarkus.container-image.group=quarkus ❶
quarkus.container-image.name=greeting-app
quarkus.container-image.tag=1.0-SNAPSHOT
quarkus.kubernetes.env-vars.greeting-message.value=greeting ❷
quarkus.kubernetes.env-vars.greeting-message.configmap=greeting-config ❸
quarkus.kubernetes.image-pull-policy=if-not-present
```

❶ Configures Docker image

❷ Sets the environment variable to override the `greeting.message` property

❸ Sets the config map resource name to load

The generation of the Kubernetes file will contain a new entry defining the key-value pairs in the container definition called `configMapKeyRef`.

To deploy the application, open a new terminal window, package the application, create the Docker container, and apply the generated Kubernetes resources:

```
./mvnw clean package -DskipTests

docker build -f src/main/docker/Dockerfile.jvm \
    -t quarkus/greeting-app:1.0-SNAPSHOT .
kubectl apply -f target/kubernetes/kubernetes.yml

kubectl patch svc greeting-app --type='json' \
    -p '[{"op":"replace","path":"/spec/type","value":"NodePort"}]'
curl $(minikube service greeting-app --url)/hello
```

Discussion

`ConfigMap` consists of key-value pairs that Kubernetes injects into pods' containers in the form of files or environment variables so the application can read them and configure accordingly. With `ConfigMaps`, you can decouple the configuration of the application from the business logic, making it portable across environments.

 `ConfigMaps` are meant to be used for storing and sharing non-sensitive configuration properties.

The MicroProfile Config spec permits the override of any configuration property using the equivalent environment variable (in uppercase and changing dots [.] to underscores [_]). The `ConfigMap` contains the configuration properties. In *application.properties*, the Kubernetes extension is configured to generate a deployment descriptor that sets these properties as environment variables so that when the container is started inside the Kubernetes cluster, the specific configuration applied to this cluster is used.

See Also

To learn more about `ConfigMaps` in Kubernetes, visit the following website:

- Kubernetes: Configure a Pod to Use a ConfigMap (*https://oreil.ly/BPmo5*)

10.8 Configuring an Application from Kubernetes with Config Extension

Problem

You want to configure your application through (or via) Kubernetes instead of the configuration file using the MicroProfile Config specification.

Solution

Quarkus has a Kubernetes Configuration extension that can read the secrets and config maps elements from the Kubernetes API Server and inject them using `@Config Property` annotation.

To enable the generation of Kubernetes resources, you need to register the `quarkus-kubernetes-config` extension.

The extension supports injecting `ConfigMaps`, either as a single key/value form or in the form in which the key is a filename (where only `application.properties` or `application.yaml` is supported) and the value is the content of that file.

Let's create a config map with a single key/value:

```
apiVersion: v1
kind: ConfigMap
metadata:
    name: my-config ❶
data:
    greeting: "Kubernetes"
```

❶ Config name is important for the extension

Then register the previous `ConfigMap` resource:

```
kubectl apply -f src/main/kubernetes/my-config.yaml
```

For this example, an *application.properties* file as `ConfigMap` is also registered.

The configuration file added contains the following:

```
some.property1=prop1
some.property2=prop2
```

Then register the previous file in a `ConfigMap` named `my-file-config`:

```
kubectl create configmap my-file-config \
    --from-file=./src/main/kubernetes/application.properties
```

The last step before you can inject these values is to configure the extension to read values from these `ConfigMaps`:

```
quarkus.kubernetes-config.enabled=true ❶
quarkus.kubernetes-config.config-maps=my-config,my-file-config ❷
```

❶ Enables the extension

❷ Sets the `ConfigMap` names

These configuration values are injected like any other configuration value:

```
@ConfigProperty(name = "greeting") ❶
String greeting;

@ConfigProperty(name = "some.property1") ❷
String property1;

@ConfigProperty(name = "some.property2")
String property2;
```

❶ Simple key is injected

❷ Keys from the *application.properties* file are injected too

To deploy the application, open a new terminal window, package the application, create the Docker container, and apply the generated Kubernetes resources:

```
./mvnw clean package -DskipTests

docker build -f src/main/docker/Dockerfile.jvm \
    -t quarkus/greeting-app:1.0-SNAPSHOT .
kubectl apply -f target/kubernetes/kubernetes.yml

kubectl patch svc greeting-app-config-ext --type='json' \
    -p '[{"op":"replace","path":"/spec/type","value":"NodePort"}]'

curl $(minikube service greeting-app-config-ext --url)/hello
Kubernetes

curl $(minikube service greeting-app-config-ext --url)/hello/p1
prop1
```

```
curl $(minikube service greeting-app-config-ext --url)/hello/p2
prop2
```

10.9 Interacting with a Kubernetes Cluster Programmatically

Problem

You want to interact with a Kubernetes API server programmatically.

Solution

Use the kubernetes-client extension to start watching and reacting to changes on Kubernetes resources.

To add the kubernetes-extension, run the following:

```
./mvnw quarkus:add-extension -Dextensions="kubernetes-client"
```

The main class to connect to the Kubernetes cluster is io.fabric8.kubernetes.cli ent.KubernetesClient. The extension produces this instance so it can be injected in the code. The client can be configured using various properties, setting them in *application.properties*.

The example developed here is an endpoint that returns the name of all deployed pods on the given namespace:

```
package org.acme.quickstart;

import java.util.List;
import java.util.stream.Collectors;

import javax.inject.Inject;
import javax.ws.rs.GET;
import javax.ws.rs.Path;
import javax.ws.rs.PathParam;
import javax.ws.rs.Produces;
import javax.ws.rs.core.MediaType;

import io.fabric8.kubernetes.client.KubernetesClient;

@Path("/pod")
public class PodResource {

    @Inject ❶
    KubernetesClient kubernetesClient;

    @GET
    @Produces(MediaType.APPLICATION_JSON)
    @Path("/{namespace}")
```

```
public List<String> getPods(@PathParam("namespace") String namespace) {
    return kubernetesClient.pods() ❷
                    .inNamespace(namespace) ❸
                    .list().getItems()
                    .stream()
                    .map(p -> p.getMetadata().getGenerateName()) ❹
                    .collect(Collectors.toList());
    }
}
```

❶ The KubernetesClient is injected like any other CDI bean

❷ Select all pods

❸ From given namespace

❹ Gets only the generated name of the pod

The recommended way to access the REST API of Kubernetes is by using kubectl in proxy mode because no man-in-the-middle attack is possible.

The other way is by providing the location and the credentials directly, but to avoid man-in-the-middle attacks you might need to import the root certificate.

Because the proxy mode is the recommended way, this is the method used for this example.

Pointing kubectl to the cluster that the application must connect with, open a new terminal window and run the next command:

```
kubectl proxy --port=8090
```

This command runs kubectl as a reverse proxy, exposing the remote Kubernetes API server at *http://localhost:8090*.

Configure KubernetesClient to connect to *http://localhost:8090* by using the quarkus.kubernetes-client.master-url property in *application.properties*:

```
%dev.quarkus.kubernetes-client.master-url=http://localhost:8090 ❶
```

❶ Sets the URL of the Kubernetes API server

Finally, run the service and make a request to the /pod/default endpoint to get all the pods deployed in the default namespace:

```
./mvnw compile quarkus:dev

curl http://localhost:8080/pod/default
["getting-started-5cd97ddd4d-"]
```

Discussion

In some circumstances, you need to create new Kubernetes resources programmatically or get some information about Kubernetes clusters/resources (what pods are deployed, configuration parameters, set secrets, and so on). Where `kubernetes-client` really shines is in implementing a *Kubernetes Operator* in Java. Thanks to the capabilities of Quarkus to generate a native executable, this is a great way to implement Kubernetes Operators in Java.

In this example, the service was deployed outside the Kubernetes cluster, and you connect to it using the Kubernetes API server.

If the service was deployed into the Kubernetes cluster that needs to be accessed, then the `quarkus.kubernetes-client.master-url` property must be set to `https://kubernetes.default.svc`.

The creation of `KubernetesClient` can be overridden by simply declaring a CDI provider factory method returning the configured instance of `KubernetesClient`:

```
@ApplicationScoped
public class KubernetesClientProducer {

    @Produces
    public KubernetesClient kubernetesClient() {
        Config config = new ConfigBuilder()
                            .withMasterUrl("https://mymaster.com")
                            .build(); ❶
        return new DefaultKubernetesClient(config); ❷
    }
}
```

❶ Configures the client

❷ Creates an instance of `KubernetesClient`

In most cases, to access the Kubernetes API server, a `ServiceAccount`, `Role`, and `Role Binding` are necessary. The following might be a starting point to work the example provided in this section:

```
---
apiVersion: v1
kind: ServiceAccount
metadata:
  name: greeting-started
  namespace: default
---
apiVersion: rbac.authorization.k8s.io/v1
kind: Role
metadata:
  name: greeting-started
```

```
    namespace: default
rules:
  - apiGroups: [""]
    resources: ["pods"]
    verbs: ["list"]
---
apiVersion: rbac.authorization.k8s.io/v1
kind: RoleBinding
metadata:
  name: greeting-started
  namespace: default
roleRef:
  kind: Role
  name: greeting-started
  apiGroup: rbac.authorization.k8s.io
subjects:
  - kind: ServiceAccount
    name: greeting-started
    namespace: default
```

See Also

To learn more about Fabric8 Kubernetes Client, visit the following page on GitHub:

- Kubernetes & OpenShift Java Client (*https://oreil.ly/_QNSL*)

10.10 Testing Kubernetes Client Interactions

Problem

You want to test Kubernetes Client code.

Solution

Quarkus implements a Quarkus Test Resource that launches a mock of the Kubernetes API server and sets the correct configuration to make the Kubernetes Client use the mock server instance instead of the value provided in *application.properties*. Moreover, you can set up the mock server to respond to any canned request required for any particular test:

```
package org.acme.quickstart;

import io.fabric8.kubernetes.api.model.Pod;
import io.fabric8.kubernetes.api.model.PodBuilder;
import io.fabric8.kubernetes.api.model.PodListBuilder;
import io.fabric8.kubernetes.client.server.mock.KubernetesMockServer;
import io.quarkus.test.common.QuarkusTestResource;
import io.quarkus.test.junit.QuarkusTest;
```

```
import io.quarkus.test.kubernetes.client.KubernetesMockServerTestResource;
import io.quarkus.test.kubernetes.client.MockServer;

import org.junit.jupiter.api.BeforeEach;
import org.junit.jupiter.api.Test;

import static io.restassured.RestAssured.given;
import static org.hamcrest.CoreMatchers.is;

@QuarkusTest
@QuarkusTestResource(KubernetesMockServerTestResource.class) ❶
public class PodResourceTest {

    @MockServer ❷
    KubernetesMockServer mockServer;

    @BeforeEach ❸
    public void prepareKubernetesServerAPI() {
        final Pod pod1 = new PodBuilder()
                .withNewMetadata()
                .withName("pod1")
                .withNamespace("test")
                .withGenerateName("pod1-12345")
                .and()
                .build(); ❹

        mockServer
                .expect()
                  .get()
                    .withPath("/api/v1/namespaces/test/pods")
                    .andReturn(200, new PodListBuilder()
                        .withNewMetadata()
                        .withResourceVersion("1")
                        .endMetadata()
                        .withItems(pod1).build()) ❺
                .always();

    }

    @Test
    public void testHelloEndpoint() {
        given()
          .when().get("/pod/test")
          .then()
            .statusCode(200)
            .body(is("[\"pod1-12345\"]"));
    }

}
```

❶ Sets Kubernetes Test Resource mock server

❷ Injects Kubernetes mock server instance to record any interaction

❸ To maintain test isolation, before every test, the interaction is recorded again

❹ Builds the pod to be returned

❺ The pod is returned as a result of querying all pods from `test` namespace

10.11 Implementing a Kubernetes Operator

Problem

You want to implement a Kubernetes Operator to extend Kubernetes using custom resources to manage applications in Java.

Solution

Use the `kubernetes-client` extension and Quarkus to implement a Kubernetes operator in Java and compile it into a native executable.

One of the use cases for an operator is to create a template (*custom resource*) where some values are set in the creation time. The biggest difference between a file template and an operator is that the common content (in the case of a *template*) is static, whereas in an operator it is set programmatically, which means that you've got the freedom to change the definition of the common part dynamically. This is known as a *custom resource*, in which, instead of using a well-known Kubernetes resource, you implement your own custom Kubernetes resource with your own fields.

Another use case might be to react/operate when something happens inside the cluster. Suppose you've got some in-memory data grids deployed on the cluster, and one of these instances dies. Maybe in this case what you want is to notify all living instances that one of the elements of the data grid cluster has been stopped.

As you can see, it is about not only the creation of a resource but also applying some tasks that are specific to your application that need to be done atop one of the tasks that Kubernetes is already doing.

The Kubernetes Operator uses Kubernetes API to decide when and how to run some of these customizations.

The following simple example does not make a lot of sense from the point of view of the logic it implements, but it will help you understand the basics of writing a

Kubernetes Operator. Use it as a starting point for implementing your own Kubernetes Operators.

To write a Kubernetes Operator, the following elements may be needed:

1. Classes that parse custom resources.
2. Factory method that registers and generates a client to operate with custom resources.
3. A watcher that reacts when a custom resource is applied to the cluster. You can think of it as the operator controller or the operator implementation.
4. Docker image with all previous code.
5. YAML/JSON file to define the custom resource (`CustomResourceDefinition`).
6. Deployment file to deploy the custom operator.

Let's implement a simple Kubernetes Operator that configures the command to run in the container and instantiates the pod with this configuration.

The base image used for the example is Whalesay (*https://oreil.ly/98T7t*), which basically prints in the container console the message you passed as argument in the run command, like this:

```
docker run docker/whalesay cowsay boo
```

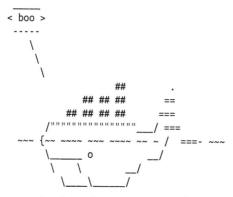

An example of a pod resource using this image could look like the following:

```
apiVersion: v1
kind: Pod
metadata:
  name: whalesay
spec:
  containers:
  - name: whalesay
    image: docker/whalesay
```

```
      imagePullPolicy: "IfNotPresent"
      command: ["cowsay","Hello Alex"] ❶
```

❶ Sets the output message

The goal of this operator is that only the message to be printed must be provided. The rest of the content (e.g., Docker image, container configuration, etc.) is set by the Kubernetes Operator automatically.

To create a custom operator, the Kubernetes Client and Jackson dependencies are required:

```
./mvnw quarkus:add-extension \
-Dextensions="io.quarkus:quarkus-kubernetes-client, io.quarkus:quarkus-jackson"
```

The first thing to do is define what the custom resource looks like. For this example, it looks like the following:

```
apiVersion: acme.org/v1alpha1
kind: Hello ❶
metadata:
  name: example-hello
spec:
  message: Hello Alex ❷
```

❶ Uses custom kind schema (defined later in this recipe)

❷ Sets the message to print

An object model is required to parse the custom resource. In this case, the Jackson library is used to map from YAML to Java Object. Three classes are required, one for the whole resource, another one for the spec section, and another one for the status section, which is empty but required because it might be filled automatically by the cluster.

Create all of them at *src/main/java* inside package org.acme.quickstart.cr:

```
package org.acme.quickstart.cr;

import com.fasterxml.jackson.databind.annotation.JsonDeserialize;

import io.fabric8.kubernetes.client.CustomResource;

@JsonDeserialize ❶
public class HelloResource extends CustomResource { ❷

    private HelloResourceSpec spec; ❸
    private HelloResourceStatus status; ❹

    public HelloResourceStatus getStatus() {
        return status;
```

```
        }

        public void setStatus(HelloResourceStatus status) {
            this.status = status;
        }

        public HelloResourceSpec getSpec() {
            return spec;
        }

        public void setSpec(HelloResourceSpec spec) {
            this.spec = spec;
        }

        @Override
        public String toString() {
            return "name=" + getMetadata().getName()
                    + ", version=" + getMetadata().getResourceVersion()
                    + ", spec=" + spec;
        }
    }
```

❶ Sets POJO as deserializable

❷ Inherits common custom resource fields like `kind`, `apiVersion`, or `metadata`

❸ Custom `spec` section

❹ `status` section

The **spec** section is mapped as follows:

```
package org.acme.quickstart.cr;

import com.fasterxml.jackson.annotation.JsonProperty;
import com.fasterxml.jackson.databind.annotation.JsonDeserialize;

@JsonDeserialize
public class HelloResourceSpec {

    @JsonProperty("message") ❶
    private String message;

    public String getMessage() {
        return message;
    }

    public void setMessage(String message) {
        this.message = message;
    }
```

```
    @Override
    public String toString() {
        return "HelloResourceSpec [message=" + message + "]";
    }

}
```

❶ The custom spec contains only a `message` field

And the empty `status` section is mapped as follows:

```
package org.acme.quickstart.cr;

import com.fasterxml.jackson.databind.annotation.JsonDeserialize;

@JsonDeserialize
public class HelloResourceStatus {
}
```

Still, two classes are required from the model point of view.

One class is used when, instead of applying a single custom resource (as shown previously) to the cluster, a list of the custom resources is provided (using the `items` array):

```
package org.acme.quickstart.cr;

import com.fasterxml.jackson.databind.annotation.JsonDeserialize;

import io.fabric8.kubernetes.client.CustomResourceList;

@JsonDeserialize
public class HelloResourceList extends CustomResourceList<HelloResource> { ❶
}
```

❶ `CustomResourceList` inherits all fields required to support a list of custom resources

The other class is used to make the custom resource editable from the operator implementation:

```
package org.acme.quickstart.cr;

import io.fabric8.kubernetes.api.builder.Function;
import io.fabric8.kubernetes.client.CustomResourceDoneable;

public class HelloResourceDoneable
        extends CustomResourceDoneable<HelloResource> { ❶
    public HelloResourceDoneable(HelloResource resource, Function<HelloResource,
                                 HelloResource> function) {
        super(resource, function);
```

```
        }
    }
```

❶ `CustomResourceDoneable` class makes the resource editable

The next big thing that is required is a CDI factory bean that provides all the machinery required by the operator. Create this class at *src/main/java* inside package `org.acme.quickstart`:

```
package org.acme.quickstart;

import java.io.IOException;
import java.nio.file.Files;
import java.nio.file.Paths;

import javax.enterprise.inject.Produces;
import javax.inject.Named;
import javax.inject.Singleton;

import org.acme.quickstart.cr.HelloResource;
import org.acme.quickstart.cr.HelloResourceDoneable;
import org.acme.quickstart.cr.HelloResourceList;

import io.fabric8.kubernetes.api.model.apiextensions.CustomResourceDefinition;
import io.fabric8.kubernetes.client.DefaultKubernetesClient;
import io.fabric8.kubernetes.client.KubernetesClient;
import io.fabric8.kubernetes.client.dsl.MixedOperation;
import io.fabric8.kubernetes.client.dsl.Resource;
import io.fabric8.kubernetes.internal.KubernetesDeserializer;

public class KubernetesProducer {

  @Produces
  @Singleton
  @Named("namespace")
  String findMyCurrentNamespace() throws IOException { ❶
    return new String(Files.readAllBytes(
          Paths
            .get("/var/run/secrets/kubernetes.io/serviceaccount/namespace")));
  }

  @Produces
  @Singleton
  KubernetesClient makeDefaultClient(@Named("namespace") String namespace) {
    return new DefaultKubernetesClient().inNamespace(namespace); ❷
  }

  @Produces
  @Singleton
  MixedOperation<HelloResource,
                 HelloResourceList,
                 HelloResourceDoneable,
```

```
        Resource<HelloResource, HelloResourceDoneable>>
  makeCustomHelloResourceClient(KubernetesClient defaultClient) { ❸
    KubernetesDeserializer
        .registerCustomKind("acme.org/v1alpha1",
                            "Hello", HelloResource.class); ❹
    CustomResourceDefinition crd = defaultClient.customResourceDefinitions()
                                    .list()
                                    .getItems()
                                    .stream()
                                    .findFirst()
        .orElseThrow(RuntimeException::new); ❺
    return defaultClient.customResources(crd, HelloResource.class,
        HelloResourceList.class,
        HelloResourceDoneable.class); ❻
    }
}
```

❶ Gets the namespace where the operator is running

❷ Configures `KubernetesClient` with the current namespace; defaults fit for Kubernetes Operator development

❸ `MixedOperation` is used for watching events about the custom resource (e.g., when a new custom resource is applied)

❹ Registers the `apiVersion` and `Kind` to be parsed by `org.acme.quick start.cr.HelloResource`

❺ Gets the definition of the custom resource; because there is only one (i.e., the one we are developing), `findFirst` can be used

❻ Registers for the customer resource, the parser, the list parser, and the doneable class

The last Java class to implement is the controller. This controller (or watcher/operator) is responsible for inspecting what's going on inside the cluster and reacting to the subscribed events—for example, a new pod has been created/destroyed or a custom resource of kind `Hello` has been applied.

In this implementation, the controller is watching when a new resource of kind `Hello` is added. When the custom resource is applied, then the message is retrieved from the model, and the pod definition is created using all the builders provided by the Kubernetes Client API. Finally, the pod is deployed into the Kubernetes cluster.

Create this class at *src/main/java* inside package `org.acme.quickstart`:

```
package org.acme.quickstart;
```

```
import java.util.HashMap;
import java.util.Map;

import javax.enterprise.event.Observes;
import javax.inject.Inject;

import org.acme.quickstart.cr.HelloResource;
import org.acme.quickstart.cr.HelloResourceDoneable;
import org.acme.quickstart.cr.HelloResourceList;

import io.fabric8.kubernetes.api.model.ContainerBuilder;
import io.fabric8.kubernetes.api.model.HasMetadata;
import io.fabric8.kubernetes.api.model.ObjectMetaBuilder;
import io.fabric8.kubernetes.api.model.Pod;
import io.fabric8.kubernetes.api.model.PodBuilder;
import io.fabric8.kubernetes.api.model.PodSpecBuilder;
import io.fabric8.kubernetes.client.KubernetesClient;
import io.fabric8.kubernetes.client.KubernetesClientException;
import io.fabric8.kubernetes.client.Watcher;
import io.fabric8.kubernetes.client.dsl.MixedOperation;
import io.fabric8.kubernetes.client.dsl.Resource;
import io.quarkus.runtime.StartupEvent;

public class HelloResourceWatcher {

  @Inject
  KubernetesClient defaultClient;    ❶

  @Inject
  MixedOperation<HelloResource,
    HelloResourceList,
    HelloResourceDoneable,
    Resource<HelloResource,
    HelloResourceDoneable>> crClient;    ❷

  void onStartup(@Observes StartupEvent event) {    ❸
    crClient.watch(new Watcher<HelloResource>() {    ❹
      @Override
      public void eventReceived(Action action, HelloResource resource) {
        System.out.println("Received " + action
            + " event for resource " + resource);
        if (action == Action.ADDED) {
          final String app = resource.getMetadata().getName();    ❺
          final String message = resource.getSpec().getMessage();

          final Map<String, String> labels = new HashMap<>();    ❻
          labels.put("app", app);

          final ObjectMetaBuilder objectMetaBuilder =
            new ObjectMetaBuilder().withName(app + "-pod")
            .withNamespace(resource.getMetadata()
                .getNamespace())
```

```
    .withLabels(labels);

final ContainerBuilder containerBuilder =
  new ContainerBuilder().withName("whalesay")
  .withImage("docker/whalesay")
  .withCommand("cowsay", message); ❼

final PodSpecBuilder podSpecBuilder =
  new PodSpecBuilder()
  .withContainers(containerBuilder.build())
  .withRestartPolicy("Never");

final PodBuilder podBuilder =
  new PodBuilder()
  .withMetadata(objectMetaBuilder.build())
  .withSpec(podSpecBuilder.build());

final Pod pod = podBuilder.build(); ❽
HasMetadata result = defaultClient
  .resource(pod)
  .createOrReplace(); ❾

if (result == null) {
  System.out.println("Pod " + pod
      + " couldn't be created");
} else {
  System.out.println("Pod " + pod + " created");
}
  }
}

@Override
public void onClose(KubernetesClientException e) { ❿
  if (e != null) {
    e.printStackTrace();
    System.exit(-1);
  }
  }
});
  }
}
```

❶ Injects KubernetesClient

❷ Injects operations specific to the developed custom resource

❸ Executes logic when the application is started

❹ Watches for any operation that HelloResource is implied

❺ Gets the information provided in the custom resource

❻ Starts the creation of the pod definition programmatically

❼ Sets the message provided by the custom resource

❽ Builds the pod

❾ Adds the pod to the cluster

❿ If there is any critical error when closing, then stop the container

Discussion

On the Java side, this is all you need to do; however, there are still some remaining parts, such as packaging and containerizing the operator, or defining the custom operator inside the cluster.

The first thing to take into consideration when developing a Kubernetes Operator is that the communication with the Kubernetes API server is done through HTTPS, and this means that crypto libraries must be provided in the Docker image if they are not provided by default.

At the time of writing, the *Dockerfile.jvm* file provided by Quarkus does not contain the crypto libraries required to communicate to the Kubernetes server. To fix this, just open *src/main/docker/Dockerfile.jvm* and add the nss (Network Security Services) package:

```
FROM fabric8/java-alpine-openjdk8-jre

RUN apk add --no-cache nss
```

Then containerize the operator by running Maven and Docker:

```
./mvnw clean package

docker build -f src/main/docker/Dockerfile.jvm \
  -t lordofthejars/quarkus-operator-example:1.0.0 .
```

Then register the custom resource definition into the Kubernetes cluster so that it is aware of the new kind, the scope of the custom resource, or the group name, among other things.

Create a new file at *src/main/kubernetes* with name *custom-resource-definition.yaml* that defines all the information required by the cluster to register a new resource:

```
apiVersion: apiextensions.k8s.io/v1beta1
kind: CustomResourceDefinition
metadata:
  name: hellos.acme.org  ❶
spec:
```

```
group: acme.org ❷
names:
  kind: Hello ❸
  listKind: HelloList ❹
  plural: hellos ❺
  singular: hello ❻
scope: Namespaced ❼
subresources:
  status: {}
version: v1alpha1 ❽
```

❶ plural plus group

❷ Sets the group of the custom resource (used in the `apiVersion` field of the custom resource)

❸ Name of the `kind`

❹ Name when the kind is a list of this custom resource

❺ The plural name

❻ The singular name

❼ Scope of the resource

❽ The version of the resource (used in the `apiVersion` field of the custom resource)

And the last thing to create is a deployment file that deploys the operator. Create a new file named *deploy.yaml* at *src/main/kubernetes*:

```
apiVersion: rbac.authorization.k8s.io/v1
kind: ClusterRole ❶
metadata:
  name: quarkus-operator-example
rules:
- apiGroups:
  - ''
  resources:
  - pods ❷
  verbs:
  - get
  - list
  - watch
  - create
  - update
  - delete
  - patch
- apiGroups:
```

```
      - apiextensions.k8s.io
      resources:
      - customresourcedefinitions
      verbs:
      - list
    - apiGroups:
      - acme.org ❸
      resources:
      - hellos
      verbs:
      - list
      - watch
    ---
    apiVersion: v1
    kind: ServiceAccount
    metadata:
      name: quarkus-operator-example
    ---
    apiVersion: rbac.authorization.k8s.io/v1
    kind: ClusterRoleBinding
    metadata:
      name: quarkus-operator-example
    subjects:
    - kind: ServiceAccount
      name: quarkus-operator-example
      namespace: default
    roleRef:
      kind: ClusterRole
      name: quarkus-operator-example
      apiGroup: rbac.authorization.k8s.io
    ---
    apiVersion: apps/v1
    kind: Deployment ❹
    metadata:
      name: quarkus-operator-example
    spec:
      selector:
        matchLabels:
          app: quarkus-operator-example
      replicas: 1
      template:
        metadata:
          labels:
            app: quarkus-operator-example
        spec:
          serviceAccountName: quarkus-operator-example ❺
          containers:
          - image: lordofthejars/quarkus-operator-example:1.0.0 ❻
            name: quarkus-operator-example
            imagePullPolicy: IfNotPresent
```

❶ Defines a cluster role for the role-based access control (RBAC) for Kubernetes resources

❷ Adds rights to get, list, watch, create, update, delete, and patch pods

❸ For the custom resource (`hellos.acme.org`), the required operations are `list` and `watch`

❹ An operator is deployed with a `Deployment`

❺ Sets the service account linked to the cluster role defined in the file

❻ Sets the container image containing the operator

The last step before having the operator up and running is to apply all these created resources:

```
kubectl apply -f src/main/kubernetes/custom-resource-definition.yaml
kubectl apply -f src/main/kubernetes/deploy.yaml

kubectl get pods
```

```
NAME                                       READY   STATUS    RESTARTS   AGE
quarkus-operator-example-fb77dc468-8v9xk   1/1     Running   0          5s
```

The operator is now installed and running. To test the operator, just create a custom resource of kind `Hello` with the message to show:

```
apiVersion: acme.org/v1alpha1
kind: Hello ❶
metadata:
  name: example-hello
spec:
  message: Hello Alex ❷
```

❶ Uses custom `kind` schema

❷ Sets the message to print

And apply it as follows:

```
kubectl apply -f src/main/kubernetes/custom-resource.yaml

kubectl get pods
```

```
NAME                                       READY   STATUS      RESTARTS   AGE
example-hello-pod                          0/1     Completed   0          2m57s
quarkus-operator-example-fb77dc468-8v9xk   1/1     Running     0          3m24s
```

When it's completed, check the pod logs to validate that the message has been printed on the console:

```
kubectl logs example-hello-pod
```

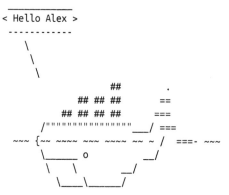

Although an operator and a custom resource are usually related, an operator without a custom resource definition is still possible—for example, to create a watcher class to intercept any event that affects a pod and apply some logic.

See Also

To learn more about operators, check out the following websites:

- CoreOS: Operators (*https://oreil.ly/NV2dN*)
- Kubernetes: Operator pattern (*https://oreil.ly/6Z77K*)

10.12 Deploying and Managing Serverless Workloads with Knative

Problem

You want to deploy and manage serverless workloads.

Solution

Use Knative, the Kubernetes-based platform to deploy and manage modern serverless workloads.

The `quarkus-kubernetes` extension provides support for generating Knative resources automatically with sane defaults and optional user-supplied configuration.

To enable the generation of Kubernetes resources, you need to register the `quarkus-kubernetes` extension:

```
./mvnw quarkus:add-extension \
  -Dextensions="quarkus-kubernetes, quarkus-container-image-docker"
```

For this example, the `quarkus-container-image-docker` extension is used to build the container image using `docker` binary, so the image is built directly inside the `minikube` cluster and registered inside the internal registry, so no external registry is required.

You need to run `eval $(minikube docker-env)` to configure `docker` to use the minikube docker host.

Then you need to set the `quarkus.kubernetes.deployment-target` property to `knative` and set it to build a Docker container during package phase, among other configuration properties regarding container image creation:

```
quarkus.kubernetes.deployment-target=knative ❶
quarkus.container-image.build=true ❷
quarkus.container-image.group=lordofthejars
quarkus.container-image.registry=dev.local ❸
```

❶ Sets target deployment to `knative`

❷ Builds the container image with `lordofthejars` group

❸ Sets to `dev.local` when deploying local container images

The Knative controller resolves image tags to digests in order to guarantee the immutability of revisions. This works well when using a normal registry; however, it can cause problems when used with minikube and local images.

By default, the Knative controller skips resolving digests with images prefixed with `dev.local` or `ko.local`. If you are running this example in minikube, you must set the registry property to any of these two options to make Knative find the images to deploy.

To generate the Kubernetes resources, execute in a new terminal `./mvnw package`. Then, among the usual files generated by the build tool in the *target* directory, two new files are created inside the *target/kubernetes* directory named *knative.json* and *knative.yaml* containing a Knative service definition:

```
{
  "apiVersion" : "v1",
  "kind" : "ServiceAccount",
  "metadata" : {
    "annotations" : {
      "app.quarkus.io/vcs-url" :
```

```
          "https://github.com/lordofthejars/quarkus-cookbook.git",
          "app.quarkus.io/build-timestamp" : "2020-03-10 - 22:55:08 +0000",
          "app.quarkus.io/commit-id" : "17b19a409c41cc933770b20009f635a65f69440e"
        },
        "labels" : {
          "app.kubernetes.io/name" : "greeting-knative",
          "app.kubernetes.io/version" : "1.0-SNAPSHOT"
        },
        "name" : "greeting-knative"
      }
    }{
      "apiVersion" : "serving.knative.dev/v1alpha1",
      "kind" : "Service",
      "metadata" : {
        "annotations" : {
          "app.quarkus.io/vcs-url" :
            "https://github.com/lordofthejars/quarkus-cookbook.git",
          "app.quarkus.io/build-timestamp" : "2020-03-10 - 22:55:08 +0000",
          "app.quarkus.io/commit-id" : "17b19a409c41cc933770b20009f635a65f69440e"
        },
        "labels" : {
          "app.kubernetes.io/name" : "greeting-knative",
          "app.kubernetes.io/version" : "1.0-SNAPSHOT"
        },
        "name" : "greeting-knative"
      },
      "spec" : {
        "runLatest" : {
          "configuration" : {
            "revisionTemplate" : {
              "spec" : {
                "container" : {
                  "image" :"dev.local/lordofthejars/greeting-knative:1.0-SNAPSHOT",
                  "imagePullPolicy" : "IfNotPresent"
                }
              }
            }
          }
        }
      }
    }
  }
```

Then deploy the generated Knative service:

```
kubectl apply -f target/kubernetes/knative.json

serviceaccount/greeting-knative created
service.serving.knative.dev/greeting-knative created

kubectl get ksvc
NAME                    URL                                                    \
greeting-knative        http://greeting-knative.default.127.0.0.1.nip.io      \
```

```
LATESTCREATED          LATESTREADY                  READY    REASON
greeting-knative-j8n76  greeting-knative-j8n76      True
```

It can take a few seconds to move the `ready` state from Unknown to True. If there is a
failure, which means that `ready` state remains in `false`, you can check the reason and
the sequence of events by running the following:

```
kubectl get events --sort-by=.metadata.creationTimestamp
```

To test that the service has been deployed correctly, open a new terminal window and
do a port forward between the local machine and Knative gateway:

```
kubectl port-forward --namespace kourier-system $(kubectl get pod \
  -n kourier-system -l "app=3scale-kourier-gateway" \
  --output=jsonpath="{.items[0].metadata.name}") \
  8080:8080 19000:19000 8443:8443

Forwarding from 127.0.0.1:8080 -> 8080
Forwarding from [::1]:8080 -> 8080
Forwarding from 127.0.0.1:19000 -> 19000
Forwarding from [::1]:19000 -> 19000
Forwarding from 127.0.0.1:8443 -> 8443
Forwarding from [::1]:8443 -> 8443
Handling connection for 8080
Handling connection for 8080
```

Notice that this is required only because the service is deployed in minikube.
Depending on the Kubernetes platform on which you are deploying the service, you
might need to do different things.

Finally, you can send a request to the service:

```
curl -v -H "Host: greeting-knative.default.127.0.0.1.nip.io" \
  http://localhost:8080/greeting

hello
```

To undeploy the example, you need to run the following:

```
kubectl delete -f target/kubernetes/knative.json

serviceaccount "greeting-knative" deleted
service.serving.knative.dev "greeting-knative" deleted
```

Discussion

You can combine the `container-image` and `kubernetes` extensions to build the container image and push it to Kubernetes automatically, as shown in Recipe 10.6, so no
manual steps are required.

See Also

To learn more, visit the following web pages:

- Knative Serving (*https://oreil.ly/RBv52*)
- GitHub: Kourier (*https://oreil.ly/3bSDL*)

CHAPTER 11

Authentication and Authorization

In this chapter, you will learn about how authorization and authentication, the backbone of application security, work within a Quarkus application. We'll discuss the following topics:

- File-backed authentication and authorization schemes
- Databased-backed authentication and authorization schemes
- External-service-backed authentication and authorization schemes

Quarkus Security Basics

Before we get to our first recipe, this section will show you the basics of Quarkus and security, the security extensions you will use to load authentication sources, and how to protect resources using a *role-based access control* (RBAC) approach.

The examples shown in this section are not meant to be runnable, but they will be the basis for the upcoming recipes in which we are going to see the security extensions in action.

The following are the two main concepts regarding security:

Authentication
  Validate your credentials (i.e., username/password) to verify your identity so that the system knows who you are.

Authorization
  Verify your rights to be granted access to a protected resource. This happens after the authentication process.

Authentication

Quarkus provides two authenticating mechanisms for HTTP, the well-known `BASIC` and `FORM` methods. These mechanisms can be extended by any Quarkus extension to provide a custom authentication method. An example of these mechanisms is found in the form of the Quarkus extension to authenticate against an OpenID Connect server such as Keycloak. We are going to explore how to do this in this section.

To use authentication, an identity provider is required to validate the credentials (i.e., username/password) provided by the user. Quarkus provides the following identity providers out of the box, but you can implement your own, too:

Elytron properties file
> Provides a mapping between user/password/role in the form of the properties file. The information can be embedded either in *application.properties* file or in a specific file for this purpose.

Elytron JDBC
> Provides a mapping between user/password/role based on JDBC queries.

JPA
> Provides support for authenticating via JPA.

SmallRye JWT
> Provides authentication using JSON Web Tokens (JWT) spec.

OIDC
> Provides authentication using an OpenID Connect (OIDC) provider like Keycloak.

Keycloak authorization
> Provides support for a policy enforcer using Keycloak Authorization Services.

Basic authentication

To authenticate using *basic* access authentication, the `quarkus.http.auth.basic` configuration property must be set to `true`.

Form-based authentication

The `quarkus.http.auth.form.enabled` configuration property must be set to `true` in order to authenticate using *form* access authentication.

> Quarkus does not store the authenticated user in an HTTP session because there is no clustered HTTP session support. Instead, the authentication information is stored in an encrypted cookie.

The encryption key can be set using the `quarkus.http.auth.session.encryption-key` property, and it must be at least 16 characters long. The key is hashed using SHA-256, and the result is used as a key for AES-256 encryption of the cookie value. This cookie contains an expiry time as part of the encrypted value, generating a new cookie in one-minute intervals with an updated expiry time if the session is in use.

Authorization

Quarkus integrates with Java EE Security annotations (*https://oreil.ly/ATPpq*) to define RBAC on RESTful web endpoints and CDI beans.

Moreover, you can define the authorization of RESTful Web Endpoints using a configuration file (*application.properties*) instead of annotations.

Both approaches can coexist in the same application, but configuration file checks are executed before any annotation check and are not mutually exclusive, which means that in case of overlap, both checks must pass.

The following snippet shows how to secure a JAX-RS endpoint using the Java EE Security annotations:

```
package org.acme.quickstart;

import javax.annotation.security.DenyAll;
import javax.annotation.security.PermitAll;
import javax.annotation.security.RolesAllowed;

import io.quarkus.security.Authenticated;

import javax.ws.rs.GET;
import javax.ws.rs.Path;

@Path("/hello")
public class GreetingResource {

    @GET
    @Path("/secured")
    @RolesAllowed("Tester")  ❶
    public String greetingSecured() {}

    @GET
    @Path("/unsecured")
    @PermitAll ❷
    public String greetingUnsecured() {}

    @GET
    @Path("/denied")
    @DenyAll ❸
    public String greetingDenied() {}
```

```
    @GET
    @Path("/authenticated")
    @Authenticated ❹
    public String greetingAuthenticated() {}
}
```

❶ Requires an authenticated user with role `Tester`

❷ Unauthenticated users have access to the method

❸ No user can access whether authenticated or not

❹ Permit any authenticated user to access; it is an alias of `@RolesAllowed("*")` and
    is provided by Quarkus, not the spec

The `javax.ws.rs.core.Context` annotation can be used to inject the
`javax.ws.rs.core.SecurityContext` instance to get information about the user that
was authenticated:

```
@GET
@Path("/secured")
@RolesAllowed("Tester")
public String greetingSecured(@Context SecurityContext sec) { ❶
    Principal user = sec.getUserPrincipal(); ❷
    String name = user != null ? user.getName() : "anonymous";
    return name;
}
```

❶ Injects `SecurityContext` for current request

❷ Gets the current logged user

> Security annotations are not restricted only to JAX-RS resources.
> They can be used in CDI beans to protect method calls, too.

Quarkus supports configuring RESTful web endpoints using the configuration file
instead of annotations. The equivalent security annotation example can be expressed
using the configuration file:

```
quarkus.http.auth.policy.role-policy1.roles-allowed=Tester ❶

quarkus.http.auth.permission.roles1.paths=/hello/secured   ❷
quarkus.http.auth.permission.roles1.policy=role-policy1    ❸
quarkus.http.auth.permission.roles1.methods=GET  ❹

quarkus.http.auth.permission.deny1.paths=/hello/denied
```

```
quarkus.http.auth.permission.deny1.policy=deny ❺

quarkus.http.auth.permission.permit1.paths=/hello/unsecured
quarkus.http.auth.permission.permit1.policy=permit ❻
quarkus.http.auth.permission.permit1.methods=GET

quarkus.http.auth.permission.roles2.paths=/hello/authenticated
quarkus.http.auth.permission.roles2.policy=authenticated
quarkus.http.auth.permission.roles2.methods=GET
```

❶ Defines the roles of the application; `role-policy1` is used as reference value

❷ Sets the permission to the resource; `roles1` is an arbitrary name to avoid repeating keys

❸ Sets the role policy

❹ Restricts permission to the `GET` method

❺ Denies access

❻ Permits access

It is important to note that the `paths` attribute supports multiple values separated by a comma, and also the `*` wildcard to match any subpath. For example, `quar kus.http.auth.permission.permit1.paths=/public/_,/robots.txt` sets permission for any resource placed at */public* and any of its subpaths and the file */robots.txt*.

In the same way, the `methods` attribute allows multiple values separated by a comma.

There are two configuration properties that affect the RBAC behavior:

`quarkus.security.jaxrs.deny-unannotated-endpoints`
> If it is set to `true`, then all JAX-RS endpoints not annotated with security annotations are denied by default. This property is `false` by default.

`quarkus.security.deny-unannotated-members`
> If it is set to `true`, then all JAX-RS endpoints and CDI methods not annotated with security annotations are denied by default. This property is `false` by default.

So far, you've seen that in Quarkus you can set authorization procedure (basic, form, or other provided by extension) and define the authentication roles using security annotations or specifying them in the configuration file.

The recipes in this chapter will explore the different Quarkus extensions to provide authentication and authorization identity providers.

11.1 Authentication and Authorization with Elytron Properties File Config

Problem

You want to secure the application by storing identities in files.

Solution

Quarkus security provides support to store identities in files using the Elytron properties file config as an identity provider.

You've seen how to define the authentication mechanism and how to protect the resources with RBAC, either with security annotations or in *application.properties*, but you've not seen how to register an identity provider and how to store the user information like username, password, or roles where it belongs.

Let's see how to define identity information using the Elytron properties file config extension. This extension is based on the properties file to define all identity information, and its main purpose is for development and testing. It is not recommended that this be used in production because passwords can be expressed only in plain text or in MD5 hashed.

To enable the Elytron properties file config, you need to register the `quarkus-elytron-security-properties-file` extension:

```
./mvnw quarkus:add-extension \
        -Dextensions="quarkus-elytron-security-properties-file"
```

This extension supports the mapping of users to passwords and users to roles with a combination of properties files.

Protect the endpoint with allowing only the `Tester` role to access the resource:

```
@GET
@Produces(MediaType.TEXT_PLAIN)
@RolesAllowed("Tester")
public String hello() {
    return "hello";
}
```

To register identities, two properties files are required, one for mapping user and password, and another one for mapping the user and the list of roles they belong in.

The user configuration properties file defines for each line the pair of user and password that are registered in the system:

```
alex=soto
```

In the users' properties file, the key part is the username, and the value part is the password.

 Notice that the password is in plain text. You can hash the password with MD5 following this pattern: HEX(MD5(user name:realm:password).

The roles configuration file defines for each line the pair of username and the roles (separated by commas) that the user belongs in:

```
alex=Tester
```

In the roles properties file, the key part is the username, and the value is the roles assigned to the user.

Finally, the Elytron Security properties file extension needs to be configured with the classpath locations of the users and roles properties files:

```
quarkus.http.auth.basic=true ❶

quarkus.security.users.file.enabled=true ❷
quarkus.security.users.file.plain-text=true ❸
quarkus.security.users.file.users=users.properties ❹
quarkus.security.users.file.roles=roles.properties
```

❶ Enables basic authentication method

❷ Enables security with the properties file extension

❸ Sets the password that is not hashed with MD5

❹ Sets the classpath location of the users and roles properties files

Run the generated test to validate the protection of the endpoint:

```
./mvnw clean test


...
INFO  [io.quarkus] (main) Installed features:
        [cdi, resteasy, security, security-properties-file]
[ERROR] Tests run: 2, Failures: 1, Errors: 0, Skipped: 0, Time elapsed: 8.485 s
        <<< FAILURE! - in org.acme.quickstart.GreetingResourceTest
[ERROR] testHelloEndpoint  Time elapsed: 0.076 s  <<< FAILURE!
java.lang.AssertionError:
1 expectation failed.
Expected status code <200> but was <401>.
        at org.acme.quickstart.GreetingResourceTest.testHelloEndpoint
                (GreetingResourceTest.java:17)
```

The test is failing with an HTTP 401 Unauthorized error because the test is not providing any identity using the Basic authentication method. Modify the test to authenticate with a configured username and password:

```
@Test
public void testSecuredHelloEndpoint() {
    given()
            .auth() ❶
            .basic("alex", "soto") ❷
            .when()
            .get("/hello")
            .then()
            .statusCode(200)
            .body(is("hello"));
}
```

❶ Sets authentication part

❷ Basic authentication with a given username and password

Now, with valid authenticating parameters, the test passes.

Discussion

The Elytron properties file config extension also supports embedding the mapping between user/password/roles in the Quarkus configuration file (*application.properties*) instead of using different files.

```
quarkus.security.users.embedded.enabled=true
quarkus.security.users.embedded.plain-text=true
quarkus.security.users.embedded.users.alex=soto
quarkus.security.users.embedded.roles.alex=Admin,Tester
```

Passwords stored in a file can be hashed using the formula HEX(MD5(username ":" realm ":" password)).

An embedded Elytron properties file config can be configured by using the properties listed in Table 11-1.

Table 11-1. Embeded Elytron properties

Property	Description
quarkus.security.users.embedded.realm-name	The realm name used when generating a hashed password (defaults to Quarkus).
quarkus.security.users.embedded.enabled	Enables security with the properties file extension (defaults to false).
quarkus.security.users.embedded.plain-text	Sets if the password is hashed or not. If true, the hashed password must be in the form of HEX(MD5(user name:realm:password) (defaults to false).

Property	Description
quarkus.security.users.embedded.users.<user>	The user information. The key part is the username, and the value part is the password.
quarkus.security.users.embedded.roles.<user>	The role information. The key part is the username, and the value part is the password.

11.2 Authentication and Authorization with Elytron Security JDBC Config

Problem

You want to secure the application and store user identities in a database.

Solution

Quarkus security provides support to store user identities in a data source using Elytron Security JDBC config as an identity provider.

You've seen how to define identities in properties files using the Elytron properties file config extension in Recipe 11.1. However, as noted there, this method is more for testing/dev purposes and should not be used in production environments.

The Elytron Security JDBC extension can be used to store the user identities in a database, supporting password encryption using bcrypt password mapper, and being versatile enough to not lock you into any predefined database schema.

To enable the Elytron Security JDBC extension, you need to register the `quarkus-elytron-security-jdbc` extension, the JDBC driver used to connect to the database, and optionally Flyway to populate schema and some default users:

```
./mvnw quarkus:add-extension \
    -Dextensions="quarkus-elytron-security-jdbc,quarkus-jdbc-h2,quarkus-flyway"
```

Protect the endpoint with allowing only the `Tester` role to access the resource:

```
@GET
@RolesAllowed("Tester")
@Produces(MediaType.TEXT_PLAIN)
public String hello() {
    return "hello";
}
```

The next step is to define the database schema to store all RBAC information. For the sake of simplicity, a simple table with user, password, and role is used in this example:

```
CREATE TABLE test_user (
    id INT,
    username VARCHAR(255),
    password VARCHAR(255),
```

```
    role VARCHAR(255)
);

INSERT INTO test_user (id, username, password, role)
    VALUES (1, 'alex', 'soto', 'Tester');
```

Finally, the extension must be configured to specify which query to execute to validate the user and retrieve the roles they belong in:

```
quarkus.datasource.url=jdbc:h2:mem:mydb
quarkus.datasource.driver=org.h2.Driver
quarkus.datasource.username=sa
quarkus.datasource.password=

quarkus.flyway.migrate-at-start=true

quarkus.security.jdbc.enabled=true ❶
quarkus.security.jdbc.principal-query.sql=\
    SELECT u.password, u.role FROM test_user u WHERE u.username=? ❷
quarkus.security.jdbc.principal-query.clear-password-mapper.enabled=true ❸
quarkus.security.jdbc.principal-query.clear-password-mapper\
    .password-index=1❹
quarkus.security.jdbc.principal-query.attribute-mappings.0.index=2 ❺
quarkus.security.jdbc.principal-query.attribute-mappings.0.to=groups
```

❶ Enables Elytron Security JDBC

❷ Defines the query to validate the user and get the roles; the query must contain exactly one parameter (the username) and return at least the password, and the value should be on the same line as the key

❸ The password is stored in cleartext

❹ Sets the index of the password; this should all be on the same line

❺ Sets the index of the role and specifies the field as role

Index is 1-based.

The query to retrieve the password (and optionally the roles) can be as complex as required by your model (i.e., SQL joins).

Now, the authentication and authorization data are retrieved from the database instead of a file. When the username and password are provided (e.g., using the basic auth method), the query is executed to retrieve all required information for the authentication process (matching provided password against the retrieved password from the database) and to get roles for the authorization process.

Remember to update the test (if not done before) to make it pass:

```
@Test
public void testSecuredHelloEndpoint() {
    given()
      .auth().basic("alex", "soto")
    .when()
      .get("/hello")
    .then()
      .statusCode(200)
      .body(is("hello"));
}
```

Discussion

In this recipe, you've used a cleartext password, which obviously should not be used in a production environment. The extension provides an integration to the bcrypt password mapper, so the authentication process also works for hashing passwords.

About bcrypt

bcrypt is a password hashing function designed by Niels Provos and David Mazières that incorporates several protections like a *salt* to protect against rainbow table attacks and an *iteration count* to be resistant against brute-force search attacks.

You need to extend the configuration file with some extra parameters to indicate to Elytron Security JDBC that the password is using bcrypt and should not be compared as cleartext.

Instead of configuring clear-password-mapper, the bcrypt-password-mapper is used. The following is an example of a configuration file using bcrypt:

```
quarkus.security.jdbc.enabled=true
quarkus.security.jdbc.principal-query.sql=\
    SELECT u.password, u.role, u.salt, u.iteration \
    FROM test_user u WHERE u.username=?

quarkus.security.jdbc.principal-query.clear-password-mapper.enabled=false
quarkus.security.jdbc.principal-query.bcrypt-password-mapper.enabled=true ❶
quarkus.security.jdbc.principal-query.bcrypt-password-mapper.password-index=\
    1        ❷
quarkus.security.jdbc.principal-query.bcrypt-password-mapper.hash-encoding=\
```

```
    BASE64     ❸
quarkus.security.jdbc.principal-query.bcrypt-password-mapper.salt-index=\
    3          ❹
quarkus.security.jdbc.principal-query.bcrypt-password-mapper.salt-encoding=\
    BASE64     ❺
quarkus.security.jdbc.principal-query.bcrypt-password-mapper.\
    iteration-count-index=4 ❻

quarkus.security.jdbc.principal-query.attribute-mappings.0.index=2
quarkus.security.jdbc.principal-query.attribute-mappings.0.to=groups
```

❶ Enables bcrypt

❷ Sets password index; this should be on the same line

❸ Sets password hash encoding; this should be on the same line

❹ Sets salt index; this should be on the same line

❺ Sets salt encoding; this should be on the same line

❻ Sets iteration count index; this should be on the same line

After this change, the password matching between the provided password and the password retrieved by query does not happen in cleartext. Rather, the provided password is hashed using bcrypt and then compared with the stored password:

```
quarkus.security.jdbc.enabled=true

quarkus.security.jdbc.principal-query.sql=\
    SELECT u.password FROM test_user u WHERE u.username=? ❶
quarkus.security.jdbc.principal-query.clear-password-mapper.enabled=true
quarkus.security.jdbc.principal-query.clear-password-mapper.password-index=1

quarkus.security.jdbc.principal-query.roles.sql=\
    SELECT r.role_name FROM test_role r, test_user_role ur \
    WHERE ur.username=? AND ur.role_id = r.id ❷ ❸
quarkus.security.jdbc.principal-query.roles.datasource=permissions ❹
quarkus.security.jdbc.principal-query.roles.attribute-mappings.0.index=1
quarkus.security.jdbc.principal-query.roles.attribute-mappings.0.to=groups
```

❶ Default data source is used to retrieve the password

❷ roles is used as a name to identify the second query; the query should all be on the same line

❸ Gets the role from another query

❹ Role query is executed against a data source named permissions

11.3 Authorization with MicroProfile JWT

Problem

You want to save security context in RESTful web services and stateless services in general.

Solution

Use JSON Web Tokens.

JWT (JSON Web Token) is a standard specified under RFC-7519 that is used for exchanging information between services. The particularity of JWT is that the token content is formatted in JSON instead of in plain text or any other binary format.

Quarkus integrates with the MicroProfile JWT specification (*https://oreil.ly/IU0-d*) to consume and validate JWT tokens and retrieve the claims.

A JWT token is formed by *claims*, which are the information to transmit—for example, the username, the expiration of the token, or the roles of the user. The token is digitally signed so the information contained in the token can be trusted and verified.

A JWT token is composed of three sections. All of them are encoded in the Base64 format:

Header
> It contains some metadata, like the algorithm used to sign the token; custom information of the token, like the type of token; or unencrypted claims if using JSON Web Encryption (JWE).

Claims
> Information to store inside the token. Some claims are mandatory, others are options, and some are custom to our application.

Signature
> The signature of the token.

Then the three sections are encoded to Base64 and concatenated with a period sign (.), so the final token looks like `base64(Header).base64(Claims).base64(Signature)`.

For this example, the following JWT token is used:

```
{ ❶
  "kid": "/privateKey.pem",
  "typ": "JWT",
  "alg": "RS256"
},
{ ❷
```

```
"sub": "jdoe-using-jwt-rbac",
"aud": "using-jwt-rbac",
"upn": "jdoe@quarkus.io",
"birthdate": "2001-07-13",
"auth_time": 1570094171,
"iss": "https://quarkus.io/using-jwt-rbac", ❸
"roleMappings": {
  "group2": "Group2MappedRole",
  "group1": "Group1MappedRole"
},
"groups": [ ❹
  "Echoer",
  "Tester",
  "Subscriber",
  "group2"
],
"preferred_username": "jdoe",
"exp": 2200814171,
"iat": 1570094171,
"jti": "a-123"
}
```

❶   Header part

❷   Claims part

❸   The issuer of the token

❹   Groups (or roles) that the owner of the token belongs in

The following is the serialized version of the same token:

```
eyJraWQiOiJcL3ByaXZhdGVLZXkucGVtIiwidHlwIjoiSldUIiwiYWxnIjoiUlMyNTYifQ.
eyJzdWIiOiJqZG9lLXVzaW5nLWp3dC1yYmFjIiwiYXVkIjoidXNpbmctand0LXJiYWMiLCJ
1cG4iOiJqZG9lQHF1YXJrdXMuaW8iLCJiaXJ0aGRhdGUiOiIyMDAxLTA3LTEzIiwiYXV0aF
90aW1lIjoxNTcwMDk0MTcxLCJpc3MiOiJodHRwczpcL1wvcXVhcmt1cy5pb1wvdXNpbmcta
nd0LXJiYWMiLCJyb2xlTWFwcGluZ3MiOnsiZ3JvdXAyIjoiR3JvdXAyTWFwcGVkUm9sZSIs
Imdyb3VwMSI6Ikdyb3VwMS1hcHBlZFJvbGUifSwiZ3JvdXBzIjpbIkVjaG9lciIsIlRlc3R
lciIsIlN1YnNjcmliZXIiLCJncm91cDIiXSwicHJlZmVycmVkX3VzZXJuYW1lIjoiamRvZS
IsImV4cCI6MjIwMDgxNDE3MSwiaWF0IjoxNTcwMDk0MTcxLCJqdGkiOiJhLTEyMyJ9.
Hzr41h3_uewy-g2B-sonOiBObtcpkgzqmF4bT3cO58v45AIOiegl7HIx7QgEZHRO4PdUtR3
4x9W23VJY7NJ545ucpCuKnEV1uRlspJyQevfI-mSRg1bHlMmdDt661-V3KmQES8WX2B2uqi
ryk05fCeCp3womboilzCq4VtxbmM2qgf6ag8rUNnTCLuCgEoulGwTn0F5lCrom-7dJOTryW
1KI0qUWHMMwl4TX5cLmqJLgBzJapzc5_yEfgQZ9qXzvsT8zeOWSKKPLm7LFVt2YihkXa80l
Wcjewwt61rfQkpmqSzAHL0QIs7CsM9GfnoYc0j9po83-P3GJiBMMFmn-vg
```

Notice how the sections are divided by periods.

MicroProfile JWT spec performs the following operations when a request is received:

1. Extract security token from the request, usually from the `Authorization` header.

2. Validate the token to make sure that the token is valid. These checks might involve things like verifying the signature to trust on the token or verifying that the token has not expired.

3. Extract token information.

4. Create a security context with identity information so it can be used in case of authorization (RBAC).

Moreover, the MicroProfile JWT spec sets a list of mandatory claims that every token must provide:

Claim	Description
typ	The token format. It must be JWT.
alg	Identifies the cryptographic algorithm to secure the token. It must be RS256.
kid	Indicates which key was used to secure the token.
iss	The token issuer.
sub	Identifies the principal subjected to the token.
aud	Identifies the recipients that the token is intended for.
exp	Sets the expiration time.
iat	Provides the time at which the token was issued.
jti	Unique identifier of the token.
upn	The user-principal name used in the `java.security.Principal` interface.
groups	The list of group names that have been assigned to the principal of the token. They are the roles in which the user belongs.

These are the minimal claims that are required by the MicroProfile JWT specification, but additional claims can be added, such as `preferred_username` or any other information that your application might need to transmit between services.

Register the `quarkus-smallrye-jwt` extension to start using the MicroProfile JWT specification:

```
./mvnw quarkus:add-extension -Dextensions="quarkus-smallrye-jwt"
```

Configure the extension to set the public key used to verify that the token has not been modified and that the issuer (`iss`) claim of the token the server accepts is valid.

The following are public key formats supported by the specification:

- Public Key Cryptography Standards #8 (PKCS#8) Privacy-Enhanced Mail (PEM)
- JSON Web Key (JWK)

- JSON Web Key Set (JWKS)
- JSON Web Key (JWK) Base64 URL encoded
- JSON Web Key Set (JWKS) Base64 URL encoded

For this example, we choose the JSON Web Key Set (JWKS) format to specify the public key used to validate the token.

The JWKS file containing the public key is placed inside the project directory:

```
{
    "keys": [
        {
            "kty": "RSA",
            "kid": "/privateKey.pem",
            "e": "AQAB",
            "n": "livFI8qB4D0y2jy0CfEqFyy46R0o7S8TKpsx5xbHKoU1VWg6QkQm-ntyIv1
                    p4kE1sPEQO73-HY8-Bzs75XwRTYL1BmR1w8J5hmjVWjc6R2BTBGAYRPFRho
                    r3kpM6ni2SPmNNhurEAHw7TaqszP5eUF_F9-KEBWkwVta-PZ37bwqSE4sCb
                    1soZFrVz_UT_LF4tYpuVYt3YbqToZ3pZOZ9AX2o1GCG3xwOjkc4x0W7ezbQ
                    ZdC9iftPxVHR8irOijJRRjcPDtA6vPKpzLl6CyYnsIYPd99ltwxTHjr3npf
                    v_3Lw50bAkbT4HeLFxTx4flEoZLKO_g0bAoV2uqBhkA9xnQ"
        }
    ]
}
```

The configuration file pointing to this data is the following:

```
mp.jwt.verify.publickey.location=quarkus.pub.jwk.json  ❶
mp.jwt.verify.issuer=https://quarkus.io/using-jwt-rbac  ❷
```

❶ Location of the public key

❷ The issuer accepted by the service

Apart from handling the verification process of the token, the MicroProfile JWT integrates with existing Java EE security APIs providing the data from the token. The integration happens in the following annotations:

```
javax.ws.rs.core.SecurityContext.getUserPrincipal()
javax.ws.rs.core.SecurityContext.isUserInRole(String)
javax.servlet.http.HttpServletRequest.getUserPrincipal()
javax.servlet.http.HttpServletRequest.isUserInRole(String)
javax.ejb.SessionContext.getCallerPrincipal()
javax.ejb.SessionContext.isCallerInRole(String)
javax.security.jacc.PolicyContext
  .getContext("javax.security.auth.Subject.container")
javax.security.enterprise.identitystore.IdentityStore
  .getCallerGroups(CredentialValidationResult)
@javax.annotation.security.RolesAllowed
```

Furthermore, the MicroProfile JWT spec provides two classes to accommodate JWT data inside CDI or JAX-RS classes:

`org.eclipse.microprofile.jwt.JsonWebToken`
Interface that exposes the raw token and offers methods to get the claims

`@org.eclipse.microprofile.jwt.Claim`
Annotation to provide injection of claims into classes

For example:

```java
package org.acme.quickstart;

import javax.annotation.security.RolesAllowed;
import javax.enterprise.context.RequestScoped;
import javax.inject.Inject;
import javax.ws.rs.GET;
import javax.ws.rs.Path;
import javax.ws.rs.Produces;
import javax.ws.rs.core.MediaType;

import org.eclipse.microprofile.jwt.Claim;
import org.eclipse.microprofile.jwt.Claims;
import org.eclipse.microprofile.jwt.JsonWebToken;

@Path("/hello")
@RequestScoped ❶
public class GreetingResource {

    @Inject
    JsonWebToken callerPrincipal; ❷

    @Claim(standard = Claims.preferred_username) ❸
    String username;

    @GET
    @Produces(MediaType.TEXT_PLAIN)
    public String hello() {
        return "hello " + username;
    }
}
```

❶ A JWT token is, by nature, request-scoped; if you expect to use the token, the class must be `RequestScoped` to avoid mixing tokens in classes

❷ Injects `JsonWebToken` interface that represents the full JWT token

❸ Injects the `preferred_username` claim

Claim annotation also supports the injection of private claim names. These claims are not official claim names provided by the RFC but claims that are specific to the service (custom claims). To inject a private claim, use the annotation value as the name of the claim: `@Claim("my_claim")`. Moreover, in case of nonmandatory claims, the `java.util.Optional` class can be used to indicate that the claim is nullable:

```
@Claim(standard = Claims.birthdate)
Optional<String> birthdate;
```

The ClaimValue Interface

To support beans/resources that are *not* `@RequestScoped`, the MicroProfile JWT spec introduces the `org.eclipse.microprofile.jwt.ClaimValue` interface that, used together with `@Claim`, makes the injection of the value safe from concurrent requests:

```
@Claim(standard = Claims.exp) ❶
ClaimValue<Long> username;

@Claim(standard = Claims.groups) ❷
ClaimValue<Set<String>> groups;

@Claim("raw_token") ❸
ClaimValue<String> rawToken;
```

❶ Expiration time injected

❷ Groups are injected in the form of `java.util.Set`

❸ `raw_token` is a special claim that represents the JWT token in raw format; the raw token can be used to propagate it across other services

---

Update the test to send a bearer JWT token to the defined endpoint:

```
@Test
public void testHelloEndpoint() {
    given().header("Authorization", "Bearer " + validToken) ❶
            .when().get("/hello").then().statusCode(200).body(is("hello jdoe"));
}
```

❶ JWT token is sent as bearer token in `Authorization` header

With the current solution, these assumptions are true:

- If a valid token is provided, the `preferred_username` is extracted.
- If an invalid token is provided (expired, signature not valid, modified by third party, etc.), then a 401 Unauthorized Error error code is sent back to the caller.
- If no token is provided, then the request is processed but the `preferred_user name` field is null.

The MicroProfile JWT spec also provides support for the authorization process by integrating with the @RolesAllowed annotation. The groups claim value is used any time the isCallerInRole() method is called, which effectively means that any value in groups can be used as a role in the application.

The groups claim in the JWT token used in this example contains the following values: "groups": ["Echoer", "Tester", "Subscriber", "group2"]. Protect the call to /hello by using @RolesAllowed with one of the group values present in the token:

```
@GET
@Produces(MediaType.TEXT_PLAIN)
@RolesAllowed("Tester")
public String hello() {}
```

Now, you can assume the following:

- If a valid token is provided and the groups claim contains the Tester group, then the preferred_username is extracted.
- If a valid token is provided and the groups claim does not contain the Tester group, then a 403 Forbidden error code is sent back to the caller.
- If an invalid token is provided (expired, signature not valid, modified by third party, etc.), then a 401 Unauthorized Error error code is sent back to the caller.
- If no token is provided, then a 401 Unauthorized Error error code is sent back to the caller.

Discussion

In the past, the security context was saved in the HTTP session, which works well until you start scaling up the services and things start to become more and more complicated. To avoid this problem, one of the possible solutions is to pass this information in all calls using a token, especially a JSON token.

It is important to note that the token is signed and not encrypted, which means that the information can be seen by anyone but not modified. An encryption layer can be added using JSON Web Encryption so that the claims are not in cleartext but instead are encrypted.

The intent of this section is not for you to master JWT but for you learn how to use it in Quarkus, so we are assuming that you already have some knowledge about JWT. We are also providing some links in the following "See Also" to help you become more familiar with JWT.

See Also

To learn about JWT, visit the following web pages:

- JSON Web Tokens (*https://jwt.io*)
- GitHub: JWT RBAC for MicroProfile (*https://oreil.ly/tXP9d*)
- IETF: JSON Web Token (*https://oreil.ly/p9jUC*)

11.4 Authorization and Authentication with OpenId Connect

Problem

You want to protect your RESTful Web API with OpenId Connect.

Solution

Use bearing token authorization where the token is issued by OpenId Connect.

In the previous section, you learned how to use the JWT token for protecting resources, but the generation of the token was not covered because the token was generated up front and provided in a text file.

In real-world applications, you need an identity provider that issues the token. The de facto protocol for distributed services is OpenId Connect and OAuth 2.0 and an authorization-compliant server with the protocol, such as Keycloak (*https://www.keycloak.org*).

Register the `quarkus-oidc` extension to protect resources with OpenId Connect:

```
./mvnw quarkus:add-extension -Dextensions="quarkus-oidc"
```

Configure the location of the OpenId Connect server to validate the token:

```
quarkus.oidc.auth-server-url=http://localhost:8180/auth/realms/quarkus ❶
quarkus.oidc.client-id=backend-service ❷
```

❶ The base URL of the OpenID Connect server

❷ Each application has a client ID used to identify the application

Protect the endpoint using the `@RolesAllowed` annotation:

```
@Inject
io.quarkus.security.identity.SecurityIdentity securityIdentity; ❶

@GET
```

```
@RolesAllowed("user")
@Produces(MediaType.TEXT_PLAIN)
public String hello() {
    return "hello " + securityIdentity.getPrincipal().getName();
}
```

❶ Quarkus interface that represents the currently logged in user

The test must be updated to get the access token from OpenId Connect and provide it
as the bearer token:

```
@Test
public void testHelloEndpoint() {
    System.out.println(accessToken);
    given()
      .auth().oauth2(accessToken)
      .when().get("/hello")
      .then()
        .statusCode(200)
        .body(is("hello alice"));
}
```

The access token is generated in the OpenId Connect server. To generate it, some
parameters must be provided, such as the username and password, to access the
server and to generate a token representing the user:

```
package org.acme.quickstart;

import java.net.URI;
import java.net.URISyntaxException;

import io.restassured.RestAssured;
import io.restassured.builder.RequestSpecBuilder;
import io.restassured.response.Response;
import io.restassured.response.ResponseOptions;
import io.restassured.specification.RequestSpecification;

public class RestAssuredExtension {

    public static ResponseOptions<Response> getAccessToken(String url,
                                                           String clientId,
                                                           String clientIdPwd,
                                                           String username,
                                                           String password) {
        final RequestSpecification request = prepareRequest(url);
        try {
          return request
            .auth()
            .preemptive()
            .basic(clientId, clientIdPwd)
            .contentType("application/x-www-form-urlencoded; charset=UTF-8")
            .urlEncodingEnabled(true)
```

```
        .formParam("username", username)
        .and()
        .formParam("password", password)
        .and()
        .formParam("grant_type", "password")
        .post(new URI(url));
    } catch (URISyntaxException e) {
      throw new IllegalArgumentException(e);
    }
  }

  private static RequestSpecification prepareRequest(String url) {
    final RequestSpecBuilder builder = new RequestSpecBuilder();
    final RequestSpecification requestSpec = builder.build();
    return RestAssured.given().spec(requestSpec);
  }
}
```

The code is essentially an implementation of the next `curl` command but using REST-Assured:

```
curl -X POST \
    http://localhost:8180/auth/realms/quarkus/protocol/openid-connect/token \
    --user backend-service:secret \
    -H 'content-type: application/x-www-form-urlencoded' \
    -d 'username=alice&password=alice&grant_type=password'
```

Now, when running the test, something completely different is shown than in Recipe 11.3.

First of all, the token (JWT token) is not static; it is issued by OpenID Connect (Keycloak) for the `alice` username.

The following is example of an issued token for `alice`:

```
{
  "alg": "RS256",
  "typ": "JWT",
  "kid": "cfIADN_xxCJmVkWyN-PNXEEvMUWs2r68CxtmhEDNzXU"
},
{
  "jti": "cc54b9db-5f2f-4609-8a6b-4f76026e63ae",
  "exp": 1578935775,
  "nbf": 0,
  "iat": 1578935475,
  "iss": "http://localhost:8180/auth/realms/quarkus",
  "sub": "eb4123a3-b722-4798-9af5-8957f823657a",
  "typ": "Bearer",
  "azp": "backend-service",
  "auth_time": 0,
  "session_state": "5b674175-a2a9-4a45-a3da-394923125e55",
  "acr": "1",
  "realm_access": {
```

```
      "roles": [
        "user"
      ]
    },
    "scope": "email profile",
    "email_verified": false,
    "preferred_username": "alice"
  }
```

Second, the OpenID Connect is responsible for providing everything to validate the token; the public key is not configured manually.

The following validations are performed by Keycloak when the token is provided:

- If a valid token is provided and the `roles` claim contains the `user` group, then the `preferred_username` is extracted.

- If a valid token is provided and the `roles` claim does not contain the `user` group, then a 403 Forbidden error code is sent back to the caller.

- If an invalid token is provided (expired, signature not valid, modified by third party, etc.), then a 403 Forbidden error code is sent back to the caller.

- If no token is provided, then a 401 Unauthorized Error error code is sent back to the caller.

See Also

To learn more about OpenId Connect protocol, see the following websites:

- OpenID Connect (*https://openid.net/connect*)
- Keycloak (*https://www.keycloak.org*)

11.5 Protecting Web Resources with OpenId Connect

Problem

You want to protect your web resources.

Solution

Use OpenId Connect and file-based role definitions to protect web resources.

Web resources can be protected using OpenId Connect protocol and Quarkus. The OpenId Connect extension enables authentication to web resources by implementing the well-known authorization code flow, where any unauthenticated user that is trying to access a protected resource is redirected to the OpenId Connect Provider website to authenticate. After the authentication process is completed, the user is sent back to the application.

Register the quarkus-oidc extension to protect resources with OpenId Connect:

```
./mvnw quarkus:add-extension -Dextensions="quarkus-oidc"
```

Configure the location of the OpenId Connect server to validate the token:

```
quarkus.oidc.auth-server-url=http://localhost:8180/auth/realms/quarkus ❶
quarkus.oidc.client-id=frontend ❷
quarkus.oidc.application-type=web-app ❸
quarkus.http.auth.permission.authenticated.paths=/* ❹
quarkus.http.auth.permission.authenticated.policy=authenticated
```

❶ The base URL of the OpenID Connect server

❷ Each application has a client ID used to identify the application

❸ Enables OpenID Connect Authorization Code Flow

❹ Sets permission to web resources

Start the application, open a browser, and enter the following URL: *http://localhost: 8080*:

```
./mvnw clean compile quarkus:dev
```

The default *index.html* page is not shown, but you are redirected to the authentication page of Keycloak. Enter the following valid credentials (login: **alice**, password: **alice**) to gain access to the web resource. After pushing the Login button, the page is redirected back to the login page.

CHAPTER 12

Application Secrets Management

Every application has information that needs to be kept confidential. This information could include database credentials, external service authentication, or even the location of certain resources. All of these are collectively called *secrets*. Your application needs a secure place to store these secrets both during application startup and at rest. In this chapter, we will discuss secret management using Kubernetes and Vault.

12.1 Storing Data Using Kubernetes Secrets

Problem

You want to store secrets in Kubernetes in a safer way than directly on the Pod or container.

Solution

Use Kubernetes secrets to store and retrieve sensitive data such as passwords, tokens, or SSH keys in plain text on a container. Kubernetes has the concept of `secret` objects that can be used to store sensitive data.

It is important to know that storing sensitive data in a secret object does not automatically make it secure because Kubernetes does not encrypt data but instead encodes it in Base64 by default. Using secrets gives you some features that are not provided by the standard configuration process:

- You can define the authorization policies to access the secret.
- You can configure Kubernetes to encrypt sensitive data (this is known as *encryption at rest*).
- You can grant access to a specific container instance using lists.

None of these features are enabled by default, and they require some knowledge about Kubernetes. In the book, we explain only how Quarkus integrates with other tools like Kubernetes; we do not explain the operational side of the tool.

The secrets can be injected into the container as an environment variable or as a volume. The environment variable approach is less secure because anyone with access to the container instance could dump the content easily. The volume approach, on the other hand, easily becomes complex when there are a large number of keys because Kubernetes creates one file per key to store inside the value.

Both approaches are shown, so you can choose the one that works better for your use case.

The example covers the use case in which an API token (e.g., GitHub Personal Access Token) needs to be set as secret in the application.

To enable the generation of Kubernetes resources with the `secrets` injection in the Pod, you need to register the `quarkus-kubernetes` extension:

```
./mvnw quarkus:add-extension -Dextensions="quarkus-kubernetes"
```

Create a secret by creating a Kubernetes resource of the kind `Secret` or by using the kubectl CLI tool. Open a new terminal and run the following command to register a new secret with `greeting-security` ID and a key `github.api.key.token` with a token (this token is invalid and is used only for example purposes):

```
kubectl create secret generic greeting-security \
--from-literal=github.api.key.token=eyJhbGciOiJIUzI1NiIsInR5cCI6IkpXVCJ9.\
eyJzdWIiOiIxMjM0NTY3ODkwIiwibmFtZSI6IkpvaG4gRG9lIiwiaWF0IjoxNTE2MjM5MDIyfQ.\
SflKxwRJSMeKKF2QT4fwpMeJf36POk6yJV_adQssw5c
```

Now that the secret is created, let's see how to set it as an environment variable.

A configuration property is required to get the property from the environment variable. In this case, the property is called `github.api.key.token`, but of course you could also access it directly by using `System.getenv()`. The former approach is better because it relies on the MicroProfile Config spec to read the configuration properties and not some custom solution:

```
@ConfigProperty(name = "github.api.key.token")
String githubToken;
```

Set extra properties for the Kubernetes extension in the *application.properties* so that the generated Kubernetes deployment file contains the segments needed to inject the secret as an environment variable:

```
quarkus.container-image.group=quarkus ❶
quarkus.container-image.name=greeting-started-kubernetes-secrets
```

```
quarkus.container-image.tag=1.0-SNAPSHOT
quarkus.kubernetes.image-pull-policy=if-not-present
quarkus.kubernetes.env-vars.github-api-key-token.name=github.api.key.token ❷
quarkus.kubernetes.env-vars.github-api-key-token.secret=greeting-security ❸
```

❶ Configures Docker image

❷ Sets the environment variable to override the `github.api.key.token` property

❸ Sets the secret name to load

The generation of the Kubernetes file will contain a new entry in the container definition called `secretKeyRef` that defines all the key/value pairs.

The MicroProfile Config spec permits the override of any configuration property using the equivalent environment variable (in uppercase and changing dots [.] to underscores [_]). The `Secrets` contains the configuration properties as secrets. In *application.properties*, the Kubernetes extension is configured to generate a deployment descriptor that sets these secrets as environment variables so that when the container is started inside the Kubernetes cluster, the secrets are injected into the container as environment variables and are read by MicroProfile Config as configuration properties.

To deploy the application, open a new terminal window, package the application, create the Docker container, and apply the generated Kubernetes resources:

```
./mvnw clean package -DskipTests

docker build -f src/main/docker/Dockerfile.jvm \
    -t quarkus/greeting-started-kubernetes-secrets:1.0-SNAPSHOT .
kubectl apply -f target/kubernetes/kubernetes.yml

kubectl patch svc greeting-started-kubernetes-secrets \
    --type='json' \
    -p '[{"op":"replace","path":"/spec/type","value":"NodePort"}]'
curl $(minikube service greeting-started-kubernetes-secrets --url)/hello
```

But secrets can also be mounted as volumes instead of being set as environment variables. Set the Kubernetes extension properties in the *application.properties* so that the generated Kubernetes deployment file contains the segments to mount the secret file as a volume:

```
quarkus.kubernetes.mounts.github-token.path=/deployment/github ❶ ❷
quarkus.kubernetes.mounts.github-token.read-only=true ❸
quarkus.kubernetes.secret-volumes.github-token.secret-name=greeting-security❹
quarkus.kubernetes.secret-volumes.github-token.default-mode=420 ❺
```

❶ Mounts the volume with `github-token` name

❷ Sets the path where the volume is mounted inside the container

❸ Sets the volume as read-only

❹ Sets the secret name to load

❺ Sets the mode to be readable from the process

The last step is to read the secret from the code. Since the secret is mounted in the file system, it needs to be read as any other file:

```
@GET
@Path("/file")
@Produces(MediaType.TEXT_PLAIN)
public String ghTokenFile() throws IOException {
    final byte[] encodedGHToken = Files.readAllBytes(
        Paths.get("/deployment/github/github.api.key.token"));  ❶
    return new String(encodedGHToken);
}
```

❶ The location of the secret is the mount path plus the secret key

To deploy the application, package it, create the Docker container, and apply the generated Kubernetes resources:

```
./mvnw clean package -DskipTests

docker build -f src/main/docker/Dockerfile.jvm \
    -t quarkus/greeting-started-kubernetes-secrets:1.0-SNAPSHOT .
kubectl apply -f target/kubernetes/kubernetes.yml

kubectl patch svc greeting-started-kubernetes-secrets --type='json' \
    -p '[{"op":"replace","path":"/spec/type","value":"NodePort"}]'
curl $(minikube service greeting-started-kubernetes-secrets --url=/hello/file
```

Discussion

Kubernetes secrets have some problems that need to be addressed externally. The following are some of these problems:

- Secrets are not encrypted but just encoded in Base64 by default.
- You need to use SSL to communicate with etcd. This is the place where the secrets are stored.

- The disk needs to be encrypted because `etcd` might store the data on the disk.
- You need to correctly define the RBAC to prevent anyone from accessing a secret.

See Also

To learn more about Kubernetes Secrets, visit the following pages on the Kubernetes website:

- Secrets (*https://oreil.ly/dFTgh*)
- Encrypting Secret Data at Rest (*https://oreil.ly/_auK1*)
- Authorization Overview (*https://oreil.ly/ctlyn*)
- Using RBAC Authorization (*https://oreil.ly/WrcaP*)

12.2 Store Configuration Secrets Securely with Vault

Problem

You want to store configuration secrets securely.

Solution

Use the Quarkus Vault (*https://oreil.ly/UMKuH*) extension to retrieve secrets.

The key aspects when dealing with secrets are storing them so they cannot be read by forbidden users and protecting access to them so only the services that require the secrets can access them.

Vault is a tool that simplifies these use cases by providing a unified interface for storing and consuming secrets.

About Vault

Vault (*https://oreil.ly/UMKuH*) is an open source tool for securely accessing secrets. How to run Vault in production is outside the scope of this book.

To simplify the installation of Vault, the Vault Docker container is used:

```
docker run --rm --cap-add=IPC_LOCK -e VAULT_ADDR=http://localhost:8200 \
  -p 8200:8200 --name=dev-vault vault:1.2.2
```

You may need to set the following environment variable:

```
$ export VAULT_ADDR='http://0.0.0.0:8200'
```

> The unseal key and root token are displayed below in case you want to
> seal/unseal the Vault or re-authenticate.
>
> Unseal Key: s7WbMScSOh02ERK6XEfl6ep6BReRQZzl9VekrrnyKE8=
> Root Token: s.ty3QS2uNaxPdiFsSZpCQfjpc ❶
>
> ❶ Token to initialize access to Vault
>
> Open a shell inside the Vault container to configure Vault and add a secret:
>
> ```
> docker exec -it dev-vault sh
> export VAULT_TOKEN=s.ty3QS2uNaxPdiFsSZpCQfjpc ❶
>
> vault kv put secret/myapps/vault-service/config foo=secretbar ❷
> ```
>
> ❶ Sets the token to access
>
> ❷ Creates a new secret with key foo at path *secret/myapps/vault-service/config*
>
> Create a policy that gives read access to the secret:
>
> ```
> cat <<EOF | vault policy write vault-service-policy -
> path "secret/data/myapps/vault-service/*" {
>   capabilities = ["read"]
> }
> EOF
> ```
>
> The last step is to enable credentials (userpass engine) for accessing secrets from the
> service:
>
> ```
> vault auth enable userpass
> vault write auth/userpass/users/alex password=alex \
>   policies=vault-service-policy ❶
> ```
>
> ❶ Creates a user with ID alex and password alex

Vault supports multiple authentication methods to authenticate against the Vault
service and start consuming the secrets. At the time of writing, the following authentication methods are supported by the Quarkus Vault extension:

token
  Directly pass the user token to bypass the authentication process.

user/password
  Authenticate with Vault using a username and password credentials.

approle
  Authenticate using a role_id and a secret_id. This method is oriented to auto-
  mated workflows (machines and services). role_id is usually embedded into a

Docker container, and `secret_id` is obtained by a Kubernetes cluster as a cubbyhole response, wrapping it (single use) and delivering it to the target service.

kubernetes
Authenticate with Vault using the Kubernetes Service Account Token.

To get started, register the `quarkus-vault` extension to use Vault:

```
./mvnw quarkus:add-extension -Dextensions="quarkus-vault"
```

The Quarkus Vault extension integrates with the MicroProfile Configuration spec so that a secret can be injected using the `@ConfigProperty` annotation. Configure the application to use username and password as the authentication method for Vault, and set the base path where secrets are stored:

```
quarkus.vault.url=http://localhost:8200 ❶
quarkus.vault.authentication.userpass.username=alex ❷
quarkus.vault.authentication.userpass.password=alex

quarkus.vault.kv-secret-engine-version=2 ❸
quarkus.vault.secret-config-kv-path=myapps/vault-service/config
```

❶ The base URL of the Vault server

❷ The credentials to authenticate

❸ The path where the secrets are stored

Access the secret value of the `foo` key by using the `@org.eclipse.microprofile.config.inject.ConfigProperty` annotation:

```
@ConfigProperty(name = "foo") ❶
String foo;

@GET
@Produces(MediaType.TEXT_PLAIN)
public String hello() {
    return foo;
}
```

❶ Secret value for the `foo` key is injected

Start the application and send a request to the endpoint:

```
./mvnw clean compile quarkus:dev

curl http://localhost:8080/hello
secretbar
```

Discussion

If the path is known only at runtime, secrets can also be retrieved programmatically by injecting the io.quarkus.vault.VaultKVSecretEngine interface:

```
@Inject
VaultKVSecretEngine kvSecretEngine;

final Map<String, String> secrets = kvSecretEngine
    .readSecret("myapps/vault-service/config"); ❶
final String fooSecret = secrets.get("foo");
```

❶ Provides the values stored in the Vault key/value secret engine

See Also

To learn more about Vault, visit the following website:

- Vault: Documentation (*https://oreil.ly/ke_Q5*)

12.3 Cryptography as a Service

Problem

You want to avoid spreading all cryptographic operations across all the services.

Solution

Use the *transit* engine of Vault to have all cryptographic operations executed in the same place.

Open a shell inside the Vault container created in the previous recipe to configure Vault and add keys to encrypt and sign messages:

```
docker exec -it dev-vault sh
export VAULT_TOKEN=s.ty3QS2uNaxPdiFsSZpCQfjpc ❶

vault secrets enable transit ❷

vault write -f transit/keys/my_encryption ❸
vault write transit/keys/my-sign-key type=ecdsa-p256 ❹
```

❶ Sets the token to access

❷ Enables transit engine

❸ Creates an encryption key of type AES-256-GCM96

❹ Creates a signing key of type ECDSA-P256

Create a policy that gives access to transit operations:

```
cat <<EOF | vault policy write vault-service-policy -
path "transit/*" {
  capabilities = [ "create", "read", "update" ]
}
EOF
```

The last step is to enable credentials (userpass engine) for accessing secrets from the service:

```
vault auth enable userpass
vault write auth/userpass/users/alex password=alex \
  policies=vault-service-policy ❶
```

❶ Creates a user with ID alex and password alex

Register quarkus-vault extension to use Vault:

```
./mvnw quarkus:add-extension -Dextensions="quarkus-vault"
```

Configure the application to use username and password as the authentication method for Vault:

```
quarkus.vault.url=http://localhost:8200 ❶

quarkus.vault.authentication.userpass.username=alex ❷
quarkus.vault.authentication.userpass.password=alex
```

❶ The base URL of the Vault server

❷ The credentials to authenticate

Inject the io.quarkus.vault.VaultTransitSecretEngine instance to use transit operations:

```
@Inject
VaultTransitSecretEngine transit; ❶

@GET
@Path("/encrypt")
@Produces(MediaType.TEXT_PLAIN)
public String encrypt(@QueryParam("text") String text) {
    return transit.encrypt("my_encryption", text); ❷
}

@GET
@Path("/decrypt")
@Produces(MediaType.TEXT_PLAIN)
public String decrypt(@QueryParam("text") String text) {
    return transit.decrypt("my_encryption", text).asString(); ❸
```

```
    }

    @GET
    @Path("/sign")
    @Produces(MediaType.TEXT_PLAIN)
    public String sign(@QueryParam("text") String text) {
        return transit.sign("my-sign-key", text);  ❹
    }
```

❶ Transit operations interface

❷ Encrypts using the encryption key

❸ Decrypts using the encryption key

❹ Signs the text with the given signature

Start the application and send a request to the endpoint:

```
./mvnw clean compile quarkus:dev
```

```
curl http://localhost:8080/hello/encrypt?text=Ada
vault:v1:iIunGAElLpbaNWWqZq1yf4cctkEUOFdJE1oRTaSI2g==
```

```
curl http://localhost:8080/hello/decrypt? \
     text=vault:v1:iIunGAElLpbaNWWqZq1yf4cctkEUOFdJE1oRTaSI2g==
Ada
```

```
curl http://localhost:8080/hello/sign?text=Alexandra
vault:v1:MEUCIGkgS5VY5KEU2yHqnIn9qwzgfBUv3O2H4bgNAFVrYCK3AiEAnQznfdEZI6b\
  /Xtko/wEl8WhZLuKZQ/arOYkfsnwBH3M=
```

Discussion

Cryptography operations such as encrypt, decrypt, sign, or hash-based message authentication codes (HMACs) of data are commonly required in services. These operations are usually implemented in each of the services, which means that you are duplicating this sensitive logic as well as the management of the keys in each of the services.

The Vault Transit engine handles all cryptographic functions for you without storing the resulted data. You can think of Vault as a *cryptographic-as-a-service* model in which data is sent, manipulated, and returned back without being stored internally.

Everything is managed internally by Vault, freeing developers to focus on implementing the important business logic.

The following operations are supported by the Vault extension:

encrypt
Encrypts a regular string with a Vault key configured in the transit secret engine.

decrypt
Decrypts the encrypted data with the specified key and returns unencrypted data.

rewrap
Reencrypts into a new cipher text a cipher text that was obtained from encryption using an old key version with the last key version.

sign
Signs an input string with the specified key.

verifySignature
Checks that the signature was obtained from signing the input with the specified key.

See Also

For more information, visit the following website:

- Vault: Transit Secrets Engine (*https://oreil.ly/rloOa*)

12.4 Generate Database Password as Secret

Problem

You want to store the database password securely.

Solution

Read the database password as a secret.

The database password is something that needs to be protected and should not be set directly to the configuration file. The Quarkus Vault extension integrates with persistence configuration to read the database password as a secret from Vault.

Open a shell inside the Vault container created in the previous recipe to configure Vault and add the database password as a secret:

```
docker exec -it dev-vault sh
export VAULT_TOKEN=s.ty3QS2uNaxPdiFsSZpCQfjpc ❶

vault kv put secret/myapps/vault-service/db password=alex ❷
```

❶ Sets the token to access

❷ Creates a new secret with a key `password` and the value `alex`

Create a policy that gives read access to the secret:

```
cat <<EOF | vault policy write vault-service-policy -
path "secret/data/myapps/vault-service/*" {
  capabilities = ["read"]
}
EOF
```

The last step is to enable credentials (`userpass` engine) for accessing secrets from the service:

```
vault auth enable userpass
vault write auth/userpass/users/alex password=alex \
  policies=vault-service-policy ❶
```

❶ Creates a user with ID `alex` and password `alex`

For this example, the PostgreSQL server is used as database. Start a new Docker instance in a new terminal by running the following command:

```
docker run --ulimit memlock=-1:-1 -it --rm=true --memory-swappiness=0 \
  --name postgres-quarkus-hibernate -e POSTGRES_USER=alex \
  -e POSTGRES_PASSWORD=alex -e POSTGRES_DB=mydatabase \
  -p 5432:5432 postgres:10.5
```

Notice that the password is the same as the one set in the *secret/myapps/vault-service/db* path.

Register the `quarkus-vault` and persistence extensions:

```
./mvnw quarkus:add-extension \
  -Dextensions="quarkus-vault, quarkus-hibernate-orm-panache, \
    quarkus-jdbc-postgresql, quarkus-resteasy-jsonb"
```

The datasource configuration is slightly different than the one shown in Chapter 7. Instead of having the password hardcoded in the configuration file, the password is retrieved from Vault as a secret and is used to make the connection.

Apart from Vault configuration parameters such as the URL and the authenticated method (i.e., user/password), you need to define the key/value path inside Vault, where the database configuration is stored. More specifically, it is the path where the key named `password` is stored with the database password. In the following example, to set this information into Vault, you run the command `vault kv put secret/myapps/vault-service/db password=alex`, but if you have followed this section, you've already done this when configuring Vault.

Also, overriding the credentials provider used when establishing the connection to the database is required to indicate that the password comes from Vault and not as a configuration property. This is done by using the quarkus.data source.credentials-provider property.

Configure the application with the datasource and Vault parameters and override the credentials provider:

```
quarkus.datasource.url=jdbc:postgresql://localhost:5432/mydatabase
quarkus.datasource.driver=org.postgresql.Driver
quarkus.datasource.username=alex
quarkus.datasource.credentials-provider=mydatabase    ❶
quarkus.vault.credentials-provider.mydatabase\
  .kv-path=myapps/vault-service/db    ❷
quarkus.vault.url=http://localhost:8200    ❸
quarkus.vault.authentication.userpass.username=alex
quarkus.vault.authentication.userpass.password=alex
quarkus.vault.kv-secret-engine-version=2
quarkus.hibernate-orm.database.generation=drop-and-create
%dev.quarkus.hibernate-orm.sql-load-script=import.sql
%dev.quarkus.hibernate-orm.log.sql=true
```

❶ Sets the credentials provider to a custom name (mydatabase)

❷ Sets the key/value path where the password is stored for the mydatabase provider

❸ Configures Vault parameters

It is important to note that there is no quarkus.datasource.password property because the password is retrieved from Vault.

At this time, when the Quarkus application is started, the following steps are executed:

1. Service authenticates to the Vault service.

2. Key/Value is retrieved from secret/myapps/vault-service/db path.

3. The value of the key password is used as password credentials for the database.

 The key name can be changed from password to any other key name by using the kv-key property: quarkus.vault.credentials-provider.mydatabase.kv-key=pass.

Discussion

Vault can generate database credentials dynamically and configure the database instances to use them as credentials instead of having to manually configure the credentials and set them in Vault and/or in the service that requires access to the database. This implies that no credentials are hardcoded in any place, as they are requested from Vault. The generated pair of username and password are subject to Vault's leasing mechanism, which makes the credentials invalid after a reasonable time.

Take the following steps to configure Vault to generate database credentials dynamically:

1. Enable the database secret engine.

2. Set connection parameters to the database, and set the vendor database (at this time most of SQL and NoSQL databases are supported).

3. Configure a role that maps a name in Vault to an SQL statement to create the database credential:

```
vault secrets enable database

cat <<EOF | vault policy write vault-service-policy -
path "database/creds/mydbrole" {
  capabilities = [ "read" ]
}
EOF

vault write database/config/mydb
    plugin_name=postgresql-database-plugin \
    allowed_roles=mydbrole \
    connection_url=postgresql://{{username}}:{{password}}\
        @localhost:5432/mydb?sslmode=disable \
    username=alex \
    password=alex

vault write database/roles/mydbrole \
    db_name=mydb \
    creation_statements="CREATE ROLE \"{{name}}\" WITH LOGIN PASSWORD \
                        '{{password}}' VALID UNTIL '{{expiration}}'; \
                        GRANT SELECT,INSERT, UPDATE, DELETE ON ALL \
                        TABLES IN SCHEMA public TO \"{{name}}\"; \
                        GRANT USAGE, SELECT ON ALL SEQUENCES IN \
                        SCHEMA public to \"{{name}}\";" \
    default_ttl="1h" \
    revocation_statements="ALTER ROLE \"{{name}}\" NOLOGIN;" \
    renew_statements="ALTER ROLE \"{{name}}\" VALID UNTIL '{{expiration}}';" \
    max_ttl="24h"
```

The Vault extension also supports using dynamic database credentials through the `database-credentials-role` property on the `credentials-provider`:

```
quarkus.vault.url=https://localhost:8200
quarkus.vault.authentication.userpass.username=alex
quarkus.vault.authentication.userpass.password=alex

quarkus.datasource.driver=org.postgresql.Driver
quarkus.datasource.url=jdbc:postgresql://localhost:6543/mydb
quarkus.datasource.username=postgres

quarkus.datasource.credentials-provider=dynamic-ds ❶
quarkus.datasource.credentials-provider-type=vault-credentials-provider
quarkus.vault.credentials-provider.dynamic-ds.database-credentials-role=\
   mydbrole ❷
```

❶ No password set

❷ Configures dynamic credentials

See Also

To learn more about dynamic database credentials with Vault, visit the following website:

- Vault: Databases (*https://oreil.ly/RDaes*)

12.5 Authenticating Services Using Vault Kubernetes Auth

Problem

You want to authenticate services against Vault without using a username/password.

Solution

Use the Vault Kubernetes Auth method.

So far, you've used credentials with the username/password approach to authenticating the Quarkus service against the Vault service. This method might be good in some circumstances (testing purposes, internal applications, etc.), but notice that you are introducing a new secret (the password) to get more secrets. One way to fix this problem is by using Kubernetes Secrets to set the Vault password using, for example, the `approle` authentication method. Another way is to use the Vault Kubernetes Auth, which makes it a perfect fit for authenticating services deployed in a Kubernetes cluster.

The Vault Kubernetes auth method uses the Kubernetes service account token and a defined role to authenticate against a Vault service. With this method, Vault does not store the credentials; it uses a trusted third party (the Kubernetes cluster) to validate them. When the Pod with the service is instantiated, the service account token is mounted inside the container, so it is accessible by the application. The default mounting point of the secret token is */var/run/secrets/kubernetes.io/serviceaccount/ token*.

The application then attempts to authenticate using this token by sending it to the Vault server. After that, Vault makes a call to Kubernetes API to ensure the validity of the token. If the token is valid, then an internal Vault token is returned to be used in future requests to get secrets. The process is summarized in Figure 12-1.

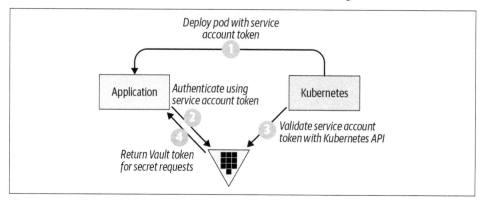

Figure 12-1. Kubernetes authentication method

To configure the Kubernetes auth mode, you need to set two parameters to Vault to connect to Kubernetes API. The first one is the token to access, and the second one is the certificate authority to validate the communication between Vault and the Kubernetes API. These values are retrieved from the secret that starts with `vault-token`. When Vault was first set up for this example, the value was `vault-token-mm5qx`.

To get the token and store it in a file, open a terminal window and run the following command:

```
kubectl get secret vault-token-mm5qx -o jsonpath='{.data.token}' \
  | base64 --decode > jwt.txt ❶ ❷

cat jwt.txt
eyJhbGciOiJSUzI1NiIsImtpZCI6Inp0WWZBcl8weW1SaTI1bjRNYVNHNmtXOUhCWDV\
yczhYandVYkVETktzRHMifQ.
```

❶ Substitute the secret name to your secret name starting with `vault-token`

❷ Secrets are stored in Base64, so they need to be decoded

To get the certificate authority and store it in a file, run the following in the terminal:

```
kubectl get secret vault-token-mm5qx -o jsonpath="{.data['ca\.crt']}" \
  | base64 --decode > ca.crt ❶ ❷

cat ca.crt

-----BEGIN CERTIFICATE-----
MIIC5zCCAc+gAwIBAgIBATANBgkqhkiG9w0BAQsFADAVMRMwEQYDVQQDEwptaW5p
-----END CERTIFICATE-----
```

❶ Pod is named `vault-0`

❷ A `vault-token` is set as a secret

Before deploying the application, you need to enable Kubernetes `auth` method, configure it, and insert some secrets to test it.

Expose the Vault service out of the Kubernetes cluster so that it can be configured from your local machine. Open a new terminal window and run the command to forward the traffic from `localhost:8200` into the Vault instance running inside the Kubernetes cluster:

```
kubectl port-forward svc/vault 8200:8200
```

Get back to the terminal window where you run the commands to get the token and the certificate authority, and run the following commands to insert a secret:

```
export VAULT_TOKEN=root ❶
export VAULT_ADDR='http://localhost:8200'

cat <<EOF | vault policy write vault-service-policy - ❷
path "secret/data/myapps/vault-service/*" {
  capabilities = ["read"]
}
EOF

vault kv put secret/myapps/vault-service/config foo=secretbar ❸
```

❶ Configure Vault connection parameters

❷ Creates a policy called `vault-service-policy` to `myapps/vault-service/*` secrets

❸ Sets a new secret

The last step is enabling the Kubernetes `auth` method and configuring it to validate the token using the Kubernetes API.

Execute the following commands:

```
vault auth enable kubernetes ❶

vault write auth/kubernetes/config \ ❷
    token_reviewer_jwt=@jwt.txt \ ❸
    kubernetes_host=https://kubernetes.default.svc \ ❹
    kubernetes_ca_cert=@ca.crt ❺

vault write auth/kubernetes/role/example \ ❻
        bound_service_account_names=vault \ ❼
        bound_service_account_namespaces=default \ ❽
        policies=vault-service-policy ❾
```

❶ Enables Kubernetes auth method

❷ Configures the auth method

❸ Sets the token file retrieved in the previous step

❹ Sets the Kubernetes API host

❺ Sets the CA file retrieved in the previous step

❻ Creates a new role (example) to authenticate from the application

❼ Sets the service account name that in our deployment is vault

❽ Sets the namespace where services are running

❾ Binds the user authenticating with this method to the created policy

Let's develop a Quarkus service that authenticates using the Vault Kubernetes auth method and get the secret named foo.

Add the Vault and Kubernetes extensions:

```
./mvnw quarkus:add-extension -Dextensions="quarkus-vault, quarkus-kubernetes"

@ConfigProperty(name = "foo")
String foo;

@GET
@Produces(MediaType.TEXT_PLAIN)
public String hello() {
    return foo;
}
```

Configure the application to use the Kubernetes Vault `auth` method and the Kubernetes extension to generate the correct deployment file:

```
quarkus.vault.url=http://vault:8200 ❶
quarkus.vault.kv-secret-engine-version=2
quarkus.vault.secret-config-kv-path=myapps/vault-service/config

quarkus.vault.authentication.kubernetes.role=example ❷
kubernetes.service-account=vault ❸

kubernetes.group=quarkus ❹
kubernetes.name=greeting-app
kubernetes.version=latest
```

❶ Configures Vault location and secrets

❷ Sets the `example` role to be used by the user (created in the previous step)

❸ Sets the `serviceaccount` name to set in the generated deployment file

❹ Sets the group name of Docker image

Notice that the `quarkus.vault.authentication.kubernetes.jwt-token-path` property is not set. The reason is that the default value (`/var/run/secrets/kuber netes.io/serviceaccount/token`) works perfectly with the defaults. If the secret was mounted on a different path, then this property should be set to the new location.

To deploy the application, open a new terminal window, package the application, create the Docker container, and apply the generated Kubernetes resources:

```
./mvnw clean package -DskipTests

docker build -f src/main/docker/Dockerfile.jvm \
  -t quarkus/greeting-started-vault-kubernetes-auth:1.0-SNAPSHOT .
kubectl apply -f target/kubernetes/kubernetes.yml

kubectl patch svc greeting-app --type='json' \
  -p '[{"op":"replace","path":"/spec/type","value":"NodePort"}]'
curl $(minikube service greeting-app --url)/hello
```

When the Pod is deployed, the application is authenticated with Vault, and Vault validates that the token is valid using the Kubernetes API. The application is then authenticated and can get the secrets from the configured path.

The big difference between this example and the previous ones is that in this case no secret like the Vault password is set, meaning that the secrets can be accessed securely but without having to add any new secret.

Discussion

Our intention isn't to show how to deploy Vault in Kubernetes for production purposes. For this reason, a deployment file is provided to deploy a Vault service with the minimal requirements to run this example.

This deployment file is located at *src/main/kubernetes/vault-dev-deployment.yaml* and provides the following elements:

- Vault with `dev` mode and root token set to `root`.
- Exposes Vault at port 8200.
- `ServiceAccount` with the name set to `vault`.
- `ClusterRoleBinding` and `ClusterRole` bound to `vault`.
- All resources applied to the `default` namespace.

Deploy the Vault service by running the following command:

```
kubectl apply -f src/main/kubernetes/vault-dev-deployment.yaml

kubectl get pods ❶
NAME       READY    STATUS     RESTARTS   AGE
vault-0    1/1      Running    0          44s

kubectl get secrets
NAME                   TYPE                                    DATA   AGE
default-token-zdw8r    kubernetes.io/service-account-token    3      2d
greeting-security      Opaque                                  1      3h9m
vault-token-mm5qx      kubernetes.io/service-account-token    3      8s ❷
```

❶ Pod is named `vault-0`

❷ A `vault-token` is set as a secret

To configure Vault, you need to install the Vault CLI locally on your computer. The Vault CLI is a single file that can be downloaded from Vault (*https://oreil.ly/fTB0x*) and set in your `PATH` variable.

Assuming you've got the Vault client installed locally and available in your PATH variable, you can configure Vault.

See Also

To learn more about Vault Kubernetes auth method, visit the following websites:

- Vault: Kubernetes Auth Method (*https://oreil.ly/AV3D_*)
- Vault Agent with Kubernetes (*https://oreil.ly/WGbUx*)

CHAPTER 13

Quarkus REST Clients

In Chapter 3, you learned about developing RESTful services, but in this chapter, you'll learn about communication between RESTful web services.

Using any service-based architecture inevitably means that you need to communicate with external services. These services might be internal services (you control the life cycle of the service and they are usually deployed in the same cluster) or external services (third-party services).

If these services are implemented as RESTful web services, then you need a client to interact with these services. Quarkus offers two ways to do that: JAX-RS Web Client, which is the standard Java EE way of communicating with RESTful service; and MicroProfile REST Client, which is the new way of communicating with RESTful services.

This chapter will include recipes for the following:

- Communicate to other RESTful services using the JAX-RS client
- Communicate to other RESTful services using the MicroProfile Rest Client
- Secure the communication between RESTful services

13.1 Using the JAX-RS Web Client

Problem

You want to communicate with another RESTful web service.

Solution

Use JAX-RS web client to communicate with other RESTful web services.

Let's look at how to communicate with other RESTful services using the JAX-RS spec.

The external service we are going to connect with, the World Clock API (*https://oreil.ly/wl2IE*), returns the current date/time by time zone. You'll need to get the current date/time exposed by the API (*https://oreil.ly/7M0tf*).

You need to add extensions for using a REST client and the JAX-B/Jackson for marshalling/unmarshalling JSON and Java objects:

```
./mvnw quarkus:add-extension -Dextensions="resteasy-jsonb, rest-client"
```

Or, if you are creating from empty directory, run the following:

```
mvn io.quarkus:quarkus-maven-plugin:1.4.1.Final:create \
    -DprojectGroupId=org.acme.quickstart \
    -DprojectArtifactId=clock-app \
    -DclassName="org.acme.quickstart.WorldClockResource" \
    -Dextensions="resteasy-jsonb, rest-client"
    -Dpath="/now"
```

You can start using the JAX-RS REST Client for communicating with an external Rest API. Let's see what the interaction with the world clock service looks like.

Open `org.acme.quickstart.WorldClockResource.java` and add the following code:

```
package org.acme.quickstart;

import javax.ws.rs.GET;
import javax.ws.rs.Path;
import javax.ws.rs.PathParam;
import javax.ws.rs.Produces;
import javax.ws.rs.client.Client;
import javax.ws.rs.client.ClientBuilder;
import javax.ws.rs.core.MediaType;
import javax.ws.rs.core.Response;

import org.eclipse.microprofile.config.inject.ConfigProperty;
import org.eclipse.microprofile.rest.client.inject.RestClient;

@Path("/now")
public class WorldClockResource {

  @ConfigProperty(name = "clock.host",
  defaultValue = "http://worldclockapi.com")
    String clockHost; ❶

  private Client client = ClientBuilder.newClient(); ❷

  @GET
```

```
@Path("{timezone}")
@Produces(MediaType.APPLICATION_JSON)
public WorldClock getCurrentTime(@PathParam("timezone") String timezone) {
  WorldClock worldClock = client.target(clockHost) ❸
    .path("api/json/{timezone}/now") ❹
    .resolveTemplate("timezone", timezone) ❺
    .request(MediaType.APPLICATION_JSON)
    .get(WorldClock.class); ❻ ❼

  return worldClock;
  }
}
```

❶ Makes service host configurable

❷ Creates a new REST Client

❸ Sets the host

❹ Sets the path to the service

❺ Resolves the timezone placeholder to the one provided

❻ Executes a GET HTTP method

❼ Transforms the JSON output to the provided POJO

Try it by opening a new terminal window, starting the Quarkus application, and sending a request to the GET method:

```
./mvnw clean compile quarkus:dev
```

```
curl localhost:8080/now/cet
{"currentDateTime":"2019-11-13T13:29+01:00","dayOfTheWeek":"Wednesday"}%
```

Discussion

In similar way, you can make requests to other HTTP methods. For example, to do a POST request, you call the post method:

```
target(host)
    .request(MediaType.APPLICATION_JSON)
    .post(entity);
```

You can also use the javax.ws.rs.core.Response to get all the response details instead of just the body:

```
@GET
@Path("{timezone}/raw")
@Produces(MediaType.APPLICATION_JSON)
```

```
    public Response getCurrentTimeResponse(@PathParam("timezone")
        String timezone) {
      javax.ws.rs.core.Response responseWorldClock = client.target(clockHost)
        .path("api/json/{timezone}/now")
        .resolveTemplate("timezone", timezone)
        .request(MediaType.APPLICATION_JSON)
        .get(Response.class);

      System.out.println(responseWorldClock.getStatus());
      System.out.println(responseWorldClock.getStringHeaders());
      // ... more methods

      return responseWorldClock;
    }
```

See Also

You can further explore the JAX-RS REST Client at the following pages on Oracle's website:

- Accessing REST Resources with the JAX-RS Client API (*https://oreil.ly/7neQm*)
- Using the Client API in the JAX-RS Example Applications (*https://oreil.ly/QA8lA*)

13.2 Using the MicroProfile REST Client

Problem

You want to communicate with another RESTful web service without going into low-level details.

Solution

Use MicroProfile REST Client to communicate with other RESTful web services.

So far, you've seen how to use the JAX-RS Web Client to communicate with other REST APIs, but it is not type-safe, and you need to deal with low-level parameters instead of focusing on message communication.

The MicroProfile REST Client provides a type-safe approach to invoke RESTful services over HTTP using as much of the JAX-RS 2.0 spec as possible. The REST client is defined as a Java interface, making it type-safe and providing the network configuration using JAX-RS annotations.

We will use the same World Clock API that was used in the previous section here, too. Remember to get the current date/time (*https://oreil.ly/7M0tf*).

Create the org.acme.quickstart.WorldClockService interface that is responsible for interacting with the external service:

```
package org.acme.quickstart;

import javax.enterprise.context.ApplicationScoped;
import javax.ws.rs.GET;
import javax.ws.rs.Path;
import javax.ws.rs.PathParam;
import javax.ws.rs.Produces;
import javax.ws.rs.core.MediaType;

import org.eclipse.microprofile.rest.client.inject.RegisterRestClient;

@Path("/api")  ❶
@ApplicationScoped
@RegisterRestClient  ❷
public interface WorldClockService {

    @GET  ❸
    @Path("/json/{timezone}/now")  ❹
    @Produces(MediaType.APPLICATION_JSON)  ❺
    WorldClock getNow(@PathParam("timezone") String timezone);  ❻

}
```

❶ The global path

❷ Sets the interface as REST client

❸ The request uses the GET HTTP method

❹ The subpath with a path parameter

❺ The media type requested

❻ The path parameter is resolved with the passed argument

Open org.acme.quickstart.WorldClockResource.java and add the following code:

```
@RestClient  ❶
WorldClockService worldClockService;

@GET
@Path("{timezone}/mp")
@Produces(MediaType.APPLICATION_JSON)
public WorldClock getCurrentTimeMp(@PathParam("timezone") String timezone) {
    return worldClockService.getNow(timezone);  ❷
}
```

❶ Injects the REST client

❷ Calls the external service

You still need to set the host of the external service. MicroProfile REST Client has a configuration property to set it.

Open *application.properties*:

```
org.acme.quickstart.WorldClockService/mp-rest/url=http://worldclockapi.com
```

The attribute name uses the following format: *fully_qualified_name_rest_client/* mp-rest/url, and the value is the hostname (or the root of the URL):

```
./mvnw clean compile quarkus:dev
```

```
curl localhost:8080/now/cet/mp
{"currentDateTime":"2019-11-13T16:46+01:00","dayOfTheWeek":"Wednesday"}%
```

Discussion

You can also convert a response with a status code equal to or greater than 400 into an exception by implementing the org.eclipse.microprofile.rest.cli ent.ex.ResponseExceptionMapper interface. If multiple mappers are registered, then you need to set a priority with javax.annotation.Priority annotation.

Create the following ResponseExecptionMapper class to have it registered, and have the application throw IOExecptions for status codes in the 400s:

```
package org.acme.quickstart;

import java.io.IOException;
import javax.ws.rs.core.MultivaluedMap;
import javax.ws.rs.core.Response;
import org.eclipse.microprofile.rest.client.ext.ResponseExceptionMapper;

public class CustomResponseExceptionMapper
            implements ResponseExceptionMapper<IOException> { ❶

    @Override
    public IOException toThrowable(Response response) { ❷
        return new IOException();
    }

    @Override
    public boolean handles(int status,
                        MultivaluedMap<String, Object> headers) { ❸
        return status >= 400 && status < 500;
    }

}
```

❶ Implements the mapper interface

❷ Does the conversion to an exception

❸ Default is to transform any response with status code ≥ 400, but you can override the method to provide a smaller range

ResponseExceptionMapper is an extension point specifically from the MicroProfile REST Client specification, but you can also use the extension model provided by the JAX-RS specification:

ClientRequestFilter
: The filter invoked when the request is made to the external service.

ClientResponseFilter
: The filter invoked when the response is received from the external service.

MessageBodyReader
: Reads the entity after invocation.

MessageBodyWriter
: Writes a request body in the operations that support bodies.

ParamConverter
: Converts a parameter in the resource to a format to be used in a request or response.

ReadInterceptor
: The listener fired when the response is received from the external service.

WriteInterceptor
: The listener fired when the request is sent on the external service.

You can also mock the WorldClockService interface by using the @InjectMock together with @RestClient:

```
@InjectMock
@RestClient
WorldClockService worldClockService;
```

See Also

The MicroProfile Rest Client specification can be found at the following website:

- Eclipse REST Client for MicroProfile (*https://oreil.ly/7D0Zv*)

13.3 Implementing a CRUD Client

Problem

You want to communicate with another RESTful web service with CRUD operations exposed.

Solution

Use MicroProfile REST Client and JAX-RS annotations to implement a CRUD client.

So far, you've seen how to use MicroProfile REST Client to get information from external services. When the service is an internal service, more often than not you need to implement more operations like insert, delete, or update.

To implement these operations, you can use JAX-RS annotations on a MicroProfile REST Client. Let's see an example:

```
package org.acme.quickstart;

import java.util.List;

import javax.ws.rs.BeanParam;
import javax.ws.rs.Consumes;
import javax.ws.rs.CookieParam;
import javax.ws.rs.DELETE;
import javax.ws.rs.GET;
import javax.ws.rs.HEAD;
import javax.ws.rs.HeaderParam;
import javax.ws.rs.POST;
import javax.ws.rs.PUT;
import javax.ws.rs.Path;
import javax.ws.rs.PathParam;
import javax.ws.rs.Produces;
import javax.ws.rs.core.Response;

import org.eclipse.microprofile.rest.client.inject.RegisterRestClient;

@Path("/developer")
@RegisterRestClient
@Consumes("application/json")  ❶
@Produces("application/json")
public interface DeveloperService {

    @HEAD  ❷
    Response head();

    @GET
    List<Developer> getDevelopers();
```

```
@POST ❸
Response createDeveloper(
    @HeaderParam("Authorization") String authorization, ❹
    Developer developer); ❺

@DELETE ❻
@Path("/{userId}")
Response deleteUser(@CookieParam("AuthToken") String authorization, ❼
    @PathParam("developerId") Long developerId);
}
```

❶ Requests and responses are in JSON format

❷ Uses the HEAD HTTP method

❸ Uses the POST HTTP method

❹ Sets Authorization header

❺ Developer content is sent as the body

❻ Uses the DELETE HTTP method

❼ Sets AuthToken cookie

Discussion

Notice how the JAX-RS annotations are used to configure how the requests are sent to the other services. You never need to do anything programmatically.

This approach is developer-friendly and helps to reduce the boilerplate code that you might end up using with the JAX-RS Web Client.

Of course, it also has some drawbacks. For example, methods can contain a huge number of parameters because of the number of path parameters, headers to set, and cookies. To fix this, pass a POJO with all of the required fields (instead of setting them in the method).

Let's create a Java class for the PUT requirements (i.e., an authorization header and a path parameter):

```
package org.acme.quickstart;

import javax.ws.rs.HeaderParam;
import javax.ws.rs.PathParam;

public class PutDeveloper {
```

```
@HeaderParam("Authorization")  ❶
private String authorization;

@PathParam("developerId")  ❷
private String developerId;

public String getAuthorization() {
    return authorization;
}

public void setAuthorization(String authorization) {
    this.authorization = authorization;
}

public String getDeveloperId() {
    return developerId;
}

public void setDeveloperId(String developerId) {
    this.developerId = developerId;
}

}
```

❶ Sets the Authorization header

❷ Sets the path parameter to resolve

The interface method using the previous class is the following:

```
@PUT
@Path("/{developerId}")
Response updateUser(@BeanParam PutDeveloper putDeveloper,  ❶
    Developer developer);
```

❶ The BeanParam is used to indicate that this class is a *parameter aggregator*

13.4 Manipulating Headers

Problem

You want to manipulate and propagate headers from the incoming request to the outgoing service (service-to-service authentication).

Solution

Use the MicroProfile REST Client feature that manipulates headers.

When you need to communicate to other RESTful web services, you might want to pass through some headers from the incoming request to the outgoing/downstream service. One of these typical cases is the Authorization header to do service-to-service authentication. Authentication and authorization in services architecture are usually solved by propagating a token, often a JWT token, through all services that compose the application. You can see the idea in Figure 13-1.

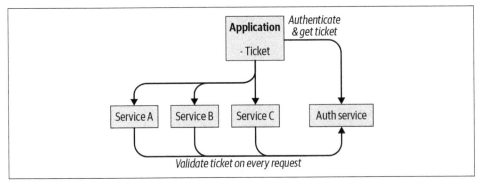

Figure 13-1. Service-to-service authentication

The MicroProfile REST Client simplifies all these operations by allowing you to propagate and manipulate headers either at a static level by using annotations or at a programmatic level by implementing ClientHeadersFactory interface.

To set a header on a method or on all the methods defined in an interface, you can use the org.eclipse.microprofile.rest.client.annotation.ClientHeaderParam annotation at method level or class level to set a header with a static value:

```
@Path("/somePath")
@ClientHeaderParam(name="user-agent", value="curl/7.54.0") ❶
Response get();
```

❶ Sets user-agent to the request

The value can be a method invocation where the return value would be the header's value:

```
@ClientHeaderParam(name="user-agent", value="{determineHeaderValue}") ❶
Response otherGet();

default String determineHeaderValue(String headerName) { ❷
    return "Hi-" + headerName;
}
```

❶ Sets the method to invoke

❷ The header name is the first argument of the method

These approaches offer a basic manipulation of headers but don't help in propagating headers from the incoming request to the outgoing service. It is also possible to add or propagate headers by implementing the ClientHeadersFactory interface and registering it with the RegisterClientHeaders annotation.

Suppose that your service receives the authentication token from your upstream service in a header named x-auth, and your downstream service requires that this value is set to the Authorization header. Let's implement this rename of headers in a MicroProfile REST Client:

```
package org.acme.quickstart;

import java.util.List;

import javax.ws.rs.core.MultivaluedHashMap;
import javax.ws.rs.core.MultivaluedMap;

import org.eclipse.microprofile.rest.client.ext.ClientHeadersFactory;

public class CustomClientHeadersFactory implements ClientHeadersFactory {

  @Override
  public MultivaluedMap<String, String> update(
      MultivaluedMap<String, String> incomingHeaders,     ❶
      MultivaluedMap<String, String> clientOutgoingHeaders) {     ❷

    final MultivaluedMap<String, String> headers =
      new MultivaluedHashMap<String, String>(incomingHeaders);
    headers.putAll(clientOutgoingHeaders);     ❸

    final List<String> auth = headers.get("x-auth");     ❹
    headers.put("Authorization", auth);
    headers.remove("x-auth");

    return headers;
  }
}
```

❶ The headers from the inbound JAX-RS request

❷ The headers parameters specified on the client interface

❸ Adds all headers

❹ Renames the header value

Finally, you need to register this factory in the client by using the RegisterClient Headers annotation:

```
@RegisterClientHeaders(CustomClientHeadersFactory.class) ❶
public interface ConfigureHeaderServices {
```

❶ Registers the headers factory for this client

Discussion

If you want to propagate the headers only as is, without any modification, you can do it by just annotating the REST client with `@RegisterClientHeaders` without specifying any factory. Then the default headers factory is used.

This default factory will propagate specified headers from the inbound JAX-RS request to the outbound request. To configure which headers are propagated, you need to set them as comma-separated values under the `org.eclipse.micropro file.rest.client.propagateHeaders` property:

```
org.eclipse.microprofile.rest.client.propagateHeaders=Authorization,\
                                                    MyCustomHeader
```

13.5 Using REST Client for Multipart Messages

Problem

You want to send multipart content to interact with the REST APIs requiring it.

Solution

Use RESTEasy multipart support to deal with multipart messages.

Sometimes the service you need to connect with requires that you send multiple content bodies embedded into one message, usually using the `multipart/form-data` MIME-type. The easiest way to work with multipart mime-types is using the REST-Easy multipart provider, which integrates with the MicroProfile REST client.

 This feature is specific of RESTEasy/Quarkus and is not under MicroProfile REST client spec.

Before you start developing, you need to add the `resteasy-multipart-provider` dependency in your build tool:

```
<dependency>
    <groupId>org.jboss.resteasy</groupId>
    <artifactId>resteasy-multipart-provider</artifactId>
</dependency>
```

Then you need to create the model object that defines the payload of the message. Let's define a multipart message with two parts, one as a binary content and another one as a string:

```
package org.acme.quickstart;

import java.io.InputStream;

import javax.ws.rs.FormParam;
import javax.ws.rs.core.MediaType;

import org.jboss.resteasy.annotations.providers.multipart.PartType;

public class MultipartDeveloperModel {

    @FormParam("avatar") ❶
    @PartType(MediaType.APPLICATION_OCTET_STREAM) ❷
    public InputStream file;

    @FormParam("name")
    @PartType(MediaType.TEXT_PLAIN)
    public String developerName;

}
```

❶ JAX-RS annotation to define the form parameter contained inside the request

❷ RESTEasy annotation to define the content type of the part

Finally, you need to declare a new method using the `MultipartDeveloperModel` object as a parameter annotated with `org.jboss.resteasy.annotations.provid ers.multipart.MultipartForm`:

```
@POST
@Consumes(MediaType.MULTIPART_FORM_DATA) ❶
@Produces(MediaType.TEXT_PLAIN)
String sendMultipartData(@MultipartForm ❷
                         MultipartDeveloperModel data); ❸
```

❶ Sets the output mime-type as multipart

❷ Defines the parameter as a `multipart/form-type` mime-type

❸ Multipart data

13.6 Using REST Client to Configure SSL

Problem

You want to configure REST client to use SSL.

Solution

The MicroProfile REST Client provides a way to configure SSL for communication with other services.

By default, the MicroProfile REST Client uses the JVM trust store to verify the certificates when HTTPS connections are used. But sometimes, especially in cases of internal services, the certificates cannot be validated using the JVM trust store and you need to provide your custom trust store.

The MicroProfile REST Client accepts setting custom trust stores by using the trust Store configuration property:

```
org.acme.quickstart.FruityViceService/mp-rest/trustStore= \
    classpath:/custom-truststore.jks ❶
org.acme.quickstart.FruityViceService/mp-rest/trustStorePassword=acme ❷
org.acme.quickstart.FruityViceService/mp-rest/trustStoreType=JKS ❸
```

❶ trustStore sets the trust store location; this can be a class path resource (class path:) or a file (file:)

❷ trustStorePassword sets the password for the trust store

❸ trustStoreType sets the type of trust store

Keystores are also provided, which are really useful in two-way SSL connections.

MicroProfile REST Client accepts setting custom key stores by using the keyStore configuration property.

```
org.acme.quickstart.FruityViceService/mp-rest/keyStore= \
    classpath:/custom-keystore.jks ❶
org.acme.quickstart.FruityViceService/mp-rest/keyStorePassword=acme ❷
org.acme.quickstart.FruityViceService/mp-rest/keyStoreType=JKS ❸
```

❶ keyStore sets the key store location; this can be a class path resource (class path:) or a file (file:)

❷ keyStorePassword sets the password for the trust store

❸ keyStoreType sets the type of key store

Finally, you can implement `javax.net.ssl.HostnameVerifier` to override the behavior when the URL's hostname and the server's identification hostname mismatch. Then the implementation of this interface can determine whether this connection should be allowed.

The following is an example of hostname verifier:

```
package org.acme.quickstart;

import javax.net.ssl.HostnameVerifier;
import javax.net.ssl.SSLSession;

public class FruityHostnameVerifier implements HostnameVerifier {

    @Override
    public boolean verify(String hostname, SSLSession session) {
        if ("fruityvice.com".equals(hostname)) {
            return true;
        }

        return false;
    }

}
```

You need to enable it in the configuration file:

```
org.acme.quickstart.FruityViceService/mp-rest/hostnameVerifier=\
org.acme.quickstart.FruityHostnameVerifier
```

Discussion

Most of the time, when you are running tests locally, you might not have installed all the trust stores or key stores required to connect to an external service. In these cases, you might run tests against the HTTP version of the service. This is not always possible, however, and in some third-party services, only the HTTPS protocol is enabled.

One possible solution to this problem is to configure the MicroProfile REST Client to trust any certificate. To do this, you need to configure the client and provide a custom trust manager:

```
package org.acme.quickstart;

import java.net.Socket;
import java.net.URI;
import java.security.KeyManagementException;
import java.security.NoSuchAlgorithmException;
import java.security.cert.CertificateException;
import java.security.cert.X509Certificate;

import javax.enterprise.context.ApplicationScoped;
```

```
import javax.net.ssl.HttpsURLConnection;
import javax.net.ssl.SSLContext;
import javax.net.ssl.SSLEngine;
import javax.net.ssl.TrustManager;
import javax.net.ssl.X509ExtendedTrustManager;

import org.apache.http.conn.ssl.NoopHostnameVerifier;
import org.eclipse.microprofile.rest.client.RestClientBuilder;

@ApplicationScoped ❶
public class TrustAllFruityViceService {

  public FruityVice getFruitByName(String name) {
    FruityViceService fruityViceService = RestClientBuilder.newBuilder()
      .baseUri(URI.create("https://www.fruityvice.com/"))
      .hostnameVerifier(NoopHostnameVerifier.INSTANCE) ❷
      .sslContext(trustEverything()) ❸
      .build(FruityViceService.class);

    return fruityViceService.getFruitByName(name);
  }

  private static SSLContext trustEverything() { ❹

    try {
      SSLContext sc = SSLContext.getInstance("SSL");
      sc.init(null, trustAllCerts(), new java.security.SecureRandom());
      HttpsURLConnection.setDefaultSSLSocketFactory(sc.getSocketFactory());
      return sc;
    } catch (KeyManagementException | NoSuchAlgorithmException e) {
      throw new IllegalStateException(e);
    }
  }

  private static TrustManager[] trustAllCerts() {
    return  new TrustManager[]{
      new X509ExtendedTrustManager(){

        @Override
        public X509Certificate[] getAcceptedIssuers() {
          return null;
        }

        @Override
        public void checkServerTrusted(X509Certificate[] chain,
                                       String authType)
          throws CertificateException {
        }

        @Override
        public void checkClientTrusted(X509Certificate[] chain,
                                       String authType)
```

```
            throws CertificateException {
        }

        @Override
        public void checkServerTrusted(X509Certificate[] chain,
                                       String authType,
                                       SSLEngine sslEngine)
            throws CertificateException {
        }

        @Override
        public void checkServerTrusted(X509Certificate[] chain,
                                       String authType,
                                       Socket socket)
            throws CertificateException {
        }

        @Override
        public void checkClientTrusted(X509Certificate[] chain,
                                       String authType,
                                       SSLEngine sslEngine)
            throws CertificateException {
        }

        @Override
        public void checkClientTrusted(X509Certificate[] chain,
                                       String authType,
                                       Socket socket)
            throws CertificateException {
        }
      }
    };
  }
}
```

❶ Creates a CDI bean; you need to use @Inject instead of @RestClient to make use of it

❷ Disable host verification

❸ Trust all certificates without doing any verification

❹ Customize SSLContext with an empty trust manager, effectively negating all SSL checks

Then if you inject this instance instead of the production one, every HTTPS request is valid independently of the certificate used by the external service.

CHAPTER 14

Developing Quarkus Applications Using Spring APIs

Up to this point, you've seen that every example was developed using CDI annotations such as @Inject or @Produces, JAX-RS annotations, or Java EE Security annotations. But Quarkus also offers a compatibility layer for some of the most-used Spring libraries, so you can use all your knowledge about Spring Framework to develop Quarkus applications.

This chapter will include recipes for the following:

- Spring Dependency Injection
- Spring REST Web
- Spring Data JPA
- Spring Security
- Spring Boot Configuration

14.1 Using Spring Dependency Injection

Problem

You want to use the Spring Dependency Injection (DI) API to develop with Quarkus.

Solution

Quarkus offers an API compatibility layer (using an extension) to use Spring DI annotations.

Although we encourage you to use CDI annotations, you are free to use the Spring annotations as well because the final application will behave in exactly the same way.

A greeting service is developed, as it was at the beginning of the book. If you are familiar with the Spring Framework, a lot of things will look familiar to you.

To add the Spring DI extension, run the following command:

```
./mvnw quarkus:add-extension -Dextensions="spring-di"
```

Or, you can create a project with the Spring DI extension by running the following:

```
mvn io.quarkus:quarkus-maven-plugin:1.4.1.Final:create \
    -DprojectGroupId=org.acme.quickstart \
    -DprojectArtifactId=spring-di-quickstart \
    -DclassName="org.acme.quickstart.GreeterResource" \
    -Dpath="/greeting" \
    -Dextensions="spring-di"
```

Open the *application.properties* file and add a new property:

```
greetings.message=Hello World
```

To inject this configuration value to any class, use the `@org.springframe work.beans.factory.annotation.Value` Spring annotation:

```
package org.acme.quickstart;

import java.util.function.Function;

import org.springframework.context.annotation.Bean;
import org.springframework.context.annotation.Configuration;

@Configuration ❶
public class AppConfiguration {

    @Bean(name = "suffix") ❷
    public Function<String, String> exclamation() {
        return new Function<String, String>() { ❸
            @Override
            public String apply(String t) {
                return t + "!!";
            }
        };
    }
}
```

❶ Uses the `@Configuration` annotation to define the class as a configuration object

❷ Creates a bean that adds the suffix to the given message

❸ Implements the service

It is important to notice that in both cases the Spring annotations are used.

The bean can be injected using the @org.springframework.beans.factory.annota
tion.Autowired and @org.springframework.beans.factory.annotation.Quali
fier annotations:

```
package org.acme.quickstart;

import org.springframework.stereotype.Service;

@Service ❶
public class PrefixService {

    public String appendPrefix(String message) {
        return "- " + message;
    }

}
```

❶ Sets this class as a service

And it can be injected using the constructor instead of @Autowired:

```
private PrefixService prefixService;

public GreetingResource(PrefixService prefixService) { ❶
    this.prefixService = prefixService;
}
```

❶ Injects the instance using the constructor; notice that @Autowired is not required

Finally, all these operations can be combined to produce the following output:

```
@GET
@Produces(MediaType.TEXT_PLAIN)
public String hello() {
    String prefixed = prefixService.appendPrefix(message);
    return this.suffixComponent.apply(prefixed);
}
```

If you run the project, you'll be able to see that all the objects are created and injected correctly, even though the Spring DI annotations are used:

```
./mvnw compile quarkus:dev

curl http://localhost:8080/greeting

- Hello World!!
```

Discussion

It is important to note that Quarkus does not start a Spring Application Context instance. That's because its integration is only at the API level (annotations, return types, etc.), which means the following:

- Using any other Spring library will not have any effect. You'll see later that Quarkus offers integrations to other Spring libraries.

- `org.springframework.beans.factory.config.BeanPostProcessor` will not be executed.

Table 14-1 shows the equivalent annotations between MicroProfile/CDI and Spring.

Table 14-1. Equivalent annotations in MicroProfile/CDI and Spring

Spring	CDI / MicroProfile
@Autowired	@Injecct
@Qualifier	@Named
@Value	@ConfigProperty. The expression language of typical use cases is supported.
@Component	@Singleton
@Service	@Singleton
@Repository	@Singleton
@Configuration	@ApplicationScoped
@Bean	@Produces

14.2 Using Spring Web

Problem

You want to use the Spring Web API to develop with Quarkus.

Solution

Quarkus offers an API compatibility layer (using an extension) to use Spring Web annotations/classes.

To add the Spring Web extension, run the following command:

```
./mvnw quarkus:add-extension -Dextensions="spring-web"
```

Create a new resource using only Spring Web annotations:

```
package org.acme.quickstart;

import org.springframework.http.ResponseEntity;
import org.springframework.web.bind.annotation.GetMapping;
```

```
import org.springframework.web.bind.annotation.PathVariable;
import org.springframework.web.bind.annotation.RequestMapping;
import org.springframework.web.bind.annotation.RestController;

@RestController ❶
@RequestMapping("/greeting") ❷
public class SpringController {

  @GetMapping ❸
  public ResponseEntity<String> getMessage() { ❹
    return ResponseEntity.ok("Hello");
  }

  @GetMapping("/{name}")
  public String hello(@PathVariable(name = "name") String name) { ❺
    return "hello " + name;
  }
}
```

❶ REST resource definition

❷ Maps the root path

❸ Sets GET HTTP method

❹ Returns Spring's `ResponseEntity`

❺ Gets path information

Only Spring annotations and classes are used to implement the resource. There are no traces of the JAX-RS API.

Discussion

You've seen how to use Spring Dependency Injection annotations in a Quarkus application. Quarkus integrates with Spring Web via an extension.

Although we encourage you to use JAX_RS annotations, you are free to use the Spring Web classes and annotations. Regardless of which is used, the final application will behave the same way.

Quarkus supports only the REST-related features of Spring Web. In summary, all `@RestController` features are supported except the ones related to the generic `@Controller`.

The following Spring Web annotations are supported: `@RestController`, `@RequestMapping`, `@GetMapping`, `@PostMapping`, `@PutMapping`, `@DeleteMapping`, `@PatchMapping`, `@RequestParam`, `@RequestHeader`, `@MatrixVariable`, `@PathVariable`,

@CookieValue, @RequestBody, @ResponseStatus, @ExceptionHandler (only to be used in a @RestControllerAdvice class), and @RestControllerAdvice (only the @ExceptionHandler capability is supported).

The following are return types that are supported out of the box for REST controllers: primitives, String (as a literal, not as an MVC support), POJO, and org.springfra mework.http.ResponseEntity.

The following are method parameters that are supported out of the box, for REST controllers: primitives, String, POJO, javax.servlet.http.HttpServletRequest, and javax.servlet.http.HttpServletResponse.

The following are return types that are supported out of the box for exception handlers: org.springframework.http.ResponseEntity and java.util.Map

The following are method parameters that are supported out of the box for exception handlers: java.lang.Exception or any other subtype, javax.serv let.http.HttpServletRequest, and javax.servlet.http.HttpServletResponse.

> To use the javax.servlet classes you need to register the quarkus-undertow dependency.

Table 14-2 shows the equivalent annotations between JAX-RS and Spring Web.

Table 14-2. Equivalent annotations in JAX-RS and Spring Web

Spring	JAX-RS
@RequestController	
@RequestMapping(path="/api")	@Path("/api")
@RequestMapping(consumes="applica tion/json")	@Consumes("application/json")
@RequestMapping(produces="applica tion/json")	@Produces("application/json")
@RequestParam	@QueryParam
@PathVariable	@PathParam
@RequestBody	
@RestControllerAdvice	
@ResponseStatus	Use javax.ws.rs.core.Response class
@ExceptionHandler	Implements javax.ws.rs.ext.ExceptionMapper interface

14.3 Using Spring Data JPA

Problem

You want to use the Spring Data JPA API to develop the persistent layer in Quarkus.

Solution

Quarkus offers an API compatibility layer (using an extension) to use Spring Data JPA classes.

To add the Spring Web extension, run the following command:

```
./mvnw quarkus:add-extension -Dextensions="spring-data-jpa"
```

The big difference between using Panache or the Spring Data JPA is that your repository class must implement the Spring Data `org.springframe work.data.repository.CrudRepository` class instead of `io.quarkus.hiber nate.orm.panache.PanacheRepository`. But the rest of the parts, like defining the entity or configuring the data source in *application.properties*, are exactly the same.

Create a new class with the name `org.acme.quickstart.DeveloperRepository`:

```
package org.acme.quickstart;

import java.util.List;

import org.springframework.data.repository.CrudRepository;

public interface DeveloperRepository extends CrudRepository<Developer, Long> { ❶
    List<Developer> findByName(String name); ❷
}
```

❶ Defines a Spring Data JPA CRUD repository

❷ Derived query method

Run the project and send some requests to validate that the objects are persisted using the Spring Data interface. To do so, run the following in a terminal:

```
./mvnw compile quarkus:dev

curl -d '{"name":"Ada"}' -H "Content-Type: application/json" \
    -X POST http://localhost:8080/developer -v

< HTTP/1.1 201 Created
< Content-Length: 0
< Location: http://localhost:8080/developer/1
<
* Connection #0 to host localhost left intact
```

Discussion

In Chapter 7, you learned how to develop persistent code with Quarkus, and in particular, using the Panache framework. Quarkus also integrates with Spring Data JPA via an extension.

Although we encourage you to use the Panache framework, you are free to use the Spring Data JPA classes as well because the final application will behave in exactly the same way.

Quarkus supports a subset of Spring Data JPA's features, which are basically the most commonly used features.

The following interfaces are supported to define a repository:

- `org.springframework.data.repository.Repository`
- `org.springframework.data.repository.CrudRepository`
- `org.springframework.data.repository.CrudRepository`
- `org.springframework.data.repository.PagingAndSortingRepository`
- `org.springframework.data.jpa.repository.JpaRepository`

 The methods that update the database are automatically annotated with `@Transactional`. If you are using `@org.springframe work.data.jpa.repository.Query`, then you need to annotate the method with `@org.springframework.data.jpa.repository.Modi fying` to make it transactional.

At the time of writing, the following features are unsupported:

- Methods of the `org.springframework.data.repository.query.QueryByExam pleExecutor`
- QueryDSL support
- Customizing the base repository for all repository interfaces in the codebase
- `java.util.concurrent.Future` or classes extending it as return types of repository methods
- Native and named queries when using `@Query`

These limitations might be fixed in the near future.

14.4 Using Spring Security

Problem

You want to use the Spring Security API to protect resources.

Solution

Quarkus offers an API compatibility layer (using an extension) to use Spring Security classes.

To add the Spring Security extension (and the identity provider), run the following command:

```
./mvnw quarkus:add-extension \
    -Dextensions="quarkus-spring-security, quarkus-spring-web, \
                   quarkus-elytron-security-properties-file"
```

From this point, the code can be protected using the Spring Security annotations (org.springframework.security.access.annotation.Secured and org.springfra mework.security.access.prepost.PreAuthorize) instead of the Java EE ones (@javax.annotation.security.RolesAllowed):

```
package org.acme.quickstart;

import org.springframework.security.access.annotation.Secured;
import org.springframework.security.access.prepost.PreAuthorize;
import org.springframework.web.bind.annotation.GetMapping;
import org.springframework.web.bind.annotation.RequestMapping;
import org.springframework.web.bind.annotation.RestController;

@RestController
@RequestMapping("/hello")
public class GreetingController {
    @GetMapping
    @Secured("admin") ❶
    public String helloAdmin() {
        return "hello from admin";
    }

    @PreAuthorize("hasAnyRole('user')") ❷
    @GetMapping
    @RequestMapping("/any")
    public String helloUsers() {
        return "hello from users";
    }
}
```

❶ @Secured annotation

❷ @PreAuthorize annotation to add expression support

Register valid users and roles in the *application.properties* file because the Elytron file properties extension is registered as identity provider:

```
quarkus.security.users.embedded.enabled=true
quarkus.security.users.embedded.plain-text=true
quarkus.security.users.embedded.users.alexandra=aixa
quarkus.security.users.embedded.roles.alexandra=admin,user
quarkus.security.users.embedded.users.ada=dev
quarkus.security.users.embedded.roles.ada=user
```

Only alexandra can access both endpoints, while ada can access only the user one.

Discussion

In Chapter 11, you learned how to protect RESTful web services using the Java EE security annotations (@RolwsAllowed). Quarkus integrates with Spring Security via an extension, allowing Spring Security annotations to be used as well.

It is important to note that the Spring Security integration happens at the API level and that an identity provider implementation like Elytron file properties is still required.

Quarkus supports a subset of Spring Security @PreAuthorze expression language, which is basically a collection of the most commonly used features:

```
@PreAuthorize("hasRole('admin')")
@PreAuthorize("hasRole(@roles.USER)") ❶

@PreAuthorize("hasAnyRole(@roles.USER, 'view')")

@PreAuthorize("permitAll()")
@PreAuthorize("denyAll()")

@PreAuthorize("isAnonymous()")
@PreAuthorize("isAuthenticated()")
```

❶ Where roles is a bean defined with the @Component annotation and USER is a public field of the class

Conditional expressions are also supported:

```
@PreAuthorize("#person.name == authentication.principal.username")
public void doSomethingElse(Person person){}

@PreAuthorize("@personChecker.check(#person,
                              authentication.principal.username)")
```

```
public void doSomething(Person person){}

@Component
public class PersonChecker {
    public boolean check(Person person, String username) {
        return person.getName().equals(username);
    }
}

@PreAuthorize("hasAnyRole('user', 'admin') AND #user == principal.username")
public void allowedForUser(String user) {}
```

14.5 Using Spring Boot Properties

Problem

You want to use Spring Boot to map configuration properties into Java objects.

Solution

Quarkus offers an API compatibility layer (using an extension) to use Spring Boot configuration properties.

Quarkus is integrated with Spring Boot in the form of an extension, so the `@org.springframework.boot.context.properties.ConfigurationProperties` annotation can be used to map configuration properties into a Java object.

To add the Spring Boot extension (and the other Spring integrations), run the following command:

```
./mvnw quarkus:add-extension \
    -Dextensions="quarkus-spring-di, quarkus-spring-web, \
                 quarkus-spring-boot-properties,
                 quarkus-hibernate-validator"
```

Add some configuration properties to be bound into a Java object:

```
greeting.message=Hello World
greeting.configuration.uppercase=true
```

The next step is to create the POJOs with getters/setters to bind the configuration properties from file to Java object. It is important to note that the property uppercase is defined in a subcategory named configuration, and this affects how the POJO classes are created because each subcategory must be added into its own class:

```
package org.acme.quickstart;

import javax.validation.constraints.Size;

import org.springframework.boot.context.properties.ConfigurationProperties;
```

```
@ConfigurationProperties(prefix = "greeting") ❶
public class GreetingConfiguration {

    @Size(min = 2) ❷
    private String message;
    private Configuration configuration; ❸

    public void setMessage(String message) {
        this.message = message;
    }

    public String getMessage() {
        return message;
    }

    public void setConfiguration(Configuration configuration) {
        this.configuration = configuration;
    }

    public Configuration getConfiguration() {
        return configuration;
    }

}
```

❶ Annotate the parent class with `ConfigurationProperties`, and set the prefix of the configuration properties

❷ Bean Validation annotations are supported

❸ Subcategory `configuration` is mapped in a field with the same name

Subcategory POJO is just a Java class with the `uppercase` attribute.

```
package org.acme.quickstart;

public class Configuration {

    private boolean uppercase;

    public boolean isUppercase() {
        return uppercase;
    }

    public void setUppercase(boolean uppercase) {
        this.uppercase = uppercase;
    }
}
```

The configuration object is injected in any class, as is any other bean using `@Inject` or `@Autowired`:

```
@Autowired ❶
GreetingConfiguration greetingConfiguration;

@GetMapping
public String hello() {
    if (greetingConfiguration.getConfiguration().isUppercase()) { ❷
        return greetingConfiguration.getMessage().toUpperCase();
    }
    return greetingConfiguration.getMessage();
}
```

❶ Injects configuration object with data bound to it

❷ Configuration properties are populated automatically to the Java object

CHAPTER 15

Working with a Reactive Programming Model

We are all familiar with the client-server architecture that has dominated enterprise software development for decades. However, we have recently had a shift in architecture styles. In addition to the standard client-server approach, we have message-driven applications, microservices, reactive applications, and even serverless! All of these types of applications are possible to create using Quarkus. In the follow recipes, you'll learn about reactive programming models, message buses, and streaming.

Quarkus (and this book!) makes use of SmallRye Mutiny for its reactive library. You can read more about Mutiny at SmallRye Mutiny (*https://oreil.ly/nBP7H*). There is also support for RxJava and Reactor, but they are not the preferred choice. To use either of them, you will need to use converters from Mutiny.

15.1 Creating Async HTTP Endpoints

Problem

You want to create an async HTTP endpoint.

Solution

Quarkus has integrations with Java Streams, the Eclipse MicroProfile Reactive spec, and SmallRye Mutiny. These integrations make it easy to support an asynchronous HTTP endpoint. The first thing you will need to do is determine which libraries you wish to use. If you wish to use native Streams or the MicroProfile Reactive specification, you will need to add the `quarkus-smallrye-reactive-streams-operators` extension. If you want to use SmallRye Mutiny, add the `quarkus-resteasy-mutiny` extension to your project.

 Going forward, Mutiny will be the preferred library within Quarkus for all things reactive.

Once the extension is in place, all you need to do with your HTTP endpoints is return a reactive class:

```
@GET
@PATH("/reactive")
@Produces(MediaType.TEXT_PLAIN) ❶
public CompletionStage<String> reactiveHello() { ❷
    return ReactiveStreams.of("h", "e", "l", "l", "o")
        .map(String::toUpperCase)
        .toList()
        .run()
        .thenApply(list -> list.toString());
}
```

❶ Naturally, any valid `MediaType` is valid; for simplicity, we used plain text

❷ `CompletionStage` comes from the `java.util.concurrent` package

For Mutiny, this example becomes the following:

```
@GET
@PATH("/reactive")
@Produces(MediaType.TEXT_PLAIN)
public Multi<String> helloMutiny() {
    return Multi.createFrom().items("h", "e", "l", "l", "o");
}
```

See Also

For more information, visit the following websites:

- SmallRye Mutiny (*https://oreil.ly/nBP7H*)
- SmallRye Reactive Streams Operators (*https://oreil.ly/Ab8eo*)
- Reactive Streams (*https://oreil.ly/pgyMk*)

15.2 Streaming Data Asynchronously

Problem

You want to stream data in an async way.

Solution

Very similar to creating an asynchronous HTTP endpoint, Quarkus allows you to stream events from your application using server-sent events or server-side events (SSE). What you will need to do in this case is to return a `Publisher` and tell JAX-RS that your endpoint produces `MediaType.SERVER_SENT_EVENTS`. Here's an example that streams a `long` every 500 milliseconds:

```
@GET
@Path("/integers")
@Produces(MediaType.SERVER_SENT_EVENTS) ❶
public Publisher<Long> longPublisher() { ❷
    return Multi.createFrom()
            .ticks().every(Duration.ofMillis(500));
}
```

❶ Make sure you tell JAX-RS you are using SSEs

❷ The return type for the method must be a `org.reactivestream.Publisher` from the Reactive Streams library

With Mutiny, a `Multi` is a `Publisher`, making this even easier by simply returning a `Multi`.

See Also

For more information, visit the following websites:

- Wikiwand: Server-Sent Events (*https://oreil.ly/m0cAC*)
- MDN Web Docs: Using server-sent events (*https://oreil.ly/ZIX4X*)

15.3 Using Messaging to Decouple Components

Problem

You want to use messaging to decouple components.

Solution

One of the underlying/bundled frameworks used by Quarkus is Vert.x. Vert.x is a framework for building asynchronous, event-driven, reactive applications, much like Quarkus! Quarkus makes use of the Vert.x Event Bus for sending and receiving events/messages with decoupled classes.

To make use of Vert.x, just like many features with Quarkus, you will need to add the proper extension to your application. The name for the Vert.x extension is vertx.

Handling events/messages

We'll first take a look at listening to or consuming events. The easiest way to consume events in Quarkus is to use the io.quarkus.vertx.ConsumeEvent annotation. @ConsumeEvent has attributes, which we'll get to, but let's see it in action:

```
package com.acme.vertx;

import javax.enterprise.context.ApplicationScoped;

import io.quarkus.vertx.ConsumeEvent;

@ApplicationScoped
public class GreetingService {
    @ConsumeEvent     ❶
    public String consumeNormal(String name) { ❷
        return name.toUpperCase();
    }
}
```

❶ With no value set, the address of the event is the fully qualified name of the bean; in this case, it would be com.acme.vertx.GreetingService

❷ The parameter for the consumer is the message body; if the method returns anything, it is packaged as the message response

Sending events/messages

To send an event, you will be interacting with the Vert.x Event Bus. You can obtain the instance via injection: @Inject io.vertx.axle.core.eventbus.EventBus bus. You will be primarily making use of two methods on the event bus:

send
    Sends a message and optionally expects a reply

publish
    Publishes a message to each listener

```
bus.send("address", "hello"); ❶
bus.publish("address", "hello"); ❷
bus.send("address", "hello, how are you?") ❸
    .thenAccept(msg -> {
    // do something with the message
});
```

❶ Send a message to a specific address, and a single consumer receives it, then for-
    get about the response.

❷ Publish a message to a specific address, and all consumers receive the message.

❸ Send a message to a specific address, and expect a reply.

You should have enough information to create your own version of the Greeting Service using Vert.x Eventing!

Discussion

You can also return a `CompletionStage` to handle events in asynchronous fashion.
Lastly, if you wish to use the `io.vertx.axle.core.eventbus.Message` as the method
param, you may do so and get access to the rest of the message within your event
handler.

Fire-and-forget style interactions are just as easy—simply return `void` from your
method.

> The method consuming an event is called on the Vert.x event loop.
> The first tenet of Vert.x is to never block the event loop. Your code
> *must* be nonblocking. *If* you need the method to block, set the
> `blocking` attribute on `@ConsumeEvent` to `true`.

To configure the name or address of the event handler, use the `value` parameter:

```
@ConsumeEvent(value = "greeting")
public String consumeNamed(String name) {
    return name.toUpperCase();
}
```

See Also

For more information, visit the following websites:

- Vert.x (*https://www.vertx.io*)
- Vert.x: The Event Bus (*https://oreil.ly/TAnxk*)

15.4 Reacting to Apache Kafka Messages

Problem

You want to react to Apache Kafka messages.

Solution

Quarkus makes use of Eclipse MicroProfile Reactive Messaging to interact with Apache Kafka.

The Reactive Messaging specification is built on top of three main concepts:

1. `Message`
2. `@Incoming`
3. `@Outgoing`

This recipe focuses on `Message` and `@Incoming`; see Recipe 15.5 if you need to go the other direction.

Message

In short, a `Message` is an envelope around a payload. The envelope also carries with it optional metadata, though more often than not, you care only about the payload.

@Incoming annotation

This annotation (`org.eclipse.microprofile.reactive.messaging.Incoming`) indicates that the method consumes a stream of messages. The only attribute is the name of the name of the stream or topic. Methods are annotated this way for the end of a processing chain, also known as a *sink*. The following are a couple of uses within Quarkus:

```
package org.acme.kafka;

import java.util.concurrent.CompletableFuture;
import java.util.concurrent.CompletionStage;

import javax.enterprise.context.ApplicationScoped;

import org.eclipse.microprofile.reactive.messaging.Incoming;
import org.eclipse.microprofile.reactive.messaging.Message;

@ApplicationScoped
public class CharacterReceiver {
  @Incoming("ascii-char")
  public CompletionStage<Void> processKafkaChar(Message<String> character) {
```

```
    return CompletableFuture.runAsync(() -> {
        System.out.println("Received a message from Kafka "
            + "using CompletableFuture: '" + character.getPayload() + "'");
    });
}

@Incoming("ascii-char")
public void processCharacter(String character) {
    System.out.println("Received a String from kafka: '" + character + "'");
}
}
```

You can see that either method works; however, in the case of processKafkaChar
acter it takes a Message and returns a CompletionStage. If your method receives a
Message as the parameter, it *must* return a CompletionStage.

If you are interested only in the payload, you don't need to worry about any of that
and can simply accept the type of the payload and return void, as is demonstrated in
processCharacter in the previous code.

Configuration

As expected, you will need to configure your application to talk to Apache Kafka:

```
mp.messaging.incoming.ascii-char.connector=smallrye-kafka
mp.messaging.incoming.ascii-char.value.deserializer=org.apache.kafka.common\
                                                     .serialization\
                                                     .StringDeserializer
mp.messaging.incoming.ascii-char.broadcast=true
```

In the preceding code, we have multiple subscribers, so we need to use broad
cast=true. The broadcast attribute lets MicroProfile Reactive Messaging (SmallRye
is an implementation) know that messages received can be dispatched to more than
one subscriber.

The syntax of the configuration is as follows:

```
mp.messaging.[outgoing|incoming].{channel-name}.property=value
```

The value in the channel-name segment must match the value set in @Incoming (and
@Outgoing, which is covered in the next recipe).

There are some sensible defaults that you can see in SmallRye Reactive Messaging:
Apache Kafka (*https://oreil.ly/L5WHK*).

Discussion

To get up and running quickly with Apache Kafka in a development environment,
you can visit the websites listed in "See Also" on page 312, or use the following
docker-compose.yml file along with docker-compose:

```
version: '2'

services:

  zookeeper:
    image: strimzi/kafka:0.11.3-kafka-2.1.0
    command: [
      "sh", "-c",
      "bin/zookeeper-server-start.sh config/zookeeper.properties"
    ]
    ports:
      - "2181:2181"
    environment:
      LOG_DIR: /tmp/logs

  kafka:
    image: strimzi/kafka:0.11.3-kafka-2.1.0
    command: [
      "sh", "-c",
      "bin/kafka-server-start.sh config/server.properties
      --override listeners=$${KAFKA_LISTENERS}
      --override advertised.listeners=$${KAFKA_ADVERTISED_LISTENERS}
      --override zookeeper.connect=$${KAFKA_ZOOKEEPER_CONNECT}"
    ]
    depends_on:
      - zookeeper
    ports:
      - "9092:9092"
    environment:
      LOG_DIR: "/tmp/logs"
      KAFKA_ADVERTISED_LISTENERS: PLAINTEXT://localhost:9092
      KAFKA_LISTENERS: PLAINTEXT://0.0.0.0:9092
      KAFKA_ZOOKEEPER_CONNECT: zookeeper:2181
```

See Also

For more information, visit the following:

- GitHub: Reactive Messaging for MicroProfile (*https://oreil.ly/DSu7u*)
- SmallRye Reactive Messaging (*https://oreil.ly/QlGHK*)
- Apache Kafka (*https://oreil.ly/6xsAP*)
- Apache Kafka: Consumer Configs (*https://oreil.ly/iE8aU*)
- Vert.x Kafka client (*https://oreil.ly/zFD5J*)

15.5 Sending Messages to Apache Kafka

Problem

You want to send messages to Apache Kafka.

Solution

First, you'll need to add the `quarkus-smallrye-reactive-messaging-kafka` extension to your project. In this example, we're also using SmallRye Mutiny, so add the `io.smallrye.reactive:mutiny` dependency as well.

To send messages to Apache Kafka, use the `@Outgoing` annotation from Eclipse MicroProfile Reactive Messaging.

When you generate data to send to Apache Kafka, you will annotate your methods with `org.eclipse.microprofile.reactive.messaging.Outgoing`. You can send either a stream of messages or a single message. If you wish to publish a stream of messages, you must return a `org.reactivestreams.Publisher` or a `org.eclipse.microprofile.reactive.streams.operators.PublisherBuilder`. If you wish to publish a single message, return a `org.eclipse.microprofile.reactive.messaging.Message`, `java.util.concurrent.CompletionStage`, or the corresponding type for your message payload.

The following is a basic example that creates a new ASCII character every second and sends it to the "letter-out" channel:

```
package org.acme.kafka;

import java.time.Duration;
import java.util.concurrent.ThreadLocalRandom;

import io.smallrye.mutiny.Multi;
import org.eclipse.microprofile.reactive.messaging.Outgoing;
import org.reactivestreams.Publisher;

public class CharacterGenerator {
    @Outgoing("letter-out")
    public Publisher<String> generate() {
        return Multi.createFrom()
                .ticks().every(Duration.ofSeconds(1))
                .map(tick -> {
                    final int i = ThreadLocalRandom.current().nextInt(95);
                    return String.valueOf((char) (i + 32));
                });
    }
}
```

The value attribute for @Outgoing is required and is the name of the outbound channel. In this example, we used SmallRye Mutiny, but you could use anything that returns an instance of org.reactivestreams.Publisher; a Flowable from RXJava2, for example, would also work well.

The following configuration is also necessary:

```
mp.messaging.outgoing.letter-out.connector=smallrye-kafka
mp.messaging.outgoing.letter-out.topic=ascii-char
mp.messaging.outgoing.letter-out.value.serializer=org.apache.kafka.common\
                                                  .serialization\
                                                  .StringSerializer
```

Discussion

If you find yourself needing to send a message in an imperative way, you can use an org.eclipse.microprofile.reactive.messaging.Emitter injected into your application:

```
@Inject @Channel("price-create") Emitter<Double> priceEmitter;

@POST
@Consumes(MediaType.TEXT_PLAIN)
public void addPrice(Double price) {
    priceEmitter.send(price);
}
```

See Also

For more information, check out the following:

- Recipe 15.4
- Apache Kafka: Producer Configs (*https://oreil.ly/hZ9Bm*)
- SmallRye Reactive Messaging (*https://oreil.ly/QlGHK*)

15.6 Marshalling POJOs into/out of Kafka

Problem

You want to serialize/deserialize POJOs into Kafka.

Solution

Quarkus has capabilities to work with JSON Kafka messages; you will need to select either JSONB or Jackson as an implementation. The required extensions are either quarkus-resteasy-jsonb or quarkus-resteasy-jackson, depending on your preference.

You will then need to create a deserializer. The easiest way to do this is to extend either the JsonDeserializer for JSONB or the ObjectMapperDeserializer for Jackson. Here is the Book class and its deserializer:

```
package org.acme.kafka;

public class Book {
    public String title;
    public String author;
    public Long isbn;

    public Book() {
    }

    public Book(String title, String author, Long isbn) {
        this.title = title;
        this.author = author;
        this.isbn = isbn;
    }
}
```

For JSONB, the deserializer looks like this:

```
package org.acme.kafka;

import io.quarkus.kafka.client.serialization.JsonbDeserializer;

public class BookDeserializer extends JsonbDeserializer<Book> {
    public BookDeserializer() {
        super(Book.class);
    }
}
```

For Jackson, it is also just as easy:

```
package com.acme.kafka;

import io.quarkus.kafka.client.serialization.ObjectMapperDeserializer;

public class BookDeserializer extends ObjectMapperDeserializer<Book> {
    public BookDeserializer() {
        super(Book.class);
    }
}
```

The last bit you will need to do is to add your deserializer and the default serializer to the Quarkus configuration:

```
# Configure the Kafka source (we read from it)
mp.messaging.incoming.book-in.connector=smallrye-kafka
```

```
mp.messaging.incoming.book-in.topic=book-in
mp.messaging.incoming.book-in.value.deserializer=com.acme\
                                        .kafka.BookDeserializer

# Configure the Kafka sink (we write to it)
mp.messaging.outgoing.book-out.connector=smallrye-kafka
mp.messaging.outgoing.book-out.topic=book-out
mp.messaging.outgoing.book-out.value.serializer=io.quarkus.kafka\
                                        .client.serialization\
                                        .JsonbSerializer
```

Or, for Jackson:

```
# Configure the Kafka source (we read from it)
mp.messaging.incoming.book-in.connector=smallrye-kafka
mp.messaging.incoming.book-in.topic=book-in
mp.messaging.incoming.book-in.value.deserializer=com.acme\
                                        .kafka.BookDeserializer

# Configure the Kafka sink (we write to it)
mp.messaging.outgoing.book-out.connector=smallrye-kafka
mp.messaging.outgoing.book-out.topic=book-out
mp.messaging.outgoing.book-out.value.serializer=io.quarkus.kafka.client\
                                        .serialization\
                                        .ObjectMapperSerializer
```

Discussion

If you are using JSONB and you do not wish to create a deserializer for each POJO sent over the wire, you can use the generic io.vertx.kafka.client.serialization.JsonObjectDeserializer. The resulting object returned will be a javax.json.JsonObject. Here, we have chosen to use the default serializers.

You can also create your own serializers if you need something more than the basic functionality.

15.7 Using Kafka Streams API

Problem

You want to use the Kafka Streams API for querying data.

Solution

The Apache Kafka extension in Quarkus (quarkus-smallrye-reactive-messaging-kafka) has integration with the Apache Kafka Streams API. This example is a bit in depth and requires some additional moving parts. You'll of course need an Apache Kafka instance up and running. We recommend you set up an Apache Kafka instance using Kubernetes if you don't already have one available. If you simply need something for development, you can use the following *docker-compose.yml* file:

```yaml
version: '3.5'

services:
  zookeeper:
    image: strimzi/kafka:0.11.3-kafka-2.1.0
    command: [
      "sh", "-c",
      "bin/zookeeper-server-start.sh config/zookeeper.properties"
    ]
    ports:
      - "2181:2181"
    environment:
      LOG_DIR: /tmp/logs
    networks:
      - kafkastreams-network
  kafka:
    image: strimzi/kafka:0.11.3-kafka-2.1.0
    command: [
      "sh", "-c",
      "bin/kafka-server-start.sh config/server.properties
      --override listeners=$${KAFKA_LISTENERS}
      --override advertised.listeners=$${KAFKA_ADVERTISED_LISTENERS}
      --override zookeeper.connect=$${KAFKA_ZOOKEEPER_CONNECT}
      --override num.partitions=$${KAFKA_NUM_PARTITIONS}"
    ]
    depends_on:
      - zookeeper
    ports:
      - "9092:9092"
    environment:
      LOG_DIR: "/tmp/logs"
      KAFKA_ADVERTISED_LISTENERS: PLAINTEXT://kafka:9092
      KAFKA_LISTENERS: PLAINTEXT://0.0.0.0:9092
      KAFKA_ZOOKEEPER_CONNECT: zookeeper:2181
      KAFKA_NUM_PARTITIONS: 3
    networks:
      - kafkastreams-network
```

The next part in this solution is to create a producer that generates values and sends those generated values to a Kafka topic. We'll be using the idea of a jukebox for this. Our jukebox will contain a number of songs and their artists, as well as the number of times a song was played. Each of those will be sent to a different topic and then aggregated together by another service:

```java
package org.acme.kafka.jukebox;

import java.time.Duration;
import java.time.Instant;
import java.util.Arrays;
```

```
import java.util.Collections;
import java.util.List;
import java.util.concurrent.ThreadLocalRandom;

import javax.enterprise.context.ApplicationScoped;

import io.smallrye.mutiny.Multi;
import io.smallrye.reactive.messaging.kafka.KafkaRecord;
import org.eclipse.microprofile.reactive.messaging.Outgoing;
import org.jboss.logging.Logger;

@ApplicationScoped
public class Jukebox {
    private static final Logger LOG = Logger.getLogger(Jukebox.class);

    private ThreadLocalRandom random = ThreadLocalRandom.current();

    private List<Song> songs = Collections.unmodifiableList(
            Arrays.asList(
                new Song(1, "Confessions", "Usher"),
                new Song(2, "How Do I Live", "LeAnn Rimes"),
                new Song(3, "Physical", "Olivia Newton-John"),
                new Song(4, "You Light Up My Life", "Debby Boone"),
                new Song(5, "The Twist", "Chubby Checker"),
                new Song(6, "Mack the Knife", "Bobby Darin"),
                new Song(7, "Night Fever", "Bee Gees"),
                new Song(8, "Bette Davis Eyes", "Kim Carnes"),
                new Song(9, "Macarena (Bayside Boys Mix)", "Los Del Rio"),
                new Song(10, "Yeah!", "Usher")
            )
    );

    @Outgoing("song-values")
    public Multi<KafkaRecord<Integer, String>> generate() {
        return Multi.createFrom().ticks().every(Duration.ofMillis(500))
                .onOverflow().drop()
                .map(tick -> {
                    Song s = songs.get(random.nextInt(songs.size()));
                    int timesPlayed = random.nextInt(1, 100);

                    LOG.infov("song {0}, times played: {1,number}",
                            s.title, timesPlayed);
                    return KafkaRecord.of(s.id, Instant.now()
                                                + ";" + timesPlayed);
                });
    }

    @Outgoing("songs")
    public Multi<KafkaRecord<Integer, String>> songs() {
        return Multi.createFrom().iterable(songs)
                .map(s -> KafkaRecord.of(s.id,
                        "{\n" +
```

```
                    "\t\"id\":\""+ s.id + "\",\n" +
                    "\t\"title\":\"" + s.title + "\",\n" +
                    "\t\"artist\":\"" + s.artist + "\"\n" +
                    "}"
                ));
    }

    private static class Song {
        int id;
        String title;
        String artist;

        public Song(int id, String title, String artist) {
            this.id = id;
            this.title = title;
            this.artist = artist;
        }
    }
}
```

Every 500 milliseconds, a new message containing the song and the times it was played, along with a time stamp, is sent out to the songs topic. We'll forgo the extra configuration—you can see steps for that in the Recipe 15.5 recipe.

Next, we need to build the pipeline. The first step is to create some value holders:

```
package org.acme.kafka.jukebox;

public class Song {
    public int id;
    public String title;
    public String artist;
}
```

Now we need a holder for a play count:

```
package org.acme.kafka.jukebox;

import java.time.Instant;

public class PlayedCount {
    public int count;
    public String title;
    public String artist;
    public int id;
    public Instant timestamp;

    public PlayedCount(int id, String title, String artist,
                       int count, Instant timestamp) {
        this.count = count;
        this.title = title;
        this.artist = artist;
        this.id = id;
```

```
        this.timestamp = timestamp;
    }
}
```

Last, for the value holders is an object to track the aggregation of values while the
messages are processed in the pipeline:

```
package org.acme.kafka.jukebox;

import java.math.BigDecimal;
import java.math.RoundingMode;

public class Aggregation {
    public int songId;
    public String songTitle;
    public String songArtist;
    public int count;
    public int sum;
    public int min;
    public int max;
    public double avg;

    public Aggregation updateFrom(PlayedCount playedCount) {
        songId = playedCount.id;
        songTitle = playedCount.title;
        songArtist = playedCount.artist;

        count++;
        sum += playedCount.count;
        avg = BigDecimal.valueOf(sum / count)
                .setScale(1, RoundingMode.HALF_UP).doubleValue();
        min = Math.min(min, playedCount.count);
        max = Math.max(max, playedCount.count);

        return this;
    }
}
```

Now, on to the magic! The last part of the puzzle is streaming the query implementation. We only need to define a method that is a CDI producer that returns an Apache
Kafka Stream Topology. Quarkus will take care of the configuration, and the life cycle
will take care of the Kafka Streams engine:

```
package org.acme.kafka.jukebox;

import java.time.Instant;

import javax.enterprise.context.ApplicationScoped;
import javax.enterprise.inject.Produces;

import io.quarkus.kafka.client.serialization.JsonbSerde;
import org.apache.kafka.common.serialization.Serdes;
import org.apache.kafka.streams.StreamsBuilder;
```

```java
import org.apache.kafka.streams.Topology;
import org.apache.kafka.streams.kstream.Consumed;
import org.apache.kafka.streams.kstream.GlobalKTable;
import org.apache.kafka.streams.kstream.Materialized;
import org.apache.kafka.streams.kstream.Produced;
import org.apache.kafka.streams.state.KeyValueBytesStoreSupplier;
import org.apache.kafka.streams.state.Stores;

@ApplicationScoped
public class TopologyProducer {
    static final String SONG_STORE = "song-store";

    private static final String SONG_TOPIC = "songs";
    private static final String SONG_VALUES_TOPIC = "song-values";
    private static final String SONG_AGG_TOPIC = "song-aggregated";

    @Produces
    public Topology buildTopology() {
        StreamsBuilder builder = new StreamsBuilder();

        JsonbSerde<Song> songSerde = new JsonbSerde<>(Song.class);
        JsonbSerde<Aggregation> aggregationSerde =
                new JsonbSerde<>(Aggregation.class);

        KeyValueBytesStoreSupplier storeSupplier =
                Stores.persistentKeyValueStore(SONG_STORE);

        GlobalKTable<Integer, Song> songs = builder.globalTable(SONG_TOPIC,
                Consumed.with(Serdes.Integer(), songSerde));

        builder.stream(SONG_VALUES_TOPIC, Consumed.with(Serdes.Integer(),
                Serdes.String()))
                .join(
                        songs,
                        (songId, timestampAndValue) -> songId,
                        (timestampAndValue, song) -> {
                            String[] parts = timestampAndValue.split(";");
                            return new PlayedCount(song.id, song.title,
                                    song.artist,
                                    Integer.parseInt(parts[1]),
                                    Instant.parse(parts[0]));
                        }
                )
                .groupByKey()
                .aggregate(
                        Aggregation::new,
                        (songId, value, aggregation) ->
                                aggregation.updateFrom(value),
                        Materialized.<Integer, Aggregation> as(storeSupplier)
                            .withKeySerde(Serdes.Integer())
                            .withValueSerde(aggregationSerde)
                )
```

```
                .toStream()
                .to(
                        SONG_AGG_TOPIC,
                        Produced.with(Serdes.Integer(), aggregationSerde)
                );
        return builder.build();
    }
}
```

Explaining all of what is happening is beyond the scope of this recipe, but the Kafka Streams site, linked to in "See Also" on page 322, has entire tutorials and videos dedicated to this topic. In a nutshell, this connects to the previous songs and song-values topic then merges the values together based on song ID. The play count values then have some aggregation performed on them, and the output is sent back to Apache Kafka on a new topic.

Discussion

We recommend using the kafkacat utility for seeing the messages as they are sent to the topics.

 In both of the examples with Apache Kafka we connected with only a single client and machine. This is not a limitation of Quarkus but something we have done to help simplify the examples.

See Also

For more information, visit the following websites:

- Apache Kafka: Kafka Streams (*https://oreil.ly/gNAof*)
- Confluent: kafkacat Utility (*https://oreil.ly/bgIT_*)

15.8 Using AMQP with Quarkus

Problem

You want to use AMQP (Advanced Message Queuing Protocol) as the messaging system.

Solution

Use the quarkus-smallrye-reactive-messaging-amqp extension.

Just like the Kafka integration, Quarkus uses Eclipse MicroProfile Reactive Messaging as the facade around all messaging interactions. By adding the `quarkus-smallrye-reactive-messaging-amqp` extension to your project, you will get the SmallRye AMQP connector and associated dependencies. This will allow @Outbound, @Inbound, @Broadcast, and other Eclipse MicroProfile Reactive Messaging annotations and concepts to work with AMQP.

 These annotations work with AMQP 1.0, not 0.9.x.

You will also need to set the channel connector to `smallrye-amqp` in the *application.properties* file. Remember that the syntax for those configurations is the following:

```
mp.messaging.[outgoing|incoming].[channel-name].property=value
```

You can also set the username and password for AMQP connections globally via the following:

```
amqp-username=[my-username]
amqp-password=[my-secret-password]
```

Or, if you need to talk to different instances with their own credentials, you may set those on a per-channel basis. Please see the SmallRye documentation for further properties.

The code from Recipe 15.5 will work exactly the same with AMQP as it will with Kafka, assuming that the channels are the same name and that the rest of the AMQP setup and connection information are correct.

See Also

For more information, visit the following website:

- SmallRye Reactive Messaging: AMQP 1.0 (*https://oreil.ly/ViPyo*)

15.9 Using MQTT

Problem

You want to use MQTT (MQ Telemetry Transport) as the messaging system.

Solution

Use the `quarkus-smallrye-reactive-messaging-mqtt` extension.

Just like the Kafka and AMQP integration, Quarkus uses Eclipse MicroProfile Reactive Messaging as the facade around all messaging interactions. By adding the `quarkus-smallrye-reactive-messaging-mqtt` extension to your project, you will get the SmallRye MQTT connector and associated dependencies. This will allow `@Out bound`, `@Inbound`, `@Broadcast`, and other Eclipse MicroProfile Reactive Messaging annotations and concepts to work with MQTT.

You will also need to set the channel connector to `smallrye-mqtt` in the *application.properties* file. Remember, the syntax for those configurations is the following:

```
mp.messaging.[outgoing|incoming].[channel-name].property=value
```

Connection and credentials can be set on a channel-by-channel basis. Please see the SmallRye documentation for further properties.

The code from Recipe 15.4 will work exactly the same with MQTT as it will with Kafka, assuming that the channels have the same name and that the rest of the MQTT setup is correct along with the connection information.

Discussion

There is also support for acting as an MQTT server; however, it is not a fully featured MQTT server. For example, it will handle only publish requests and their acknowledgment; it does not handle subscription requests.

See Also

For more information, visit the following website:

- SmallRye Reactive Messaging: MQTT (*https://oreil.ly/QmkVY*)

15.10 Query Using Reactive SQL

Problem

You want to query data using the PostgreSQL reactive client.

Solution

Quarkus integrates with the Vert.x Reactive SQL client, which works with MySQL/MariaDB, and PostgreSQL. In this recipe, we will be demonstrating this with PostgreSQL; in the following recipe we will use MariaDB.

Naturally, you will need to add an extension to utilize the reactive SQL client. Currently, there are two of them: quarkus-reactive-pg-client and quarkus-reactive-mysql-client, respective to the two databases. You will also need to ensure that the following extensions are in your project (if you are using JAX-RS):

- quarkus-resteasy
- quarkus-resteasy-jsonb or quarkus-resteasy-jackson
- quarkus-resteasy-mutiny

Just as with any data store, you will need to configure access:

```
quarkus.datasource.db-kind=postgresql
quarkus.datasource.username=quarkus_test
quarkus.datasource.password=quarkus_test
quarkus.datasource.reactive.url=postgresql://localhost:5432/quarkus_test
```

Now you can use the client:

```
package org.acme.pg;

import io.smallrye.mutiny.Multi;
import io.smallrye.mutiny.Uni;
import io.vertx.mutiny.pgclient.PgPool;
import io.vertx.mutiny.sqlclient.Row;
import io.vertx.mutiny.sqlclient.Tuple;

public class Book {
    public Long id;
    public String title;
    public String isbn;

    public Book() {
    }

    public Book(String title, String isbn) {
        this.title = title;
        this.isbn = isbn;
    }

    public Book(Long id, String title, String isbn) {
        this.id = id;
        this.title = title;
        this.isbn = isbn;
    }

    public static Book from(Row row) {
        return new Book(row.getLong("id"),
                        row.getString("title"),
                        row.getString("isbn"));
    }
}
```

```java
    public static Multi<Book> findAll(PgPool client) {
        return client.query("SELECT id, title, isbn " +
                            "FROM books ORDER BY title ASC") ❶
                .onItem().produceMulti(Multi.createFrom()::iterable) ❷
                .map(Book::from); ❸
    }
}
```

❶   Query the database, returning a Uni<RowSet<Row>>

❷   Create a Multi<Row> once the query returns

❸   Map each row into a Book instance

To complete the exercise, you can use the RESTful endpoint:

```java
package org.acme.pg;

import javax.annotation.PostConstruct;
import javax.inject.Inject;
import javax.ws.rs.Consumes;
import javax.ws.rs.GET;
import javax.ws.rs.Path;
import javax.ws.rs.Produces;
import javax.ws.rs.core.MediaType;
import javax.ws.rs.core.Response;

import io.smallrye.mutiny.Uni;
import io.vertx.mutiny.pgclient.PgPool;
import org.eclipse.microprofile.config.inject.ConfigProperty;

@Path("/books")
@Produces(MediaType.APPLICATION_JSON)
@Consumes(MediaType.APPLICATION_JSON)
public class BookResource {

    @Inject
    PgPool client;
    @GET
    public Uni<Response> get() {
        return Book.findAll(client)
                .collectItems().asList()
                .map(Response::ok)
                .map(Response.ResponseBuilder::build);
    }
}
```

Discussion

You can also use prepared queries by using the `preparedQuery` method and the `Tuple` class:

```
public static Uni<Boolean> delete(PgPool client, Long id) {
    return client.preparedQuery("DELETE FROM books " +
                                "WHERE id = $1", Tuple.of(id))
            .map(rowSet -> rowSet.rowCount() == 1); ❶
}
```

❶ Using metadata, return from the `RowSet` instance to verify the row was deleted

See Also

The underlying implementation can be found at Vert.x: Reactive PostgreSQL Client (*https://oreil.ly/0nuDM*).

15.11 Insert Using Reactive SQL Client

Problem

You want to insert data using the MySQL reactive client.

Solution

Similar to the previous recipe using PostgreSQL, data insertion can be done with a reactive MySQL client. The same extensions need to be used to changed the `quarkus-reactive-pg-client` for `quarkus-reactive-mysql-client`:

- `quarkus-resteasy`
- `quarkus-resteasy-jsonb` or `quarkus-resteasy-jackson`
- `quarkus-resteasy-mutiny`

You will, of course, need to set up the datasource:

```
quarkus.datasource.db-kind=mysql
quarkus.datasource.username=quarkus_test
quarkus.datasource.password=quarkus_test
quarkus.datasource.reactive.url=mysql://localhost:3306/quarkus_test
```

You will see very similar themes in the `Book.save` method as you did in the previous recipe:

```
public Uni<Long> save(MySQLPool client) {
    String query = "INSERT INTO books (title,isbn) VALUES (?,?)";
    return client.preparedQuery(query, Tuple.of(title, isbn))
```

```
                .map(rowSet -> rowSet
                       .property(MySQLClient.LAST_INSERTED_ID));  ❶
    }
```

❶   Use the property from the RowSet to get the inserted ID.

By now, you should be able to put together the appropriate POST method for the
BookResource endpoint, calling the save method on the new Book instance received
from the user.

See Also

For more information, visit the following website:

- Vert.x: Reactive MySQL Client (*https://oreil.ly/UHxfh*)

15.12 Using the Reactive MongoDB Client

Problem

You want to use the Reactive MongoDB client.

Solution

The MongoDB Quarkus extension also includes a reactive MongoDB client. As was
shown in Recipe 7.21, you will need to add the quarkus-mongodb-client. You will
also need to add the following extensions to your project:

quarkus-resteasy-mutiny
    To return and interact with Mutiny for endpoint returns.

quarkus-smallrye-context-propagation
    This allows things like injection and transactions to work with async code.

The rest of the integration is pretty straightforward. Here are the versions of the service and the resource classes from the previous MongoDB recipe, but written in a
reactive way:

```
    package org.acme.mongodb;

    import java.util.List;
    import java.util.Objects;

    import javax.enterprise.context.ApplicationScoped;
    import javax.inject.Inject;

    import com.mongodb.client.model.Filters;
```

```java
import io.quarkus.mongodb.reactive.ReactiveMongoClient;
import io.quarkus.mongodb.reactive.ReactiveMongoCollection;
import io.smallrye.mutiny.Uni;
import org.bson.Document;

@ApplicationScoped
public class ReactiveBookService {
    @Inject
    ReactiveMongoClient mongoClient;

    public Uni<List<Book>> list() {
        return getCollection().find()
                .map(Book::from).collectItems().asList();
    }

    public Uni<Void> add(Book b) {
        Document doc = new Document()
                .append("isbn", b.isbn)
                .append("title", b.title)
                .append("authors", b.authors);

        return getCollection().insertOne(doc);
    }

    public Uni<Book> findSingle(String isbn) {
        return Objects.requireNonNull(getCollection()
                .find(Filters.eq("isbn", isbn))
                .map(Book::from))
                .toUni();
    }

    private ReactiveMongoCollection<Document> getCollection() {
        return mongoClient.getDatabase("book")
                .getCollection("book");
    }
}
```

Besides imports and moving from an imperative to a reactive approach with Mutiny, nothing has changed. The same can be seen for the REST endpoint:

```java
package org.acme.mongodb;

import java.util.List;

import javax.inject.Inject;
import javax.ws.rs.Consumes;
import javax.ws.rs.GET;
import javax.ws.rs.POST;
import javax.ws.rs.Path;
import javax.ws.rs.PathParam;
import javax.ws.rs.Produces;
import javax.ws.rs.core.MediaType;
import javax.ws.rs.core.Response;
```

```
import io.smallrye.mutiny.Uni;

@Path("/reactive_books")
@Produces(MediaType.APPLICATION_JSON)
@Consumes(MediaType.APPLICATION_JSON)
public class ReactiveBookResource {
    @Inject
    ReactiveBookService service;

    @GET
    public Uni<List<Book>> getAll() {
        return service.list();
    }

    @GET
    @Path("{isbn}")
    public Uni<Book> getSingle(@PathParam("isbn") String isbn) {
        return service.findSingle(isbn);
    }

    @POST
    public Uni<Response> add(Book b) {
        return service.add(b).onItem().ignore()
                .andSwitchTo(this::getAll)
                .map(books -> Response.status(Response.Status.CREATED)
                                  .entity(books).build());
    }
}
```

See Also

For more information, visit the following website:

- Quarkus: Context Propagation in Quarkus (*https://oreil.ly/bd9hA*)

15.13 Using the Reactive Neo4j Client

Problem

You want to use the reactive Neo4j client.

Solution

The Neo4j Quarkus extension has support for the reactive driver.

You will need to use version 4 or higher of Neo4j to go fully reactive. You will also need to add the quarkus-resteasy-mutiny extension to your project. Following up from Recipe 7.23, there isn't much that has changed, besides using an RxSession from the driver and using Mutiny:

```java
package org.acme.neo4j;

import java.util.stream.Collectors;

import javax.inject.Inject;
import javax.ws.rs.Consumes;
import javax.ws.rs.GET;
import javax.ws.rs.POST;
import javax.ws.rs.Path;
import javax.ws.rs.Produces;
import javax.ws.rs.core.MediaType;
import javax.ws.rs.core.Response;

import io.smallrye.mutiny.Multi;
import io.smallrye.mutiny.Uni;
import org.neo4j.driver.Driver;
import org.neo4j.driver.Record;
import org.neo4j.driver.Value;
import org.neo4j.driver.Values;
import org.neo4j.driver.reactive.RxResult;
import org.reactivestreams.Publisher;

@Path("/reactivebooks")
@Produces(MediaType.APPLICATION_JSON)
@Consumes(MediaType.APPLICATION_JSON)
public class ReactiveBookResource {
    @Inject
    Driver driver;

    @GET
    @Produces(MediaType.SERVER_SENT_EVENTS) ❸
    public Publisher<Response> getAll() {
        return Multi.createFrom().resource( ❷
                driver::rxSession,
                rxSession -> rxSession.readTransaction(tx -> { ❶
                    RxResult result = tx.run("MATCH (b:Book) RETURN " +
                                             "b ORDER BY b.title");
                    return Multi.createFrom().publisher(result.records())
                            .map(Record::values)
                            .map(values -> values.stream().map(Value::asNode)
                                    .map(Book::from)
                                    .map(Book::toJson))
                            .map(bookStream ->
                                    Response.ok(bookStream
                                            .collect(Collectors.toList()))
                                    .build());
                }))
                .withFinalizer(rxSession -> { ❹
                    return Uni.createFrom().publisher(rxSession.close());
```

```
                                    });
            }

            @POST
            public Publisher<Response> create(Book b) {
                return Multi.createFrom().resource(
                        driver::rxSession,
                        rxSession -> rxSession.writeTransaction(tx -> {
                            String query = "CREATE " +
                                            "(b:Book {title: $title, isbn: $isbn," +
                                            " authors: $authors}) " +
                                            "RETURN b";
                            RxResult result = tx.run(query,
                                    Values.parameters("title", b.title,
                                            "isbn", b.isbn, "authors", b.authors));
                            return Multi.createFrom().publisher(result.records())
                                    .map(record -> Response.ok(record
                                            .asMap()).build());
                        })
                ).withFinalizer(rxSession -> {
                    return Uni.createFrom().publisher(rxSession.close());
                });
            }
        }
```

❶ Get an RxSession from the driver

❷ Use Mutiny to interact with the ReactiveStreams Publisher

❸ Stream the results back to the user

❹ Close the session at the very end

CHAPTER 16

Additional Quarkus Features

This chapter contains features of Quarkus that don't fit into any other chapter. That, of course, doesn't make them any less useful! In this chapter, you'll learn about the following topics:

- Quarkus's templating solution, Qute
- OpenAPI integration
- Sending emails
- Scheduling functions
- Application data caching

16.1 Creating Templates with the Qute Template Engine

Problem

You want to create templates and render them with specific data.

Solution

Use the Qute template engine.

Qute is a templating engine designed specifically to meet the Quarkus needs of minimizing the usage of reflection and supporting the imperative and reactive style of coding.

Qute can be used as a standalone library (generating reports to disk or generating e-mail body messages) or together with JAX-RS to deliver HTML content.

To start using Qute with JAX-RS, add the `resteasy-qute` extension:

```
./mvnw quarkus:add-extension -Dextensions="quarkus-resteasy-qute"
```

By default, templates are stored at the *src/main/resources/templates* directory and its subdirectories.

The following might be a simple template as a plain-text file:

```
Hello {name}!
```

The template is a simple sentence parametrized with the `name` parameter.

To render the template with concrete data, you just need to inject the `io.quarkus.qute.Template` instance and provide the template parameters:

```
@Inject
io.quarkus.qute.Template hello; ❶ ❷

@GET
@Produces(MediaType.TEXT_PLAIN)
public TemplateInstance hello() { ❸
    final String name = "Alex";
    return hello.data("name", name); ❹
}
```

❶ `Template` instance defines the operations to do in a template

❷ By default, the field name is used to locate the template; in this case, the template path is *src/main/resources/templates/hello.txt*

❸ Rendering is not necessary because RESTEasy integrates with the `TemplateInstance` object to render the content

❹ `data` method is used to set the template parameters

If you run the project, you'll be able to see how the template is rendered:

```
./mvnw compile quarkus:dev

curl http://localhost:8080/hello

Hello Alex!
```

Discussion

Qute supports more syntax (e.g., `include` and `insert` fragments, injecting CDI beans directly, or variant templates) as well as integration with other Quarkus parts like email or schedule tasks.

See Also

Visit the following website to learn more about Qute:

- Quarkus: Qute Reference Guide (*https://oreil.ly/R1A1S*)

16.2 Rending HTML Using Qute

Problem

You want to render HTML using Qute.

Solution

Qute will render HTML just as easily as text. All that needs to happen is for Quarkus to find the template that matches your injection. The actual content of the template doesn't matter much.

Let's render an HTML page with more complex structures on the template. A simple HTML report is rendered in this case. Create a POJO class containing the parameters of the report:

```
package org.acme.quickstart;

import java.util.ArrayList;
import java.util.List;

import io.quarkus.qute.TemplateData;

@TemplateData ❶
public class Movie {

    public String name;
    public int year;
    public String genre;
    public String director;
    public List<String> characters = new ArrayList<>();
    public float ratings;

    public int getStars() { ❷
        return Math.round(ratings);
    }
}
```

❶ This annotation allows Quarkus to avoid using reflection to access the object at runtime

❷ Custom method

Discussion

The following are some details of the HTML template that are worth explaining.

The first part to look at is an optional header that you can put in any template to help Quarkus validate all the expressions at compile time:

```
{@org.acme.quickstart.Movie movie} ❶
<!DOCTYPE html>
<html>
```

❶ Parameter declaration; this is not mandatory, but it helps Quarkus to validate your template for type safety

Basic syntax like conditionals or loops are supported:

```
<div class="col-sm-12">
    <dl>
        {#if movie.year == 0} ❶
            <dt>Year:</dt> Not Known
        {#else} ❷
            <dt>Year:</dt> {movie.year}
        {/if}
        {#if movie.genre is 'horror'} ❸
        <dt>Genre:</dt> Buuuh
        {#else}
        <dt>Genre:</dt> {movie.genre}
        {/if}
        <dt>Director:</dt> {movie.director ?: 'Unknown'} ❹
        <dt>Main Characters:</dt>
        {#for character in movie.characters} ❺
            {character} ❻
            {#if hasNext} ❼
            -
            {/if}
        {/for}
        <dt>Rating:</dt>
        <font color="red">
        {#for i in movie.stars} ❽
            <span class="fas fa-xs fa-star"></span>
        {/for}
        </font>
    </dl>
</div>
```

❶ Conditional with a numeric type

❷ Else part

❸ Conditional with a string type using is

❹ Elvis operator; if the parameter is `null`, the default value is used

❺ Iterate over all characters

❻ Show the character info

❼ `hasNext` is a special attribute that checks if there are more elements

❽ Method call defined in the POJO; iterates the number of times defined in the call

Inside a loop, the following implicit variables can be used: `hasNext`, `count`, `index`, `odd`, and `even`.

At this time, it is possible to use only `Iterable`, `Map.Entry`, `Set`, `Integer`, and `Stream`.

16.3 Changing the Location of Qute Templates

Problem

You want to change the location Qute uses to find templates.

Solution

You can customize the template location (still within *src/main/resources/templates* and output to the *templates* directory in your application deployable) by using the `io.quarkus.qute.api.ResourcePath` annotation:

```
@ResourcePath("movies/detail.html") ❶
Template movies;
```

❶ Sets the path of the template to *src/main/resources/templates/movies/detail.html*

Run the application again (or if already running, let live reloading do its job), and then open a browser and enter this URL: *http://localhost:8080/movie*.

16.4 Extending Qute Data Classes

Problem

You want to extend the functionality of a Qute data class.

Solution

A template extension method must follow the following rules:

- Must be static.

- Must not return void.

- Must contain at least one parameter. The first parameter is used to match the base data object.

 You can use *template extensions* to add methods specifically for reporting purposes when you do not have access to data object source code.

You can implement *template extension methods* by using the @io.quarkus.qute.Tem plateExtension annotation. In this case, let's implement a method that rounds the rating number:

```
@TemplateExtension
static double roundStars(Movie movie, int decimals) { ❶ ❷
    double scale = Math.pow(10, decimals);
    return Math.round(movie.ratings * scale) / scale;
}
```

❶ First parameter is the POJO data object

❷ Custom parameters can be set

From the template engine, movie has a roundStars method with one argument, which is the number of decimals to round.

In a template you can now call the following:

```
({movie.roundStars(2)}) ❶
```

❶ Movie class doesn't define a roundStars method, but it is accessible because it is a template extension

Run the application again (or if already running, let live reloading do its job), and then open a browser and enter the URL: *http://localhost:8080/movie*.

The output should be similar to the output shown in Figure 16-1.

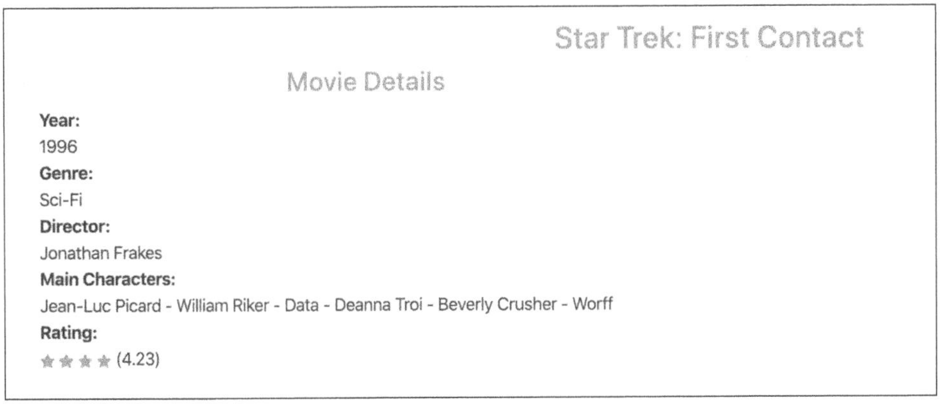

Figure 16-1. HTML output

16.5 Describing Endpoints with OpenAPI

Problem

You want to describe your REST API with OpenAPI.

Solution

Use the SmallRye OpenAPI extension.

Once you have a RESTful API created with Quarkus, all you need to do is add the openapi extension:

```
./mvnw quarkus:add-extension -Dextensions="openapi"
```

Then restart the application for everything to take effect:

```
./mvnw compile quarkus:dev
```

The specification of the API is available at */openapi* by default. To change this, use the quarkus.smallrye-openapi.path configuration:

```
quarkus.smallrye-openapi.path=/rest-api
```

You can get to the specification at *http://localhost:8080/openapi*:

```
openapi: 3.0.1
info:
  title: Generated API
  version: "1.0"
```

```yaml
paths:
  /task:
    get:
      responses:
        200:
          description: OK
          content:
            application/json:
              schema:
                $ref: '#/components/schemas/SetTask'
    post:
      requestBody:
        content:
          application/json:
            schema:
              $ref: '#/components/schemas/Task'
      responses:
        200:
          description: OK
          content:
            application/json:
              schema:
                $ref: '#/components/schemas/SetTask'
    delete:
      requestBody:
        content:
          application/json:
            schema:
              $ref: '#/components/schemas/Task'
      responses:
        200:
          description: OK
          content:
            application/json:
              schema:
                $ref: '#/components/schemas/SetTask'
components:
  schemas:
    Task:
      type: object
      properties:
        complete:
          type: boolean
        description:
          type: string
        reminder:
          format: date-time
          type: string
    SetTask:
      type: array
      items:
        type: object
```

```
properties:
  complete:
    type: boolean
  description:
    type: string
  reminder:
    format: date-time
    type: string
```

Based on the previous spec, there are GET, POST, and DELETE endpoints. You can also see that there is a task object required for DELETE and POST. The task requires a boolean, string, and a date-time. This is simple and easy to understand.

Discussion

It is very easy to create an OpenAPI specification using the SmallRye OpenAPI extension in Quarkus. This gives you an easy-to-use and easy-to-read view into your RESTful APIs.

SmallRye OpenAPI is an implementation of the Eclipse MicroProfile OpenAPI. The OpenAPI Specification is a standard, language-agnostic means of describing and discovering RESTful APIs. It is readable by both humans and machines. An OpenAPI document is defined either as JSON or YAML.

See Also

For more information, visit the following pages on GitHub:

- Eclipse MicroProfile OpenAPI (*https://oreil.ly/hczN4*)
- MicroProfile OpenAPI Specification (*https://oreil.ly/ufzr6*)
- OpenAPI Specification (*https://oreil.ly/uslyb*)

In Recipe 16.6 you will learn how to use the annotations from SmallRye OpenAPI to customize the resulting spec.

16.6 Customizing OpenAPI Spec

Problem

You want to customize the generated API spec.

Solution

Use OpenAPI annotations from the SmallRye OpenAPI extension.

Reusing the task API created in the previous recipe, Recipe 16.5 it is easy to make use of the OpenAPI annotations to add customizations and further documentation to your API:

```java
package org.acme.openapi;

import java.time.LocalDateTime;
import java.util.Collections;
import java.util.LinkedHashMap;
import java.util.Set;

import javax.ws.rs.Consumes;
import javax.ws.rs.DELETE;
import javax.ws.rs.GET;
import javax.ws.rs.POST;
import javax.ws.rs.Path;
import javax.ws.rs.Produces;
import javax.ws.rs.core.MediaType;

import org.eclipse.microprofile.openapi.annotations.Operation;
import org.eclipse.microprofile.openapi.annotations.media.Content;
import org.eclipse.microprofile.openapi.annotations.media.Schema;
import org.eclipse.microprofile.openapi.annotations.parameters.Parameter;

@Path("/task")
@Produces(MediaType.APPLICATION_JSON)
@Consumes(MediaType.APPLICATION_JSON)
public class TaskResource {

  Set<Task> tasks = Collections.newSetFromMap(
      Collections.synchronizedMap(new LinkedHashMap<>()));

  public TaskResource() {
    tasks.add(new Task("First task",
        LocalDateTime.now().plusDays(3), false));
    tasks.add(new Task("Second task",
        LocalDateTime.now().plusDays(6), false));
  }

  @GET
  @Operation(summary = "Get all tasks",
            description = "Get the full list of tasks.")
  public Set<Task> list() {
    return tasks;
  }

  @POST
  @Operation(summary = "Create a new task")
  public Set<Task> add(
      @Parameter(required = true, content =
        @Content(schema = @Schema(implementation = Task.class))) Task task) {
    tasks.add(task);
```

```
        return tasks;
    }

    @DELETE
    @Operation(summary = "Remove the specified task")
    public Set<Task> delete(
        @Parameter(required = true,
        content = @Content(schema = @Schema(implementation = Task.class)))
        Task task) {
      tasks.removeIf(existingTask -> existingTask.equals(task));
      return tasks;
    }
  }
}
package org.acme.openapi;

import java.time.LocalDateTime;
import java.util.Objects;

import javax.json.bind.annotation.JsonbDateFormat;

import org.eclipse.microprofile.openapi.annotations.enums.SchemaType;
import org.eclipse.microprofile.openapi.annotations.media.Schema;

public class Task {
    public String description;

    @Schema(description = "Flag indicating the task is complete")
    public Boolean complete;

    @JsonbDateFormat("yyyy-MM-dd'T'HH:mm")
    @Schema(example = "2019-12-25T06:30", type = SchemaType.STRING,
            implementation = LocalDateTime.class,
            pattern = "yyyy-MM-dd'T'HH:mm",
            description = "Date and time for the reminder.")
    public LocalDateTime reminder;

    public Task() {
    }

    public Task(String description,
                LocalDateTime reminder,
                Boolean complete) {
      this.description = description;
      this.reminder = reminder;
      this.complete = complete;
    }

    @Override
    public boolean equals(Object o) {
      if (this == o) return true;
      if (o == null || getClass() != o.getClass()) return false;
      Task task = (Task) o;
```

```
        return Objects.equals(description, task.description) &&
                Objects.equals(reminder, task.reminder) &&
                Objects.equals(complete, task.complete);
    }

    @Override
    public int hashCode() {
        return Objects.hash(description, reminder, complete);
    }
}
```

The previous code will create the following spec:

```
---
openapi: 3.0.1
info:
  title: Generated API
  version: "1.0"
paths:
  /task:
    get:
      summary: Get all tasks
      description: Get the full list of tasks.
      responses:
        200:
          description: OK
          content:
            application/json:
              schema:
                $ref: '#/components/schemas/SetTask'
    post:
      summary: Create a new task
      requestBody:
        content:
          application/json:
            schema:
              $ref: '#/components/schemas/Task'
      responses:
        200:
          description: OK
          content:
            application/json:
              schema:
                $ref: '#/components/schemas/SetTask'
    delete:
      summary: Remove the specified task
      requestBody:
        content:
          application/json:
            schema:
              $ref: '#/components/schemas/Task'
      responses:
        200:
```

```
              description: OK
              content:
                application/json:
                  schema:
                    $ref: '#/components/schemas/SetTask'
components:
  schemas:
    Task:
      type: object
      properties:
        complete:
          description: Flag indicating the task is complete
          type: boolean
        description:
          type: string
        reminder:
          format: date-time
          description: Date and time for the reminder.
          pattern: yyyy-MM-dd'T'HH:mm
          type: string
          example: 2019-12-25T06:30
    SetTask:
      type: array
      items:
        type: object
        properties:
          complete:
            description: Flag indicating the task is complete
            type: boolean
          description:
            type: string
          reminder:
            format: date-time
            description: Date and time for the reminder.
            pattern: yyyy-MM-dd'T'HH:mm
            type: string
            example: 2019-12-25T06:30
```

Based on the previous spec, there are GET, POST, and DELETE endpoints. You can also see that there is a task object required for DELETE and POST. The task requires a boolean, string, and a date-time. This is simple and easy to understand.

Discussion

Various OpenAPI annotations are used to provide additional information about the API, including descriptions, summaries, and examples. More information can be found about these annotations in the spec and at the links in the "See Also" section.

Further customization of the generated OpenAPI specification is very easy with Quarkus. For ultimate customization, Quarkus supports serving a static file OpenAPI spec. To do this, you need to place your valid OpenAPI spec file at

META-INF/openapi.yml or at *META-INF/openapi.json*. Quarkus will then combine the two and serve a combined static and dynamic spec. To disable the dynamic spec generation, just use the `mp.openapi.scan.disable=true` configuration in the *applications.properties* file.

See Also

For more information, visit the following pages on GitHub:

- Eclipse MicroProfile OpenAPI Specification (*https://oreil.ly/i47k_*)
- Eclipse MicroProfile OpenAPI: Annotation Samples (*https://oreil.ly/ITXQz*)
- Swagger 2.X Annotations: OpenAPI Annotations (*https://oreil.ly/ol6nb*)

16.7 Sending Email Synchronously

Problem

You want to synchronously send an email.

Solution

Make use of the Quarkus mailer extension.

Quarkus makes it very intuitive to send emails in both plain text and HTML, and to add attachments. There is also an easy-to-use method for testing whether emails have been properly sent without having to setup your own relay. Add the Email Quarkus extension to an existing project:

```
mvn quarkus:add-extensions -Dextensions="mailer"
```

Quarkus uses the Vert.x Mail client, though there are two wrappers for ease of use:

```
@Inject
Mailer mailer;

@Inject
ReactiveMailer reactiveMailer;
```

The `Mailer` class uses standard blocking and synchronous API calls, and the `ReactiveMailer`, as expected, uses nonblocking and asynchronous API calls. The `Reactive Mailer` will be discussed in the following recipe; both classes offer the same features. To send an email, simply use the `withText` or `withHtml` methods. You will need to supply a recipient, a subject, and a body. If you need to add things such as CC, BCC, and attachments, you can do so on the actual `Mail` instance.

You will also need to configure the SMTP provider (in this case, we're using Gmail TLS):

```
quarkus.mailer.from=quarkus-test@gmail.com
quarkus.mailer.host=smtp.gmail.com
quarkus.mailer.port=587
quarkus.mailer.start-tls=REQUIRED

❶
quarkus.mailer.username=YOUREMAIL@gmail.com
quarkus.mailer.password=YOURGENERATEDAPPLICATIONPASSWORD
```

❶ These can also be set with system properties and/or environment properties

Testing of the email component is done easily by making use of the MockMailbox component. It is a simple component consisting of three methods:

- getMessagesSentTo
- clear
- getTotalMessagesSent

The following test demonstrates all three of these methods:

```
package org.acme.email;

import java.util.List;

import javax.inject.Inject;

import io.quarkus.mailer.Mail;
import io.quarkus.mailer.Mailer;
import io.quarkus.mailer.MockMailbox;
import io.quarkus.test.junit.QuarkusTest;
import org.junit.jupiter.api.BeforeEach;
import org.junit.jupiter.api.Test;

import static org.assertj.core.api.Assertions.assertThat;

@QuarkusTest
public class MailerTest {
    @Inject
    Mailer mailer;

    @Inject
    MockMailbox mbox;

    @BeforeEach
    void clearMBox() {
        mbox.clear(); ❶
    }
```

```
@Test
public void assertBasicTextEmailSent() {
    final String mailTo = "test@example.org";
    final String testingSubject = "Testing email";
    final String testingBody = "Hello World!";

    mailer.send(Mail.withText(mailTo,
            testingSubject,
            testingBody));

    assertThat(mbox.getTotalMessagesSent()).isEqualTo(1); ❷
    List<Mail> emails = mbox.getMessagesSentTo(mailTo); ❸

    assertThat(emails).hasSize(1);
    Mail email = emails.get(0);

    assertThat(email.getSubject()).isEqualTo(testingSubject);
    assertThat(email.getText()).isEqualTo(testingBody);
    }
}
```

❶ We clear out the mailbox before the start of each test

❷ Use `getTotalMessagesSent` to verify how many messages Quarkus sent out

❸ Verify the messages sent to a particular address

Discussion

Both regular attachments and inline attachments are supported. Here is a simple example of an inline attachment:

```
@Test
void attachmentTest() throws Exception {
    final String mailTo = "test@example.org";
    final String testingSubject = "email with Attachment";
    final String html = "<strong>E-mail by:</strong>" + "\n" +
            "<p><img src=\"cid:logo@quarkus.io\"/></p>"; ❶

    sendEmail(mailTo, testingSubject, html);

    Mail email = mbox.getMessagesSentTo(mailTo).get(0);
    List<Attachment> attachments = email.getAttachments();

    assertThat(email.getHtml()).isEqualTo(html);
    assertThat(attachments).hasSize(1);
    assertThat(attachments.get(0).getFile())
            .isEqualTo(new File(getAttachmentURI()));
    }
```

```
private void sendEmail(String to, String subject, String body)
    throws URISyntaxException {
    final File logo = new File(getAttachmentURI());

    Mail email = Mail.withHtml(to, subject, body)
            .addInlineAttachment("quarkus-logo.svg",
                    logo,
                    "image/svg+xml",
                    "<logo@quarkus.io>");    ❷

    mailer.send(email);
}
```

❶ Be sure to reference the inline attachment by the `content-id`

❷ The `content-id` of the attachment

See Also

For more information, see the following:

- Recipe 16.8
- Vert.x Mail client (SMTP client implementation) (*https://oreil.ly/aqGZU*)

16.8 Sending Email Reactively

Problem

You want to send an email in a nonblocking, reactive fashion.

Solution

Make use of the Quarkus mailer extension.

The previous section details the basics. To do this reactively, simply inject the `Reacti veMailer` component and use it instead. The methods are the same; they simply return reactive counterparts instead of synchronous ones:

```
package org.acme.email;

import java.util.List;
import java.util.concurrent.CountDownLatch;

import javax.inject.Inject;

import io.quarkus.mailer.Mail;
import io.quarkus.mailer.MockMailbox;
```

```
import io.quarkus.mailer.reactive.ReactiveMailer;
import io.quarkus.test.junit.QuarkusTest;
import org.junit.jupiter.api.BeforeEach;
import org.junit.jupiter.api.Test;

import static org.assertj.core.api.Assertions.assertThat;

@QuarkusTest
public class ReactiveMailerTest {
    @Inject
    ReactiveMailer reactiveMailer;

    @Inject
    MockMailbox mbox;

    @BeforeEach
    void clearMbox() {
        mbox.clear();
    }

    @Test
    public void testReactiveEmail() throws Exception {
        final String mailTo = "test@example.org";
        final String testingSubject = "Testing email";
        final String testingBody = "Hello World!";
        final CountDownLatch latch = new CountDownLatch(1);

        reactiveMailer.send(Mail.withText(mailTo,
                testingSubject,
                testingBody)).subscribeAsCompletionStage().join();

        assertThat(mbox.getTotalMessagesSent()).isEqualTo(1);
        List<Mail> emails = mbox.getMessagesSentTo(mailTo);

        assertThat(emails).hasSize(1);
        Mail email = emails.get(0);

        assertThat(email.getSubject()).isEqualTo(testingSubject);
        assertThat(email.getText()).isEqualTo(testingBody);
    }
}
```

This test is exactly the same as the one in the previous section; the only difference is turning the CompletionStage to a CompletableFuture and calling join to get back to an imperative style for the test.

Discussion

Qute integrates with Mailer extension so the body content of the message is rendered from a template.

You need only the `qute` extension this time because no RESTEasy integration is required:

```
mvn quarkus:add-extensions -Dextensions="quarkus-qute"
```

The main class is the `io.quarkus.mailer.MailTemplate`, and it is used in the same way as the `io.quarkus.qute.Template`, but the first one contains methods that are specific to mail logic:

```
@ResourcePath("mail/welcome.txt") ❶
MailTemplate mailTemplate;

CompletionStage<Void> c = hello.to("to@acme.org")
    .subject("Hello from Qute template")
    .data("name", "Alex")
    .send(); ❷
```

❶ Template placed at *src/main/resources/templates/mail/welcome.txt*

❷ Sends the email rendering the body from the template file with provided data

The reactive way of sending emails follows the exact same method names and usage, instead using reactive classes. This makes it very easy to switch and understand.

See Also

For more information, see the following:

- Recipe 16.7
- Recipe 16.1

16.9 Creating Scheduled Jobs

Problem

You want some tasks to run on a schedule.

Solution

Scheduling tasks in Quarkus is fast and easy yet provides a high level of control and customization. Quarkus has a `scheduler` extension that integrates with Quartz.

Creating scheduled jobs is very easy: simply add the `@io.quarkus.scheduler.Sched uled` annotation to an application-scoped bean. There are two attributes available for specifying the schedule for the task: `cron` and `every`.

The cron attribute uses the Quartz cron syntax. If you are not familiar with Quartz, please note that there are some differences to standard cron syntax. You can learn more about this at the link in "See Also" on page 353.

The every attribute is probably the easiest to use, though it has some nuances. every parses the string using Duration#parse. If the expression starts with a digit, the PT prefix is automatically added.

Both every and cron will do a config look up for an expression started with { and ended with }.

There is a delay attribute that takes a long, and there is a delayUnit attribute that takes a TimeUnit. Used together, these will specify a delay, after which the trigger is started. By default, the trigger starts when it is registered.

Here is a demonstration of a very simple usage:

```
package org.acme.scheduling;

import java.util.concurrent.atomic.AtomicInteger;

import javax.enterprise.context.ApplicationScoped;

import io.quarkus.scheduler.Scheduled;
import io.quarkus.scheduler.ScheduledExecution;

@ApplicationScoped
public class Scheduler {

    private AtomicInteger count = new AtomicInteger();

    int get() {
        return count.get();
    }

    @Scheduled(every = "5s")
    void fiveSeconds(ScheduledExecution execution) {
        count.incrementAndGet();
        System.out.println("Running counter: 'fiveSeconds'. Next fire: "
                + execution.getTrigger().getNextFireTime());
    }
}
```

Discussion

Qute can be used to periodically generate reports.

You need only the qute extension because no RESTEasy integration is required:

```
mvn quarkus:add-extensions -Dextensions="quarkus-qute"
```

Now the `render()` method must be called manually to get the result:

```
@ResourcePath("reports/report_01.html")
Template report;

@Scheduled(cron="0 30 * * * ?")
void generate() {
    final String reportContent = report
        .data("sales", listOfSales)
        .data("now", java.time.LocalDateTime.now())
        .render();
    Files.write(reportOuput, reportContent.getBytes());
}
```

See Also

For more information, see the following:

- Quartz: Cron Trigger Tutorial (*https://oreil.ly/XdQ7r*)
- Recipe 16.1

16.10 Using Application Data Caching

Problem

You want to avoid waiting time when methods take a long time to respond.

Solution

Use application data caching.

There are some cases in which a method might take more time than expected to respond, maybe because it is making a request to an external system or because the logic being executed takes a long time to execute.

One way to improve this situation is by using application data caches. The idea is to save the result of a method call so that further calls with the same *inputs* to that method return the previously calculated result.

Quarkus integrates with Caffeine (*https://oreil.ly/1NjlX*) as a caching provider.

To start using application data caching, add the `cache` extension:

```
./mvnw quarkus:add-extension -Dextensions="cache"
```

Here is a method that simulates a long execution time:

```
@GET
@Produces(MediaType.TEXT_PLAIN)
```

```
public String hello() {
    long initial = System.currentTimeMillis();
    String msg = greetingProducer.getMessage(); ❶
    long end = System.currentTimeMillis();
    return msg + " " + (end - initial) + "ms";
}
```

❶ This logic has a random sleep time

If you run the project, you'll be able to see this delay:

```
./mvnw compile quarkus:dev
```

```
curl http://localhost:8080/hello
Hello World 4009ms
```

```
curl http://localhost:8080/hello
Hello World 3003ms
```

Let's cache the `getMessage()` method call by using the `@io.quarkus.cache.CacheRe` `sult` annotation:

```
@CacheResult(cacheName = "greeting-cache") ❶
public String getMessage() {
    try {
        TimeUnit.SECONDS.sleep(random.nextInt(4) + 1);
        return "Hello World";
    } catch (InterruptedException e) {
        throw new IllegalStateException(e);
    }

}
```

❶ Creates a new cache for this method call

Run the application again (or if it is already running, let live reloading do its job) and repeat the calls to *http://localhost:8080/hello*:

```
curl http://localhost:8080/hello
Hello World 2004ms
```

```
curl http://localhost:8080/hello
Hello World 0ms
```

The second time the method is called, the method is never invoked but is returned from the cache. Quarkus computes for every call a cache key and checks for a hit in the cache system.

To calculate the cache key, Quarkus uses all argument values by default. If there are no argument methods, the key is derived from the cache name.

Discussion

The @io.quarkus.cache.CacheKey annotation can be used in method arguments to specify exactly which arguments must be used for cache key calculation—for example the public String myMethod(@CacheKey String keyElement1, String notPartOf TheKey).

The @io.quarkus.cache.CacheKey annotation cannot be used on a method returning void.

The @io.quarkus.cache.CacheInvalidate annotation can be used to invalidate an entry from the cache. When a method annotated with @CacheInvalidate is invoked, the cache key is calculated and used to remove an existing entry from the cache.

The @io.quarkus.cache.CacheInvalidateAll annotation is used to invalidate all cache entries.

Each of the data caching options can be configured individually in the *application.properties* file:

```
quarkus.cache.caffeine."greeting-cache".initial-capacity=10 ❶
quarkus.cache.caffeine."greeting-cache".expire-after-write=5S ❷
```

❶ Minimum total size for the internal data structures of the greeting-cache cache

❷ Sets the expiration time, counting after the write operation of greeting-cache cache

Run the application again (or if it is already running, let live reloading do its job) and repeat the calls to *http://localhost:8080/hello*:

```
curl http://localhost:8080/hello
Hello World 2004ms

curl http://localhost:8080/hello
Hello World 0ms

// Wait 5 seconds

curl http://localhost:8080/hello
Hello World 1011ms
```

The `quarkus.cache.caffeine."greeting-cache".expire-after-access` property can be used to set the expiration time of the cache to an amount of time after the most recent read or write of the cache value.

Minikube

All the recipes in the book that involve a Kubernetes cluster have been tested in minikube; however, they should also work in any other Kubernetes cluster.

Minikube is a tool that makes it easy to run Kubernetes locally instead of in a remote Kubernetes cluster.

In this book, minikube 1.7.3 and Kubernetes 1.17.3 has been used; but again, any other version should be fine because no advanced techniques are used. Minikube requires a hypervisor to be installed. We recommend you use the VirtualBox hypervisor. In our experience, this is the most portable and stable way to run minikube.

How you install minikube, VirtualBox, and kubectl might depend on the system you are running, so we are providing the links where you can find the instructions to install each of these components:

- VirtualBox (*https://oreil.ly/KU2vk*)
- Minikube (*https://oreil.ly/gth-J*)
- kubectl (*https://oreil.ly/FpZzN*)

After installing all the software, you can start minikube by opening a terminal window and running the following:

```
minikube start --vm-driver=virtualbox --memory='8192mb' \
    --kubernetes-version='v1.17.3'

[serverless] minikube v1.7.3 on Darwin 10.15.3
 Using the virtualbox driver based on user configuration
 Reconfiguring existing host ...
 Starting existing virtualbox VM for "default" ...
 Preparing Kubernetes v1.17.3 on Docker 19.03.6 ...
Launching Kubernetes ...
```

```
    ⬜⬜Enabling addons: dashboard, default-storageclass, storage-provisioner
    ⬜⬜ Done! kubectl is now configured to use "default"
```

Then, configure the docker CLI to use the minikube docker host:

```
eval $(minikube docker-env)
```

Then any operation executed with docker, like docker build or docker run, happens within the minikube cluster.

Keycloak

Keycloak is an open source identity and access management system. Configuring and deploying Keycloak in production is outside the scope of this book. In the following example, a realm file is provided with all users, roles, configurations, and so on, and needs to be imported into a running Keycloak server.

To simplify the installation of Keycloak, the Keycloak Docker container is used:

```
docker run --name keycloak -e KEYCLOAK_USER=admin -e KEYCLOAK_PASSWORD=admin \
    -p 8180:8080 jboss/keycloak:8.0.1
```

Then open a browser and enter the following URL: *http://localhost:8180*.

Click Administration Console, as shown in Figure B-1.

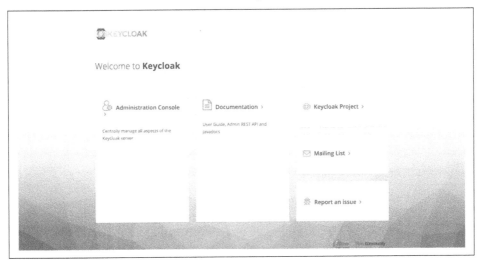

Figure B-1. Keycloak home page

Next, you will be presented with a login option similar to the one you see in Figure B-2. Use login/password admin as the credentials.

Figure B-2. Keycloak login page

In the main page, toggle the Master button to reveal the Add realm button, and click that so that your screen looks like the one shown in Figure B-3.

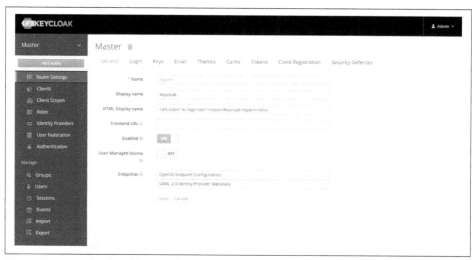

Figure B-3. Keycloak Add realm button

Finally, you should see a screen like the one shown in Figure B-4. You will need to import a Keycloak file. The file we used is in the code for the book at *https://oreil.ly/quarkus-cookbook-code*.

Figure B-4. Result of importing realm

Knative

In Chapter 10, you need to have access to a Kubernetes cluster—it can be a minikube installation or any other kind. But you also need Knative Serving installed to run the Knative recipe. For this book, Kourier is used as an Ingress for Knative.

In this book, minikube 1.7.3, Kubernetes 1.17.3, Knative 0.13.0, and Kourier 0.3.12 were used.

To install Knative Serving, you need to run the following commands:

```
kubectl apply -f \
 https://github.com/knative/serving/releases/download/v0.13.0/serving-core.yaml
kubectl apply -f \
 https://raw.githubusercontent.com/3scale/kourier/v0.3.12/deploy/\
 kourier-knative.yaml
```

Configure Knative Serving to use the proper ingress.class:

```
kubectl patch configmap/config-network \
  -n knative-serving \
  --type merge \
  -p '{"data":{"clusteringress.class":"kourier.ingress.networking.knative.dev",
               "ingress.class":"kourier.ingress.networking.knative.dev"}}'
```

Set your desired domain; in this case, 127.0.0.1 is used because it runs in minikube:

```
kubectl patch configmap/config-domain \
  -n knative-serving \
  --type merge \
  -p '{"data":{"127.0.0.1.nip.io":""}}'
```

Now, you are ready start deploying Knative services.

Index

About the Authors

Alex Soto Bueno is a Java Champion and director of developer experience at Red Hat. He first found joy with the Java world when he started coding in Java version 1.2 when swing.jar was an external library. Alex began programming with ZX Spectrum (in the good old days, using the POKE command) and had several different computers, such as an 80286. (He is grateful to his parents, Ramon and Mili, for buying them.) He is an international speaker, and he teaches at La Salle Universitat Ramon Llull. You can even listen to him on the radio.

Jason Porter has been excited about software since the early 1990s, when his family bought their first computer. It all began with QBasic's *Gorillas* and *Nibbles*. After discovering the source code for those games, he was hooked and knew exactly what he wanted to do when he grew up! Shortly after learning BASIC, he picked up *Teach Yourself Java in 21 Days*. High school and university improved upon the foundation with more Java and C/C++. After starting work after the dotcom burst, Jason eventually ended up at Red Hat, a dream job for him. He has worked on many software projects, mostly Java based, and has also done his share of web work over the years. He's very happy helping others learn and be productive. You can see him on stage at various conferences around the globe, or at the local JUG in Utah.

Colophon

The animal on the cover of *Quarkus Cookbook* is a purple-throated carib humming-bird (*Eulampis jugularis*). Named for its distinctive coloring, the purple-throated carib is found on most islands of the Lesser Antilles off the coast of Venezuela.

The purple-throated carib is a large hummingbird with shimmering green wings, a black body, and the eponymous purple throat. It also has a distinctly down-curved bill that, along with its purple throat, distinguishes it from many of its close cousins, although the bill of the female purple-throated carib is both longer and more curved than the male's bill.

These birds are found primarily in the depths of tropical forests and occasionally at the forests' edges. In the low light of their forest habitat, the birds often appear mostly black, save for some shimmer off their wings. This hummingbird emmits sharp, high-pitched calls in a variety of patterns. They also have a distinct relationship with two species of flowering Heliconia plants, which has been pointed to as evidence of co-evolution.

Though the purple-throated carib's conservation status is "Least Concern" at the time of writing, many of the animals on O'Reilly covers are endangered; all of them are important to the world.

The cover illustration is by Karen Montgomery, based on a black and white engraving from *Encyclopedie D'Histoire Naturelle*. The cover fonts are Gilroy Semibold and Guardian Sans. The text font is Adobe Minion Pro; the heading font is Adobe Myriad Condensed; and the code font is Dalton Maag's Ubuntu Mono.

O'REILLY®

There's much more where this came from.

Experience books, videos, live online training courses, and more from O'Reilly and our 200+ partners—all in one place.

Learn more at oreilly.com/online-learning

Milton Keynes UK
Ingram Content Group UK Ltd.
UKHW050758030724
445002UK00010B/541